Irish Gardens
and Demesnes
from 1830

The National Trust
33 Sheep Street
Cirencester
Glos. GL7 1QW

Irish Gardens and Demesnes from 1830

Edward Malins and Patrick Bowe

Barrie & Jenkins, London

To Mitzi and Nikki

Barrie & Jenkins Ltd
3 Fitzroy Square, London W1P 6JD

An imprint of the Hutchinson Publishing Group

Melbourne Sydney Auckland Johannesburg
and agencies throughout the world

First published 1980

© Edward Malins and Patrick Bowe 1980

Set in Baskerville

Printed in Great Britain by Ebenezer Baylis and Son Ltd,
Worcester and London and bound by The Pitman Press, Bristol

ISBN 0 214 20628 9

This book was produced with the financial assistance
of the Center for Studies in the History of Landscape
Architecture, Dumbarton Oaks Research Library
and Collection.

Contents

List of Plates

Colour

Monochrome

Endpapers:
Glasnevin, Dublin. The Curvilinear Range from a survey by K. C. Chow,
   B. O'Connell and P. V. Sweeny, 1963

Acknowledgements

We are most grateful to the Director of the Center for Studies in the History of Landscape Architecture, Dumbarton Oaks Research Library and Collection, for financial assistance towards the completion of the book. We have also received much help from many people to whom we are most indebted: to the Hon. Desmond Guinness for his initiative in suggesting our authorial collaboration; to the Knight of Glin for encouragement and advice in the writing of the book; to the late Earl of Rosse and to Dr Charles Nelson of the National Botanic Garden, Glasnevin, for reading our text and giving us incomparable guidance in matters horticultural. The recent death of Lord Rosse leaves a gap in horticultural and gardening affairs in Ireland which it will be hard to fill. He will be much missed both for his great personal qualities and for his botanical knowledge which was expressed in the gardens and tree collections at Birr Castle. As Chairman of the Heritage Gardens Committee of An Taisce, the Irish National Trust, Lord Rosse initiated and steered many successful projects: a travelling Heritage exhibition, a list of gardens in the Republic compiled on behalf of ICOMOS (The International Council of Monuments and Sites) of UNESCO; and an inventory of plants in major Irish gardens, inaugurated and financed by the Heritage Trust. Lastly, at the suggestion of Lord Rosse, An Foras Forbatha, the National Institute of Physical Planning and Research in the Republic, started a national inventory of parks and gardens. It is hoped that the work of this committee, for which he worked so selflessly, will continue to flourish as it did under his chairmanship.

Above all, we should like to thank Penelope Hobhouse for planning visits and transporting us to many gardens in Northern Ireland which we would otherwise not have seen. Her expert horticultural guidance and advice was of great value. A rich source of photographic material was revealed to us by Daniel Gillman and his late brother Sylvester who placed their collection of Irish country house material at our disposal. Without this the book would have been inadequately illustrated. Our thanks also to Lyn Gallagher, Public Relations Officer of the National Trust of Northern Ireland, to Aidan Brady of the National Botanic Garden, Glasnevin, to the Librarian of the University of Bath, to the staffs of the Lindley Library, Royal Horticultural Society, the National Library of Ireland, Trinity College Library, the Royal Irish Academy, the Ulster Museum Library, the National Trust Archive, Michael Hodson of Barrie & Jenkins, and Helen Gleadow for her hospitality.

We are beholden to all those owners of gardens who have been generous with their hospitality as well as showing us their gardens, instructing us in horticulture and discussing maps, photographs and documents with us. Without their help on these visits the book could never have been written, and we should not have been able to bring to the notice of our readers the splendid gardening heritage which, like so many earlier gardens in *Lost Demesnes*, is so worthy of preservation in our own times. If that is achieved the book will have been worth while indeed.

The Dowager Duchess of Abercorn
Charles Acton
Sir Harold Acton
Colonel C. B. C. Anderson
Mrs P. E. Anderson
William M. Anderson
Martin Anglesea
Mrs E. P. Grove Annesley
Mr and Mrs Patrick Grove Annesley

Mr and Mrs W. Bagwell
Mrs Priscilla Ballantyne
Captain and Mrs F. B. Barton
Mrs Mavis Batey
Mark Bence-Jones
Rex Beaumont

Commander Pack-Beresford
Toby Bernard
Mrs Alfred Bewley
John Bland
Miss Evelyn Booth
Aidan Brady
Cavan Browne
Kenneth Burras
Ailbhe Butler

The Earl of Caledon
Dr Elizabeth Cartwright
Miss Jane Chisholm
Mrs Harry Clifford
The late Miss Alice Coats
John Colleran
Howard Colvin
Ambrose Congreve
Adrian Cosby
Mrs B. D. Craig
Mrs A. C. Crichton
Mrs Diana Curtis

Ronald Davies
Viscount and Viscountess de Vesci
Hugh Dixon
Charles Doyne and Patrick Doyne
The Marquess of Dufferin and Ava
Lord and Lady Dunleath
The Dowager Lady Dunraven
The Earl and Countess of Dunraven
Dr John Durand

Giles Eyre

Mrs Betty Farquhar
Frances Jane French
Stanley Fyffer

Mrs W. B. Galloway
The Garden Club of Florence
Mrs Meryl Gardner
William Y. Garner
David Gilliland
Daniel and the late Sylvester Gillman
Lord and Lady Glenconner
The Knight of Glin
Antoinette Glynn
Mrs M. E. Gordon
Sir Basil and Lady Goulding
The Hon. Desmond Guinness
The Hon. Kieran and the Hon. Tamsy Guinness

C. D. H. Hamilton
John Harris
G. V. Hart
The Marquess of Headfort
Arthur Hellyer
Derek Hill
Penelope Hobhouse
Gabriel Hogan
Mrs G. Hunt and the late John Hunt
Miss Patricia Hutchins

11

The Earl and Countess of Iveagh

Mrs Ronald Kaulbeck

Dr J. G. D. Lamb
Lady Langham
Mrs I. Lecky-Watson
The late Miss Phoebe Lefroy
The Countess of Leitrim
Seymour Leslie
The Lindley Library
Raymond Lister

Mrs Frazer Mackie
Dr Elizabeth McDougall
Henry McDowell
Mrs Molly McElligott
Michael McGarvie
Ciaran McGonigal
Henry McIlhenny
Barbara Maclean
Dr Edward McParland
Sidney Maskell
Betty Massingham
Georgina Masson
Robin Mathew
The late Brian Molloy
Hilary Moran
Dr and Mrs Brian Morley

James Naper
The National Gallery of Ireland
The National Library of Ireland
The National Trust Archive
The National Trust of Northern Ireland
Dr E. C. Nelson
Diana Duchess of Newcastle
Nicholas Nicholson
The Northern Ireland Public Record Office

John O'Connell
Sean O'Criadain
The O'Donovan
Roderic More O'Ferrall
Lady O'Neill
Lady O'Neill of the Maine
Carolyn Oppenheimer (Department of Prints and Drawings, Victoria and Albert Museum)
Austin O'Sullivan

Parks Department, Dublin County Council
Lionel Perry
Colonel and Mrs David Price
Mrs Jobling Purser

Sean Rafferty
John Redmill
Mrs G. W. Reside
Lanning Roper
David Rose
The late Earl, and the Dowager Countess of Rosse
Lord Rossmore
The Royal Dublin Society

12

Mr and Mrs Jeremy Scott
David Shackleton
Denis Shannon
Nicholas Sheaff
The Earl of Shelburne
Robert Sherwood
Major Shirley
Colin Smythe
Dr H. Steadman
Dr Patricia Strong
Margaret Sweeney

An Taisce
Captain A. C. Tupper

The Ulster Museum

Mr and Mrs Ralph Walker
Mr and Mrs P. R. Walker
Robert Walpole
Mrs Michael Walsh-Kemmis
The Marquess and Marchioness of Waterford
Captain and Mrs H. P. Watt
Professor David Webb
Richard Webb
John Westby
Sally Duchess of Westminster
The Countess of Wicklow
Jeremy Williams
Mr and Mrs David Willis
Mrs B. J. Wright

The Estate of Mrs W. B. Yeats

The authors would also like to express their thanks to the following owners, institutions and photographers for permission to reproduce the following plates:

Colour
John Brookes XI; Ambrose Congreve XII; Richard Dann III; Bord Failte VII, XIII; Sir Basil Goulding VI; National Trust Archive II; Office of Public Works IV.

Monochrome
Aerofilms Ltd 28, 30, 73; Patrick Annesley 120, 121; W. E. G. Bagwell 54; Bord Failte 44, 55, 78, 90, 93, 138, 139, 149, 150, 151, 166; Pamela Browne 116; Thomas F. Cahill 56; Country Life 108; Richard Dann 36, 37, 43, 57, 64, 65, 67, 68, 71, 78, 130, 157; David Davison 57; Hugh Dixon 133; John Donat 136; William Y. Garner 30, 56, 158; Jonathan Gibson 168; The Gillman Collection 49, 50, 88, 153; *The Irish Times* 44, 80, 113, 114, 127, 160; Pat Langan 71; The National Library of Ireland 20, 22, 23, 24, 25, 27, 29, 31, 32, 35, 39, 40, 42, 44, 45, 46, 47, 50, 51, 52, 55, 56, 60, 64, 70, 74, 75, 83, 87, 95, 110, 118, 140, 148, 154, 156, 158, 166, 169; The National Trust Archive 20, 21, 34, 43, 53, 72, 84, 159; The National Trust, Committee for Northern Ireland 102, 103, 104, 130, 131, 132; The O'Donovan 29, 152, The Office of Public Works 94, 96, 98, 108, 170; Rex Roberts Studios 36; The Royal Institute of British Architects 24; Ianthe Ruthven 135; Colin Smythe 139, 142, 144, 145; The Ulster Museum 34, 36; The Victoria and Albert Museum 28, 30; R. B. Walpole 124; The Countess of Wicklow 46.

Patrick Bowe supplied photographs for the following: I, V, VIII, IX, X, XIV, 49, 162, 171.

Approximate metric equivalents

INCHES TO MILLIMETRES

$\frac{1}{32}$ in $=$	0·8 mm	$\frac{5}{8}$ in $= 15\cdot9$ mm		4 in $= 101$ mm	
$\frac{1}{16}$ $=$	1·6	$\frac{3}{4}$ $= 19\cdot1$		5 $= 127$	
$\frac{1}{8}$ $=$	3·2	$\frac{7}{8}$ $= 22\cdot2$		6 $= 152$	
$\frac{3}{16}$ $=$	4·8	1 $= 25\cdot4$		7 $= 178$	
$\frac{1}{4}$ $=$	6·4	$1\frac{1}{4}$ $= 31\cdot8$		8 $= 203$	
$\frac{5}{16}$ $=$	7·9	$1\frac{1}{2}$ $= 38\cdot1$		9 $= 229$	
$\frac{3}{8}$ $=$	9·5	$1\frac{3}{4}$ $= 44\cdot5$		10 $= 254$	
$\frac{7}{16}$ $=$	11·1	2 $= 51$		11 $= 279$	
$\frac{1}{2}$ $=$	12·7	3 $= 76$		12 $= 305$	

FEET TO METRES

2 ft $= 0\cdot61$ m	12 ft $= 3\cdot66$ m	60 ft $= 18\cdot3$ m
3 $= 0\cdot91$	15 $= 4\cdot57$	70 $= 21\cdot3$
4 $= 1\cdot22$	20 $= 6\cdot10$	80 $= 24\cdot4$
5 $= 1\cdot52$	25 $= 7\cdot62$	90 $= 27\cdot4$
6 $= 1\cdot83$	30 $= 9\cdot15$	100 $= 30\cdot5$
7 $= 2\cdot13$	35 $= 10\cdot67$	110 $= 33\cdot5$
8 $= 2\cdot44$	40 $= 12\cdot20$	120 $= 36\cdot6$
9 $= 2\cdot74$	45 $= 13\cdot72$	130 $= 39\cdot6$
10 $= 3\cdot05$	50 $= 15\cdot2$	140 $= 42\cdot7$
11 $= 3\cdot55$		150 $= 45\cdot7$

From W. J. Bean's *Trees and shrubs hardy in the British Isles*.

Foreword

The Romans christened Ireland 'Winter' (Hibernia) and left her severely alone. It was not until the Renaissance reached our shore, as late as the seventeenth century, that Italian example came to be followed in the sphere of art and architecture. As a result there are, to this day, two distinct threads running through the visual arts in Ireland, the Celtic and the Classical, each with their faithful band of devotees.

The idea of the Renaissance garden travelled through France and Holland to England; formal parterres were laid out beside the manor houses of the Tudors. These were also common in eighteenth-century Ireland, as can be seen on Rocque's map of Co. Dublin, but for a time they went out of favour when the Brownian landscape came into fashion. At this time, in both England and Ireland, the garden was divorced from the house and walled up some distance away – the further the grander, according to Elizabeth Bowen. Sheep and cattle pressed their noses against the panes of the drawing-room windows.

It is paradoxical that the romantic movement, whose protagonists would presumably have been in sympathy with this 'return to nature', should have come into being just when the 'natural' garden was going out of fashion. It must have begun to seem impracticable, by 1830, to be employing a number of men to grow flowers without having the pleasure of seeing them from the house. The Italian garden made a come-back. The Irish yew took the place of the cypress, and there was a craze for box hedges, gravel paths and wire hoops to keep people off the grass. A straitjacket was imposed on garden design that was to last until the present. The herbaceous border of the 1900s was an attempt at freedom without actually breaking bounds – the garden had become an extension of the house once more.

Chronicling the past in Ireland has ever been complicated by a widespread disdain for fact and an innate preference for fancy. The difficulty of unearthing facts about the Irish garden can well be imagined, especially as so many have vanished almost without trace. This is an account of an important part of the artistic heritage of the country. It is to be hoped that it will lead to a general understanding of the heavy burden involved in the upkeep of gardens in Ireland.

Desmond Guinness
Leixlip Castle, 1980

Introduction

This book aims to be a companion to *Lost Demesnes* by continuing the story of land-scape gardening in Ireland from 1830 to the present day. In our choice of gardens and demesnes to represent this period (many of them not lost but flourishing), we have excluded gardens which are only plant collections, whether public or private, and in particular the history of the National Botanic Garden at Glasnevin that we hope will soon be written. We have also omitted many smaller gardens, partly because cottage and farmhouse gardens play a small part in Irish gardening tradition, and also because it is with larger gardens that most of our historical material from gardening magazines, estate papers and letters deals in detail. In trying to illustrate each garden with contemporary photographs we hope the gardening styles of each period will become more evident and interesting.

After the Act of Union (1800), the shift of power from Dublin to London, and the departure of many land-owners from Ireland was only too evident. However, by 1830 a few were returning and indulging in gardening pursuits that are usually thought of as a sign of permanent residence. Then the disaster of the Great Famine (1845–49) cast its dreadful shadow over the country, yet ironically it resulted in an increase in landscaping activity as many huge works were carried out by landlords as famine relief schemes, including the creation of the lakes at Johnstown Castle, the fortifications at Birr Castle and the planting and roadbuilding at Powerscourt.

As in England, the loss of power and influence of the landed aristocracy to an industrial middle class resulted in a substitution of a unified classical style of building for a variety of different architectural fashions. The Early English, the Gothic, the Medieval and Early Renaissance were paralleled by a diversity of small flower gardens planted in a manner that the owners thought used to accompany castellated walls, bowers, parterres and topiary work. However, the rich and successful men of the High Victorian period regarded such gardens as unsophisticated and soon began to model theirs on the more elaborate gardens of Renaissance Italy or seventeenth-century France. Thus were the great gardens of Powerscourt, The Great Dublin Exhibition and Baronscourt created.

In recent times Ireland has looked more to Europe and the Common Market than to Britain; so also in the late nineteenth century Ireland became more cosmopolitan, and gardens as far apart as Villa Aloupka in the Crimea and Villa Bagheria in Sicily influenced the design of Irish gardens. Another link in this international chain was the industrial and craft exhibitions in Europe from which many of the ornaments and some sculpture still adorning Irish gardens were obtained.

With the expansion of European empires in the High Victorian period an over-whelming influx of plant material reached Ireland from all parts of the world. The Irish climate in the south-west and in many places near the sea was particularly suitable for the growth of a variety of tender subtropical plants. Thus the riches of the botanist-explorers were added to a plethora of gardening and architectural styles. Foremost in this horticultural activity were David Moore and his son Sir Frederick, successive directors of the Botanic Garden, Glasnevin for eighty-eight years, and through whom many trees and shrubs were introduced to Irish gardens. The history of the Irish landscape garden during this period is therefore a dichotomy between a series of revived architectural styles and the cultivation of exotic plants. When the styles of each matched – a castellated terrace supporting the garden of a castle, a formally planted Italianate parterre before a Renaissance-type house, a fernery adjoining a picturesque villa – then a successful synthesis results.

The cultivation of exotics was helped by the technical advances of the Industrial Revolution, especially by engineering ingenuity in the design and construction of cast iron conservatories, greenhouses and forcing houses – essential ingredients of every large Victorian garden. The new-rich as well as the aristocracy emulated the sculptural displays of French and Italian gardens with their mass-produced cast and moulded ornaments. Mass-production of a different sort also influenced current gardening styles by the economic raising of hundreds of bedding plants, often identical in colour and shape, which were then drilled into the ground like bottles on a factory production line.

In a reaction against over-mechanization William Morris and John Ruskin revived many of the arts and crafts of an earlier, simpler civilization; and a parallel reaction in the gardening world was initiated towards the end of the century by the Irish-born William Robinson. Both Morris and Ruskin were contributors to the first numbers of Robinson's *The Garden* as his view of the nineteenth century matched theirs. Robinson advocated the revival of an earlier and simpler form of gardening, choosing old-fashioned flowers from cottage gardens planted in natural conditions amongst traditionally built stone walls, while William Morris revived arts and crafts as a reaction to mass-produced ornaments.

Gertrude Jekyll's treatment of flower borders was similar to Robinson's, and examples of her work in partnership with Sir Edwin Lutyens can be seen in Ireland. There are no finer examples in garden history than the combination of Lutyens's classical formality and his use of local materials with Jekyll's eye for the planting of flowers and shrubs in Lutyens' settings. Also in the first decade of the twentieth century Japanese influences reached the British Isles, and there remains at Tully, Co. Kildare, the finest example of a small garden made by a Japanese gardener at that time. We have therefore thought it appropriate to discuss this at some length.

Although Ireland was split into two political units in 1922, it seems that landscape gardening was unaffected. On the one hand, Padraic Pearse, the hero of the Easter Rebellion (1916), included horticulture in the curriculum of St Enda's, Rathfarnham, where he was headmaster, and created there an elaborate Celtic Revival garden; on the other, Lady Londonderry, wife of Northern Ireland's first minister of education, began to plan her famous garden at Mount Stewart. In recent years forest parks and arboreta have been planted with State aid on both sides of the border, and it is excellent to find communication between them in botanical and horticultural matters. Most remarkable of all, four large private gardens have been created in Ireland in the last forty years, and these we discuss in our final chapter. In each of these the great traditions of gardening have been brought to fruition: befitting formality near the house leading to a garden of Robinsonian freedom enriched by plants of world-wide origins. Other more modest gardeners continue to create beautiful gardens in the traditions of which we write – horticultural excellence united to architectural beauty – and we hope their work will continue to flourish in Ireland.

1 J.C. Loudon and his Followers in Ireland

The garden history of the early nineteenth century is dominated by the universal genius of the great encyclopedist J. C. Loudon (1783–1843). Although a professional landscape gardener in his early career, his most important contribution later was the collection, in encyclopedic form, of others' work. His books *An Encyclopaedia of Gardening* (1822) and *Arboretum et Fruticetum Britannicum* (1838), ran to numerous editions, and he is recorded as being particularly gratified that his architectural work *The Suburban and Villa Companion* (1838) sold well in Ireland. Indeed, one of his designs illustrated in this book is extant as a gate-lodge at Red Hall, Co. Down. In the *Arboretum et Fruticetum* he mentions his work at Charleville Castle, Co. Offaly. We know that all Loudon's professional work in Ireland was carried out between 1809 and 1812:[1] he says he made a general tour of the country and was employed professionally in three or four counties.[2] It appears that he worked for the 1st Marquess of Hastings,[3] a soldier and colonial administrator, who nearly bankrupted himself in carrying out large-scale improvements on his estate in Moira, Co. Down,[4] at a time when few landlords were spending money in Ireland. Loudon's influence in Ireland was felt more strongly, however, through his pupils and friends, Alexander McLeish and James Fraser being the best known. Loudon's *Encyclopaedia* was both a symptom and a cause of the fragmentation of style in the early nineteenth century. An encyclopedia by its nature must include within its covers a description of every significant style of gardening, and Loudon's included not only a history of gardening styles and horticulture from the earliest classical times but accounts of styles in every country of Europe and other continents. Such a wide-ranging variety must have opened the eyes of readers in these islands whose horticultural and landscaping education was limited to the variation of styles within the confines of what we know as the *jardin anglais*. Loudon's influence, however, was mainly confined to the immediate setting of the house, the outer reaches of the park being designed still in the traditional English style. Many landscape gardeners during this period would design not only an extensive park which formed a general setting for a house but terraces as well; and not only flower-forcing houses in a kitchen garden but a conservatory, and, in some cases, the house itself.

Such a man of all trades was Alexander McLeish, a pupil of Loudon, who settled in Ireland at Harold's Cross, Dublin, in 1813.[5] In his work we see for the first time the breakdown of the homogeneous landscaping style of the eighteenth century. He travelled the country in a constant whirl of professional activity. By 1824 he had designed a floral parterre at Merville, Stillorgan, Co. Dublin, for Lord Chancellor Downes. It was laid out within a walled garden, where there was also an American garden[6] in front of flower-forcing houses designed by McLeish.[7] The park itself was designed by the famous Hely Dutton. James Fraser later criticized McLeish's formal layout:

The parterre in front of the greenhouses is remarkably pretty, though the figurines are rather formal. We hope ere long to see the stiff geometrical figures, which have so long held a place in the flower garden, entirely exploded, and fancy, aided by correct taste, have its flight in this part of the garden. The kaleidoscope exhibits many figurines which will greatly assist the imagination in matters of this kind.[8]

McLeish also designed the first cast-iron hothouses to be erected in Ireland, at Clonmannon, Co. Wicklow, the estate of the Rev. Dr Truell,[9] and in 1824 published a plan for the ornamentation of St Stephen's Green, Dublin. Until his death in 1829 he was exceptionally busy. A very large commission was given him by Sir Richard

KNOCKDRIN CASTLE,
CO. WESTMEATH. *The
formal gardens designed by
Alexander McLeish.
Lithograph by Augustus
Butler, c. 1850.*

Levinge Bt. to lay out gardens and grounds round his new neo-Gothic castle at Knockdrin, Co. Westmeath, which had been erected to the designs of James Shiel. Here McLeish's eclectic style flowered, for he designed round the castle a series of separate gardens *en suite* in different styles. From a conservatory one stepped on to a terrace, then down to a grass parterre in the English style, and on into a Dutch topiary parterre. From here one passed through a rosarium to the botanical grounds and the kitchen garden. The boundary walls were ornamented at the corners by pavilions and by seats, and along its length by arbours.[10] For Sir Richard's brother-in-law McLeish created the near-by seat of Reynella in its entirety, designing house, gardens and grounds, and a further seat similarly for Edward Purdon at Lisnabin, Co. Westmeath, the house, offices and conservatory all being in the Gothic style. He also designed St Lucy's, Co. Westmeath, for Sir Thomas Chapman.

It is characteristic of architects and landscape gardeners of the early nineteenth century that they were able to turn their pencils to either the Classical or Gothic styles. McLeish was no exception, for he also created settings for classical mansions designed by Francis Johnston at Ballynegall, Co. Westmeath, and by Robert Adam at Headfort, Co. Meath, where he was working in 1824.[11] James Fraser refers to his successful use of the uncommon White Spruce as a nurse for young plantations on the windy coast of Co. Sligo, and to his professional visit to Dartfield, Co. Galway, in 1819 when Fraser was employed there.[12]

LOUGH CREW, CO.
MEATH. *The house and
demesne, c. 1860.*

When McLeish was working in Co. Westmeath, C. R. Cockerell (1788–1863) was erecting for James Lenox Naper at near-by Lough Crew[13] a large mansion round which he laid out a landscape park, designed an orangery and parterre behind the house, and erected a gate-lodge in the primitive Doric style in the valley below – the whole ensemble achieving a rare unity in house, garden, park and landscape. It lies in a remote inland corner of Co. Meath, in the shadow of the bare Lough Crew hills (Slieve na Calliagh), whose silhouettes are punctuated by great mounds, megaliths and earthworks marking the burial cairns of pre-Celtic chiefs of 2,000 years ago. In 1791 James Lenox Naper, a great reforming landlord and author of many tracts on the improvement of agricultural and social conditions,[14] inherited this wild and romantic estate inhabited by the shades of the ancient world. At first a castle may have been suggested by the remote setting, but Naper's architect, C. R. Cockerell, had just returned from an extended Grand Tour in Europe, the climax of which was his spectacular discovery of the marbles from the Temple of Jupiter Panhellenius on the remote island of Aegina.[15] The hills around Lough Crew must have been for Cockerell a powerful reminder of these remote Greek sites, for his design for the new house and demesne reproduces the spirit of that ancient world. Like the temples in the sacred landscapes of Greece, his chastely classical building was placed on a high platform, giving it a sense of lonely isolation in the encircling hills – a classical gauntlet flung down before the tombs of the ancient pre-Celtic chiefs. A long drive winds up the hill from the valley floor, where a small wayside temple, built in 1825 with columns of a simple Tuscan order, boldly proclaims the classical rusticity of the demesne. The road widens in front to form a little piazza – a dramatic urban incident in this remote setting. Behind the house an orangery masqueraded as a peristyle overlooking a sunken parterre with flower-beds in patterns of linked diamonds.[16] Below the orangery a sunken atrium houses the stableyard, which is now all that remains inviolate, for the shades of the Bronze Age chiefs have won the day. This fine house, with the shadow of a curse laid on it, was thrice burned but only twice rebuilt. Strewn across the platform today are fallen capitals and immense blocks of stone below the sole surviving wall, so that now the site seems an Irish Delphi – the apotheosis of Cockerell's conceit.

In 1829, after McLeish had died, James Fraser, Loudon's friend and the Irish correspondent of *The Gardener's Magazine*, publicly assumed the profession of land-scape gardener.[17] Born in Edinburgh in 1793, Fraser came to Loudon's attention when he was employed as head gardener at Terenure, Co. Dublin, the suburban villa of Frederick Bourne, a wealthy Dublin businessman, who was making a fine

21

collection of plants judiciously arranged by Fraser. Here for the first time the barriers which had so long hemmed in the villa gardener, with his parallel beds of tulips and elliptical figures of roses, were broken down, and Fraser and Bourne led the way 'in endeavouring on natural principles to blend the decorative and the useful' in the villa garden.[18]

Loudon said in 1824 that Fraser was an excellent botanist and gardener as well as a man of general information.[19] Having arrived in Ireland as a head gardener, by his great talents he quickly achieved the position of professional landscape gardener. In the early years of his practice he supplemented his income by writing the first series of comprehensive travel guides to Ireland. His *Guide to the County of Wicklow, Guide to the Lakes of Killarney, Guide to Dublin* and his *Handbook for Travellers in Ireland* are masterpieces of topographical observation. In them one first sees that fragmentation of architectural style and the parallel break-up of the landscape-gardening style which were then taking place. The accounts of eighteenth-century travellers in Ireland tell of a cohesive social structure, based on the landed gentleman in his Georgian seat surrounded by a landscape park, outside which were his tenant farms and neat towns. Fragmentation of the social structure occurring in the early nineteenth century with the rise of a prosperous and cultured middle class led to a transformation of that simple rural scene. Fraser's *Guides* not only describe the Georgian rural seats but are peppered with references to the introduction of other architectural styles – the Early English or Tudor, the Italianate, the Manorial, the Castellated and the Abbey styles – into the canons of domestic architecture. Moreover, the text is dotted with accounts of new domestic building – the suburban villa, the marine villa, the mountain shooting-lodge and the cottage retreats of Dublin professional gentlemen. It is not surprising, therefore, that a wide range of landscape-gardening styles was assembled to answer this limitless architectural variety. During the early years of Fraser's practice all landscape artists were expected to be conversant with this extraordinary variety of styles.

One such practitioner was William Sawrey Gilpin, the English watercolourist and landscape gardener. He was first employed in Ireland in 1829 by the Earl of Caledon at Caledon, Co. Tyrone, to lay out a terrace in front of the house.[20] Gilpin, like Loudon, considered that the formal garden around the house gratified a human need for retirement and protection, where 'the scholar could take his exercise without interruption of his meditation, and the females of the house secured from every blast and every intrusive eye, could cultivate the glowing parterre'. Of an entirely different character was his work at Castle Blayney, Co. Monaghan, for Lord Caledon's uncle, the 11th Baron Blayney.[21] The house stands on a knoll above a lake with its six wooded islands. Gilpin planted each of these so that now they rise like woody knolls above the lake water. Thick belts of woodland fringe the shore, from which a series of open parklands rises to the wooded crests of the hills. The ensemble

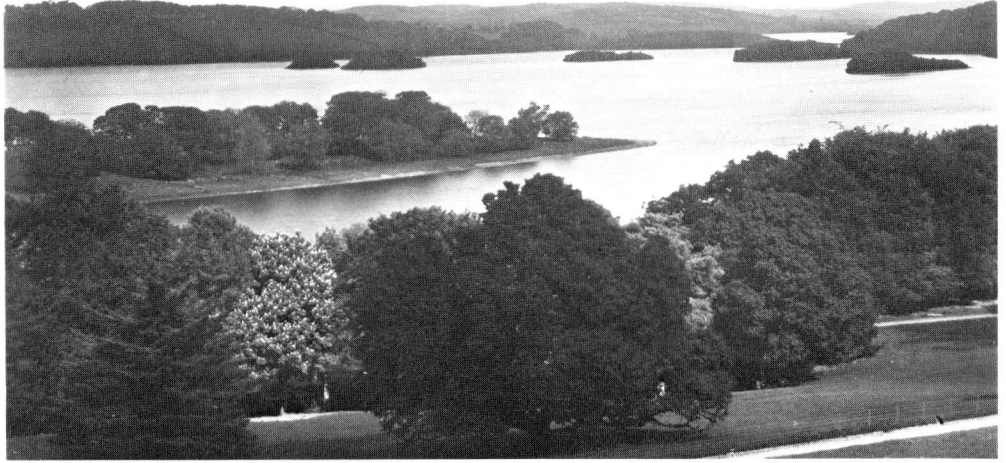

CASTLE BLAYNEY, CO. MONAGHAN. *The landscape designed by William Sawrey Gilpin, c. 1900.*

gradually merges into farmland on the distant shore of the lake, behind which rise the misty outlines of the Mourne Mountains. Later, a temple with a portico in the Ionic style was erected. The landscape is what Gilpin called 'Grand' – having a single dramatic view in front of the mansion, quite unlike the intricacy and variety of prospect which is characteristic of Picturesque landscapes, an example of which can be seen at Crom Castle, Co. Fermanagh, the seat of the Earl of Erne.

Here, in 1830, the 2nd Earl of Erne built a castle to the designs of Edward Blore, the Scottish architect, in the wondrous landscape of Upper Lough Erne, with its deep wooded promontories, inlets and islands with picturesque remains of former civilizations. On a headland almost surrounded by water, the new castle rose to look over the older and ruined Crom Castle[22] with an ancient yew tree within its bawn, a pretty schoolhouse and church on neighbouring headlands, ivy-clad ruins in the maze of wooded islands on the lough, with a folly castle then recently constructed on one of the islands. Ancient, long-abandoned monastic ruins, an Irish High Cross, and large mounds or *raths*, evidence of pre-Christian civilization, could also be seen in this spot. Oak, ash, yew, larch and pine overhang the water's edge, and in the woods on an island wild goats roam. Here, Gilpin's landscape is characterized by the subtle intricacy and variety of its parts rather than by the one dramatic view he created at Castle Blayney.

Romantic scenery is wrought upon a smaller scale than the former, with more parts, and a greater variety and quickness of transition from part to part. Intricacy seems the leading feature of the Romantic. The Grand bursts upon the eye at once and holds it in astonishment; the Romantic leads you onwards in alternate expectation and discovery.[23]

CASTLE BLAYNEY, CO. MONAGHAN. *The temple and Lough Muckno, c. 1965.*

CROM CASTLE, CO. FERMANAGH. *A broken vista of the Castle and boathouse.*

CROM CASTLE, CO. FERMANAGH. *Lough Erne, with the island castle, and its setting designed by William Sawrey Gilpin, c. 1900.*

Gilpin's idea of the relationship between house and landscape in the Romantic style, of which Crom Castle is a superb example, is recorded in his *Practical Hints on Picturesque Landscaping* (1827): 'A variety of height and projection in the general mass of the building which when broken and encircled by well-disposed planting will form a much more agreeable whole than can be produced by any single compact mass of whatever style.' And again, 'When the house is of irregular form, windows may be placed so as to command a greater variety of scenery than can be obtained by the usual rectangular building.'[24] The effect is enhanced at Crom by the planting of many large trees near the house to provide a frame and foreground to the view, which is thus broken up into a variety of separate prospects. This style presupposes a moving rather than a static observer. As one walks round Crom, or sails on the intricately patterned lake, by reason of Gilpin's planting one can never obtain a complete view of Blore's castle but rather a series of partial views – its towers, gables and wings seen in different picturesque assemblies. As one journeys, park, castle, old castle's ruins, church folly tower, schoolhouse and ancient ruins on the islands continually recompose themselves into a series of views of unmatched intricacy and variety. From the house, likewise, no single view of the landscape is obtained, but as one walks from room to room a different view unfolds from each window. The beauty of the lake is tinged with sadness: the water is shallow, meandering and sluggish; great houses and cottages stand in ruins round its shores; water-lilies and tall reeds choke the backwaters; and plaintive bird-calls in the stillness make it a remote and eerie world.

JOHNSTOWN CASTLE, CO. WEXFORD. *The castle and lake designed by Daniel Robertson, c. 1895.*

JOHNSTOWN CASTLE, CO. WEXFORD.*The Gothic pavilion and parterre, c. 1895.*

Another designer who combined a talent for landscape gardening, and indeed architecture in different styles, was Daniel Robertson (*fl.* 1821–43) who left a distinguished practice in Oxford to come to Ireland where his wife's family lived.[25] He practised principally in the counties of Wicklow and Wexford,[26] and his work at Powerscourt will be discussed in detail in Chapter 4. He also designed Johnstown Castle in Co. Wexford for Hamilton Knox Grogan-Morgan in 1840, on the site of two old Esmonde castles. It borrowed a little of their antiquity by being sited adjoining one of the keeps, so that the one might look towards the other, which would become a picturesque ruin in the park. Originally a symmetrical design, it was later given a picturesque appearance by the addition of a large irregular wing, containing, among other rooms, a laboratory for Mr Grogan-Morgan who was interested in experimental chemistry. A model of this later form of the castle was admired by the fashionable throng at the Great Exhibition (1851) in London.[27]

The landscape setting had already been begun while Johnstown Castle was being built,[28] and as there was no distant prospect of mountain or lough an inward-looking landscape round an artificial lake was created. This lake was dug at immense cost in the shape of two broad bays joined by a narrow isthmus, intended as the site for a bridge which was never built. Islands, which have now disappeared, were raised, and a circuit walk laid down round the lake shore. Opposite the castle the walk widens into an extensive terrace, on which stands a fishing turret whose arched windows frame views of the castle and landscape. From here one can also see the ruined keep draped in ivy and the castellated screen of the stable-block reflected in the water. The walk continues through woodland to the southern shore from which a distant view of the castle and its towers, with the lake as its foreground and the woodland as its sidescreens, is perfectly composed. One then returns along the western shore, passing the stable castellations, a cascade (which once fell under an elliptical Gothic arch flanked by turrets), to the lower lake, and finally by a squat tower over the servants' entrance which is appropriately half-hidden in trees and from which an underground passage led to the castle basement. A *jet d'eau* played on the castle lawn, raised on a terrace, the retaining walls of which were at a later stage swept round the lake in two great arcs, the west one becoming a site for a collection of classical statuary. Screened from the lake by a thick belt of trees, the high road runs by an enfilade of embattled gates to the demesne. On the opposite side of the road a castellated observation tower was erected on an eminence in the deer park.

Mr Knox Grogan-Morgan died in 1854, and his widow, Lady Esmonde, completed the formal garden to the west. Thomas Lacy describes it and its pavilion in the florid language of the time:

Two light and finely wrought open arches to the south, and one of the same description to the east and west. In the nearer of the open arcades an elegant alcove has been formed, furnished with chairs and loungers. The summit of this unique and fanciful structure is decorated with embattled ornaments in the subdued embattled style, and the heads of the arches are embellished with semi-circular ornaments. In the centre of the garden, a light and remarkably striking jet d'eau has been placed, which is formed by the bronze figure of a boy in a half-sitting, half-kneeling attitude who is represented in all the wantonness of playful sportiveness, blowing into the smaller end of a horn, whence from a tube in the larger end is propelled a light volume of water, which rises to a proportionate height. In its descent, the crystal stream falling upon the outstretched hand of the delightful urchin, breaks into several fragments, which in their fine fall into a brimful oval reservoir produce a pleasing effect . . .[29]

These landscaping works were undertaken by Hamilton Knox Grogan-Morgan to provide work during the desperate years of the Famine in Ireland, an enterprise which showed his characteristic awareness of his duties as a landlord. Lacy describes his happy estate:

The comfortable and substantially built slated farmhouse, with its neat garden or orchard, and its tasteful parterre will speak in language not to be misunderstood, his best eulogium. Many of the tenant farmers on his estate are frequently to be seen as well mounted as some of the surrounding gentry, following the hounds in the hunting season; while his day labourers dwell in neatly slated cottages, where the creeping woodbine, or mayhap, the sweetly scented rose declares in silent but convincing terms that comfort and refinement are not strangers to those who live within the range of his influence and his bounty.[30]

The remaining years of the nineteenth century saw the lawns at Johnstown planted with a collection of exotic trees, displaying in their varied foliage the Victorian delight in polychromy. A magnificent Japanese cedar now hangs its bronze whorls over the lake; behind it a blue Atlas cedar shows its pointed head, and a pair of cordylines enlivens the foreground. A range of false cypresses – golden *Chamaecyparis lawsoniana* 'Stewartii', bright green *C. laws.* 'Erecta', dark *C. laws.* 'Filiformis', and silver-grey *C. pisifera* squarrosa – front the woodland. Tall firs break the skyline around the towers, and a quantity of monkey-puzzles stands gauntly about the eastern lawns, where there are also rare oaks – the Californian Live Oak, *Quercus agrifolia*, Turner's Oak, *Quercus × turneri* 'Pseudoterneri', and the Makimo Oak.[31] Since the death in 1945 of Lady Maurice Fitzgerald, a great granddaughter of Hamilton Grogan-Morgan, the estate has housed the Soils Division of An Foras Taluntais (The Agricultural Institute). The formal garden is now a picnic ground, *jets d'eau* no longer play, and Lady Esmonde's lake is obscured – yet much remains of this landscape, now happily being restored and cared for, open to the public and enjoyed by many.

26

In 1838 Robertson also designed a castle in the Early English style for Henry Alcock at Wilton in the north of the county.[32] The battlemented and machicolated pile stands on a moated platform surrounded by parapet walls and sham fortifications on a natural terrace above the river Boro, which was spanned at several points by handsome bridges. A long, riverside walk led to the flower-garden, a furlong from the castle. Thomas Lacy described the scene: 'It is no uncommon thing to see a fashionable angler plying his line from the windows of the mansion, and capturing the bright unconscious inhabitant of the beautiful stream that flows beneath.' No fashionable angler now plies his line, but the winding Boro still flows below the ruins, its deep murmur soothing the ear.[33]

Eclectic as ever, Robertson later designed, in an Italianate *palazzo* style, a new seat for Lord Carew at near-by Castleboro. It was sited on the brow of a hill overlooking the ruins of the old family mansion, which had been burnt down and subsequently maintained as a picturesque ruin in the park. In between lay a stream, dammed to create a mirror of water, in which the reflection of each might be seen from the other. A tall French window led from the garden front on to the first of a series of seven terraces descending to the water-gate on the river bank. On either side were cascades over which stone bridges had been thrown, so that from the opposite bank the spectator might capture, on looking back, the glorious *coup d'oeil* of the *palazzo* and its terraces mirrored in the water at his feet. The park, of 1,000 acres undivided by a single fence, was ornamented by a classical screen fronting the stable-block, a church spire, a pretty schoolhouse, and two gate-lodges. One, in the form of a hillside temple, which has a portico reached by a dramatically long flight of steps, stands on a grassy platform above a wooded gorge to the north of the demesne; the second lodge, built in 1863 at the termination of a new drive to the near-by railway station, hid its Doric portico behind a gate of massive stone piers and elaborate ironwork which has now gone.[34] The house, burned down in 1922, now stands a ruined and awe-inspiring hulk on its overgrown terraces, its lake almost obscured by reeds, in the midst of a lost demesne. The lodges remain, as do the stables and the old castle, now in their ivied ruin more Picturesque than ever.

James Fraser had been working during these years close by at Saunders Court for the 4th Earl of Arran.[35] At the Act of Union (1800) Lord Arran's father abandoned this estate on the estuary of the Slaney in Co. Wexford. Subsequently, its noble oak-woods and hedgerow trees, which had once sheltered and adorned the country for

CASTLEBORO, CO. WEXFORD. *The house and terraced gardens designed by Daniel Robertson, c. 1895.*

27

miles around, were felled. The 4th Earl, however, set about rescuing the estate, and by about 1840 restoration was far advanced – a commodious mansion had been built, new plantations were showing the long, flowing boundary lines characteristic of a Fraser landscape, and the growth of natural coppices, encouraged by Fraser for their picturesque effect, was already beginning to adorn the glens. Now all that remains is the ruined triumphal arch which served as the entrance to the demesne.

The 4th Earl of Shannon had returned also to his Irish seat, Castlemartyr, Co. Cork, which had been neglected since his father's departure early in the nineteenth century, again as a result of the Act of Union (1800). It is said that as a boy he so loved the place that he departed with tears in his eyes. On his return he started to plant a noble pinetum and a garden of tender camellias to a design of Fraser,[36] who also laid out a circular sunken garden in front of an old Norman keep in the park. Fraser's drawing for the extension to the park at Gowran, Co. Kilkenny, for Lord Clifden in his characteristic style of broad flowing lines of woodland and pasture still exists,[37] as does his proposal for near-by Castlemorres, the seat of Lord Mount-morres, now a forestry plantation.[38] Two of his works in Co. Limerick survive. His gardens and park round the Scottish baronial house and park of Castle Oliver, designed by J. Fowler Jones for the Misses Gascoigne, were made to give employment during the Famine. The castle is surrounded by a terrace with a pierced 'Jacobethan' parapet adorned with heraldic beasts. Fraser also renovated the park of Adare round the manor erected by the 2nd Earl of Dunraven,[39] opening an

CASTLE OLIVER (CLONGHANODFOY), CO. LIMERICK. *Engraving by G. Fowler Jones.*

ADARE MANOR, CO. LIMERICK. *The park, designed by James Fraser, c. 1960.*

immensely long but broken vista to a line of distant mountains. In addition, he laid out a series of pleasure-grounds, one at Blandsfort, Co. Leix,[40] another at Ballyhyland, Co. Wexford,[41] and another at Drishane Castle, Co. Cork.[42] In 1863 he died from complications arising from a chest cold at his residence at 25 Westland Row, Dublin. His obituary speaks of his urbanity, hospitality and good will, and of the fact that in his last years his fame had spread so far that he carried out many commissions in England and Scotland.[43]

Fraser's master, Loudon, had been the first landscape gardener to publish designs for suburban villas. Fraser's *Guide* speaks of their proliferation round the cities and towns of Ireland, and McLeish, Fraser, Niven, and Sheppard all provided designs for such villas throughout the nineteenth century. Among those which showed the style in its most typical fashion were Roseville, Lismore, Co. Waterford, and The O'Donovan's villa at Douglas in Cork. Fraser's *Guide* also tells of the many old castellated buildings which were being restored as houses, and of the many new castellated residences being built. Generally speaking, they were surrounded by parterres or terrace gardens, whose walls were embattled and whose corners were given turrets to simulate an old bawn or fortified enclosure. Examples are at Flesk Castle, Co. Kerry, Charleville Castle, Co. Offaly, where the garden was later given a *patte-d'oie* of Irish yews, and Humewood Castle, Co. Wicklow, where one façade overlooks a walled garden whose walls were designed at different heights to make them appear ruined.

ROSEVILLE, LISMORE, CO. WATERFORD. *Garden with greenhouses, c. 1885.*
MONTPELLIER, DOUGLAS, CO. CORK. *The O'Donovan and his gardeners, c. 1865.*

FLESK CASTLE, CO. KERRY. *The castellated terrace walls and park.*

CHARLEVILLE CASTLE, CO. OFFALY. *The* patte-d'oie *of Irish yews, c. 1960.*

DROMORE CASTLE, CO. LIMERICK. *Engraving from architect's pencil drawing by E. W. Godwin.*

KNOCKTOPHER ABBEY, CO. KILKENNY. *The Monks' Walk, c. 1970.*

Sometimes a castle's functional aspect was emphasized by being built on a bare hillside or rock with no landscaped gardens around it as at Dromore, Co. Limerick, which represents the peak of nineteenth-century architectural Romanticism in Ireland. Among other eclectic fashions was the 'Abbey' style of architecture, in which the gardens were often laid out as a series of Monks' Walks, such as those at Knocktopher Abbey, Co. Kilkenny, and at Tynan Abbey, Co. Tyrone, where the Yew Walk leads to an ancient Celtic cross which had been discovered in the grounds.[44] A further popular style was based on the architecture of medieval Oxford and Cambridge colleges, an example of which is Lough Fea, Co. Monaghan, designed in the manner of three sides of an Oxford quadrangle. On the garden front, contemporaneous with the house,[45] is a parterre leading to a formal stepped *allée* which descends to the valley floor, where a medieval well-head was erected. From here a further stepped *allée* ascends the opposite hill to a Celtic cross, erected by

LOUGH FEA, CO.
MONAGHAN. *The
terraced* allée *from the
house, c. 1895.*

LOUGH FEA, CO.
MONAGHAN. *The
terraced* allée *from the foot
of the terraces, c. 1895.*

Mr Shirley's tenants in his honour, on the skyline. Another striking example of the Celtic influence on nineteenth-century Irish gardens was the lake made by Lord Gosford at Gosford Castle, Co. Antrim, in the shape of a shamrock, on which he then built a model of a *crannog*, or Irish lake-dwelling.

Despite the richness of Loudon's influence, landscape parks in the eighteenth-century style continued to form the background and setting for the formal garden: even some new ones were created, the last great one being made by the 1st Marquess of Dufferin and Ava in the 1860s at Clandeboye, Co. Down. He made a great lake, planted woodlands, and laid out a private avenue to the railway station at Helen's Bay in 1865, where he built a bridge for the trains to steam into his Sir Walter Scott dreams. The bridge has barbicans, arrow slits, heraldic beasts and crumbling coats of arms, and the station had a private waiting-room furnished like a Victorian parlour with coroneted curtains. On a near-by hill he erected a tower in memory of his

31

mother in 1867. In the Scotch Baronial style, Helen's Tower contains inscriptions to
her memory written by Tennyson, Kipling, Lord Houghton, and Browning, whose
verse we quote:

Browning's neat poem

> Who hears of Helen's Tower may dream perchance
> How that great beauty of the Scaean Gate
> Gazed on old friends unanimous in hate,
> Death doomed because of her fair countenance.
> Hearts would leap otherwise at thy advance;
> Lady to whom this tower is consecrate!
> Like hers, the face once made the eyes elate,
> Yet unlike hers, was blessed by every glance![46]

was considered inferior by Lord Dufferin to Tennyson's contribution:

> Helen's Tower here I stand,
> Dominant over sea and land.
> Son's love built me, and I hold
> Mother's love in lettered gold.
> Would my granite girth were strong
> As either love, to last as long.
> I should wear my crown entire
> To and thro' the Doomsday fire,
> And be found of angel eyes
> In earth's recurring Paradise.

From the musty top room with these damp-stained golden tablets containing these
verses one can pass by turret staircase to the roof-bastion. Below one the Clandeboye
demesne with its lakes and woods; to the north over Belfast Lough the hills of Antrim
rise; to the south the outlines of the Mourne Mountains; far away to the east the
coast of Scotland from the Mull of Kintyre to Ayrshire joins sky and sea. As one
closes the door on the wind and descends past three rooms, it is as if one were in a
mausoleum rather than a nobleman's folly. Such was Lord Dufferin's love for his
mother, for the tower was built six years before her death from cancer in 1867.

2 The French Taste

After the defeat of Napoleon at Waterloo, there was a moment of celebratory triumphalism in Ireland, when commemorative columns were erected,[1] trees were planted in the battlefield formations as at Lyons, Co. Kildare,[2] avenues were planted,[3] and even single specimens of wellingtonia surrounded by wreaths of clipped laurel, as at Altamont, Co. Carlow. The restoration of the French monarchy and the subsequent improvement in French relations with these islands led to a renewal of interest in French culture. This coincided with the revival in Ireland of the formal garden round the house, so that the two movements coalesced and led to a revival of the French parterre throughout the country. Only a century earlier the era of French taste in the great formal landscapes of Kilruddery and Dromoland had died in the face of the rising popularity of the English landscape garden. There were, however, important differences between these two periods of French influence, for the earlier left a legacy of formal landscape parks (see *Lost Demesnes*, Chapter 1), whereas the one under consideration became a revival of the French parterre garden only. There was a reluctance to alter the landscape park, which by this time surrounded every important house, by replanting it in formal vistas. The French-style garden in Ireland, therefore, was conceived as a foreground to a naturalistic landscape park, rather than to a formal vista as it would be in France. Furthermore, the conception of a parterre as a flat surface which would allow unimpeded views into formal vistas was exactly that which made it adaptable as the foreground to a landscape garden in the eighteenth-century style.

There are important differences between the French and Italian styles of formal gardening which are not often taken into account in descriptions of the revival of these styles in the Victorian period. The differences derive from three factors: terrain, climate and horticulture. The majority of French gardens were in the north and centre of France where the terrain is flat. The Italian villa and its garden were inhabited only in the summer, and the garden was constructed in terraces on cool hillsides where water was plentiful. The parterre developed as a pattern made in box hedging on the various terrace levels. In France the parterre was formed in sunken panels to allow views over it on to the flat terrain in the distance. In Ireland the sunken parterre was adopted to allow views over it into the landscape park. The dry Italian summers prevented the lawn from becoming an important element in garden design, whereas the *tapis vert* became of crucial importance in the French garden. Furthermore, the French adopted the Dutch method of connecting levels by shaven grass banks in preference to the Italian method of retaining walls. Climate was again responsible for the substitution by the French of living material for the architectural elements of the Italian garden: living walls of clipped trees for stone walls, clipped yew cones for statuary to act as vertical accents and, finally, flowers (made possible by the advances of Dutch horticulture in the seventeenth century), in addition to gravels for filling in the pattern of the parterre.[4]

Because of the similarity of much of Ireland's terrain and climate to that of France, the French style of formal gardening was usually preferred to the Italian, but a number of adaptations were made, of course. The discovery and subsequent propagation of the upright Irish yew at Florence Court, Co. Fermanagh, led to its substitution for the clipped cone in the Irish parterre. Its use, be it in an enfilade, *en rondelle*, in a *patte-d'oie*, or otherwise, is one of the unchanging features of the Irish nineteenth-century garden. Standard Portugal laurels were all-weather substitutions for the clipped orange trees of the great French gardens and were often planted in Versailles cases (the decorative wooden cases in which orange trees were grown at Versailles) to make the simulation even more convincing. The Irish parterre evolved, therefore, from the French rather than the Italian model, as a geometrical

arrangement of lawns and grass banks outlined by gravel paths, accented by upright Irish yews, coloured by beds of bright annuals in geometric patterns, and finally buttoned down by lines of standard Portugal laurels clipped into domes.

The Catholic Gormanston family in Co. Meath had a parterre laid out in front of the family chapel by their French chaplain towards the end of the eighteenth century,[5] but the first real indication of a revival in the French taste in Ireland was in the restoration of the formal garden of Antrim Castle by the Countess of Ferrard in the 1820s.[6] This seventeenth-century garden had a formal French canal running between tall lime hedges, a mount with an ascending spiral path, and a *bosquet*, or circular enclosure, of yew hedges with an obelisk of yew at its centre. In the garden an inscription on an urn commemorates its restoration by the Countess:

This blessed retreat, chosen, planned, formed and finished by the refined and incomparable taste of its dear departed mistress.[7]

Another restoration was carried out by Daniel Robertson in 1846 at Kilruddery in Co. Wicklow for the Earl of Meath, where the old garden had been based on Le Nôtre's design at Courances, near Paris.[8] In the same year Lady Osborne made a similar garden at Newtown Anner, Co. Tipperary. Ornamental canals ran between

NEWTOWN ANNER, CO. TIPPERARY. *The temple and the canal, c. 1860.*

34

CURRAGHMORE, CO.
WATERFORD. *The lake
and parterre, designed by
James Fraser, c. 1890.*

CURRAGHMORE, CO.
WATERFORD. *The cast-
iron fountain, c. 1895.*

shaven grass banks in a setting of high terraces and flights of steps decorated with sculpted figures. The gravel paths were lined with Portugal laurels in pots, and a Doric temple on a raised mount stood on the principal reach of water.[9]

At near-by Curraghmore, Co. Waterford, Lady Waterford,[10] who had been brought up in Paris where her father was Ambassador, laid out what was the most complete French garden in Ireland of this period. Curraghmore, although set in one of the most sublime of eighteenth-century parks, had an uncharacteristic *cour d'entrée* with *claire-voie* screen before the entrance front. On the garden front stretched a lake. Lady Waterford commissioned James Fraser to lay out a parterre between it and the house in the manner of Le Nôtre's garden at Rambouillet.[11] Fraser designed a four-panel sunken parterre round a central circular fountain. There were sentinels of Irish yew, and the grand central path was lined with standard Portugal laurels, leading to a balustrade by the lake, formalized into a stone-edged *pièce d'eau* in the French manner. It was found, however, when excavations had begun, that due to the level of the *pièce d'eau* the sunken panels filled up with water, so they were hurriedly filled in again, and the panels left level. A contemporary visitor remarked that he preferred it thus, as no bright colours detracted from the view across the parterre over the lake and the shrubberies planted on the far side, and then across the rolling woods to the Monavullagh Mountains on the horizon. The line of the parterre was later broken by an enormous circular fountain of tiered basins on pedestals in cast iron, in the style of Barbezat and Co., which was bought by the 4th Marquess at the Paris Exhibition of 1867. The basins and pedestals were ornamented with river gods and goddesses, masks, garlands and water plants, and on top were the goddesses of industry and the arts, with a central figure holding aloft a cornucopia from which a *jet d'eau* shot skyward. Because the spray from the jet showered the windows of the house on a windy day, wetting the chambermaids as they opened the windows, and as it also obscured the view of the mountains, the 5th Marquess had it taken down and sold for scrap.[12] Below the north front Fraser laid out a formal semicircular garden, from which radiated a *patte-d'oie* of three avenues. The central one ran up a smooth slope for a mile to the horizon, with dense flanking woodland on either side. In this woodland a *bosquet* was formed in the French manner, with avenues leading to secluded clearings. It was in just such clearings that *fêtes champêtres* of the French court, painted by Watteau, Lancret and Boucher, took place. Here, at Curraghmore, one *bosquet* was made as a circular garden around the delightful eighteenth-century Shell House; another was designed in the shape of an oval. To the south of the house a *parterre des fleurs* was made with a balustraded walk overlooking the American garden above the river Clodiagh.

Another garden laid out before 1845, with a similar relationship between house, parterre and lake as at Rambouillet, was at Lyons, Co. Kildare, the seat of Lord Cloncurry, who had been forced because of his political activity to spend some years in exile on the Continent.[13] This garden was an eight-panel parterre with the central crossing broken into triangular panels, having at its centre a figure of Venus supported on a tall antique column brought from Italy. It was encircled by an arcade of cast iron and overlooked from one side by a Turkish kiosk.

The introduction of the French style in Ireland owed more to the professional landscape gardener Ninian Niven (1799–1879) than to anyone else. If anyone was the Court gardener in Ireland during this period, then surely it was Niven: he conducted the ceremonial plantings of trees at the Viceregal Lodge during the visits of Her Majesty, the Prince Consort and their family to Ireland;[14] he designed the new formal gardens round the Viceregal Lodge, the Chief Secretary's Lodge and the Under Secretary's Lodge in the Phoenix Park;[15] and he was compelled, we are told, to widen the gravel sweep in front of his nursery at Glasnevin, Co. Dublin, to accommodate the Lord Lieutenant and his entourage when they came to buy

NINIAN NIVEN.
Engraving, c. 1870.

ARAS AN UACHTARAIN (THEN THE VICEREGAL LODGE), DUBLIN. *Aerial view of the parterre and yew walk designed by Ninian Niven.*

ARAS AN UACHTARAIN, DUBLIN. *The yew terraces, c. 1910.*

BOTANIC GARDENS, GLASNEVIN, CO. DUBLIN. *A view of the hothouses. Drawn and engraved by J. Kirkwood, c. 1835.*

BOTANIC GARDENS, GLASNEVIN, DUBLIN. *The chain tent. Engraving, c. 1835.*

plants.[16] He came from the Scottish Highlands to Dublin to be Head Gardener to the Chief Secretary.[17] (Many formal French gardens of the seventeenth century in Scotland, as at Drummond Castle, had survived through the eighteenth century.) In 1834, when the Royal Dublin Society was faced with the near collapse of its botanical garden, it appointed Niven as the curator. Niven was a gardener rather than a botanist, but he immediately set about reorganizing the collections, which had been arranged in a disorderly manner. In 1835 he placed before the British Association an original proposal for arranging a botanical collection, called *A Plan for the Formation of a natural arrangement of Plants for a Botanic Garden*,[18] which had as its object 'the uniting together of a British and an exotic arrangement on a serpentine walk'. To the left of the walk were to be placed the exotic plants, and to the right the native species, the different botanical families being separated by an archway over the path. Those of the native species peculiar to England, Ireland or Scotland were to be identified by distinctive labels, impressed with the rose, shamrock or thistle! Always conscious of popular appeal, Niven also included a mount with a labyrinth for the public's amusement. In the following year he wrote the first-ever popular guide to a botanical garden.[19] After four years, he magnanimously decided to hand over the now efficient gardens to a botanist, David Moore,[20] and announced the commencement of his practice as a landscape gardener, showing the life he expected to lead and the way in which a landscape gardener should cope with the difficulties of travel:

N. Niven proposes to include, under the above title the following branches of his profession: namely landscape gardening in all its details; the designing and superintending of the laying out of botanical and horticultural gardens. He will also give designs for the arrangement of public buildings, squares, promenades etc; also professional advice as to the planting and thinning of trees, and forestry operations generally, draining etc.

He also intends to make such arrangements as will enable him to take one or two annual tours through the country, one in spring, the other in autumn, when he will wait upon such noblemen and gentlemen as may wish to have his advice on their estates. In like manner, he hopes to devote a certain proportion of his time for the purposes of making periodical professional visits to places where he may be required within the immediate neighbourhood of Dublin, which he hopes will continue to be more especially the centre of his field of action.[21]

Niven's first project for a national arboretum in the Phoenix Park appears to have fallen through. He then went to France where he visited the gardens of Le Nôtre at Versailles and other places round Paris. He was so impressed that thereafter he abandoned the English style of landscape gardening, which suffered, in his opinion, from 'an extreme of curves and windings', in favour of an intermediate style in which the English and the French would be blended. On his return from France he was

37

commissioned by James Pim, a businessman and entrepreneur, to design public gardens at Monkstown, Co. Dublin.[22] They were to include an observatory to be designed in the Grecian style by Mulvany, a band arena, a horticultural exhibition ground, rock-work exemplifying the different geological strata of the country, numerous *jets d'eau*, a lake with exotic waterfowl, and other amusements. For this type of garden to which the public would throng, the French style was ideal, for its wide paths, generous open spaces, with more intimate *bosquets* for contrast, had been developed to contain the crowds of courtiers at Versailles.

At Monkstown, however, Niven modified the French style to make the principal axes curve with the contours of the land. The first swept down from the entrance gates by the ruins of old Monkstown Castle to the lake in the valley, which was crossed by a bridge, and then up again to meet the second axis – a broad terrace wrapped round the hill. Traversing this, it wound its way up between borders with herbaceous plants and annuals sown freely[23] to the Grecian observatory on top of the hill. The second axis went round the hill. Its centrepiece was a galleried Palm House with matching wings for ferns and camellias, each terminating in a semicircular aquarium, with covered arcades for tender plants continuing the architectural lines. In front of the Palm House the outer edge of the terrace widened to form an esplanade in the shape of a pair of semicircular lawns, each with a single *jet d'eau* rising from a circular stone basin. Between them was a gravelled area upon which a band would play on festive occasions. The terraces were elaborately bedecked with ornamental vases, bursting with flowers, at regular intervals on pedestals. Elsewhere in the grounds were an American garden, a rosarium, a pinetum, willow-hung islands, 'dripping cliffs', and a botanical ground. After the detailed plans and advertisement had been prepared, this extraordinarily elaborate plan also fell through. Disheartened, Niven bought a farm at Glasnevin where he began a nursery, a market garden and a school for training young gardeners, and published a number of pamphlets on the improvement of potato cultivation during the Famine.

Niven's first important commission appears to have been for Alderman Roe, the Dublin distilling magnate and philanthropist, who financed the restoration by G. E. Street of Christ Church Cathedral. Niven artfully concealed the modest extent of Nutley, Roe's suburban demesne, by laying out the boundary plantations in curves, and borrowing views from the neighbouring demesne of the Earl of Pembroke at Mount Merrion. In the park he made a lake and a tall belvedere, from the summit of which there was a panoramic view of Dublin Bay and Mountains. As a contrast to the informality of the park he laid out round the house a balustraded formal garden with level lawns, statuary alternating with Irish yews along the paths, patterned flower-beds, and at the centre a circular fountain, representing a shell resting on a rustic base, with herons perched on the edge of the shell, having, we are told, apparently invidious designs on the goldfish in the basin! On one side was a great semicircular wall, with niches set at regular intervals to contain statuary, which concealed the kitchen garden.[24]

In 1852 Niven prepared designs for a parterre in front of the courtyard of Kilkenny Castle for the Marquess of Ormonde, with enfilades of Irish yews on raised gravel walks, and sunken panels between, leading to a *rondelle* of more yews on a circular lawn. On the centre of this lawn was a circular basin with a single *jet d'eau*, and from the balustraded terrace one could look over the park.[25] Unfortunately, the Marquess died before the scheme could be carried out, but Niven's luck took a better turn in succeeding years, when he laid out one of the finest Irish Victorian gardens at Killakee, Co. Dublin, for Colonel and Mrs Samuel White.[26]

The Whites had reclaimed one of the higher slopes of the Dublin Mountains, sheltered it with trees, and built an Italianate villa with views over Dublin Bay and the eastern coastline. As a foreground to the view, Niven designed a series of grass terraces descending by shaven slopes to a classical balustrade. The great central terrace had a circular basin with a bronze Neptune in his car of shells drawn by seahorses, a pair of symmetrical araucarias to break up the view, and a suite of smaller flanking terraces, studded with flower-filled vases seen against a background of dark Irish yews. On either side of the villa were circular chain tents of cast iron in

imitation of eighteenth-century French *treillage*, surrounded by ivies trained into baskets *à la française*. One of the chain tents, festooned with climbing roses, enclosed a formal rose garden; the other, wreathed with ivies and clematis, shaded an American garden. To the south the ground fell away to a sheltered glen through which tumbled a mountain stream. Here, in a secluded spot out of reach of mountain gales, Niven designed a walled flower-garden of three shallow terraces joined by shaven grass banks. On the topmost terrace a line of clipped Portugal laurels in Versailles cases surrounded figures of Venus and Diana on either side of the central gravel path. On the middle terrace stood figures of Sappho and Flora; while on the lowest stood a pair of fountain basins in front of the central dome of the conservatory designed by Richard Turner in his curvilinear style.[27] Turner's conservatories, with their domes, barrel-vaulted galleries and semicircular apses, have their formal forebears in the light *galeries de charpenterie*, of sixteenth-century France, whose light timber frameworks were also wreathed with climbing plants. On each platform stood pairs of Irish yews and araucarias, their architectural masses reminiscent of the tonsured trees of France, their funereal colour relieved by a frivolous riot of flowers and gaily painted china vases.

Another whiskey magnate, Sir James Power Bt., had a garden laid out in Niven's 'intermediate' style at Edermine, his estate overlooking the river Slaney in Co. Wexford. It was composed of a series of formal gardens linked together like beads on a string by curving *allées* through informally planted woodland or shrubberies.[28] Between the house and the Grand Conservatory, which were joined by a *chinoiserie* aviary erected by Pugin's pupil, James Pierce, to Turner's designs, was a floral parterre encircling a figure of Terpsichore. From here walks led through a *bosquet* to a clearing with a circular terrace garden round an elegant parterre with a statue of Cupid. Meandering through the woodland one reached another clearing with an island encircled by a deep canal and approached by fanciful bridges. Swans and ducks disported themselves on its waters. On the circular island a stone figure of Ceres, holding in her hand a wheaten wreath, was surrounded by a parterre of flowers. The use in these gardens of statuary, depicting the Goddesses of Love and of the Arts of Music and Poetry, Fruitfulness and Abundance, is again reminiscent of the gardens of eighteenth-century France. Such figures had presided over the woodland trysts painted by Watteau.

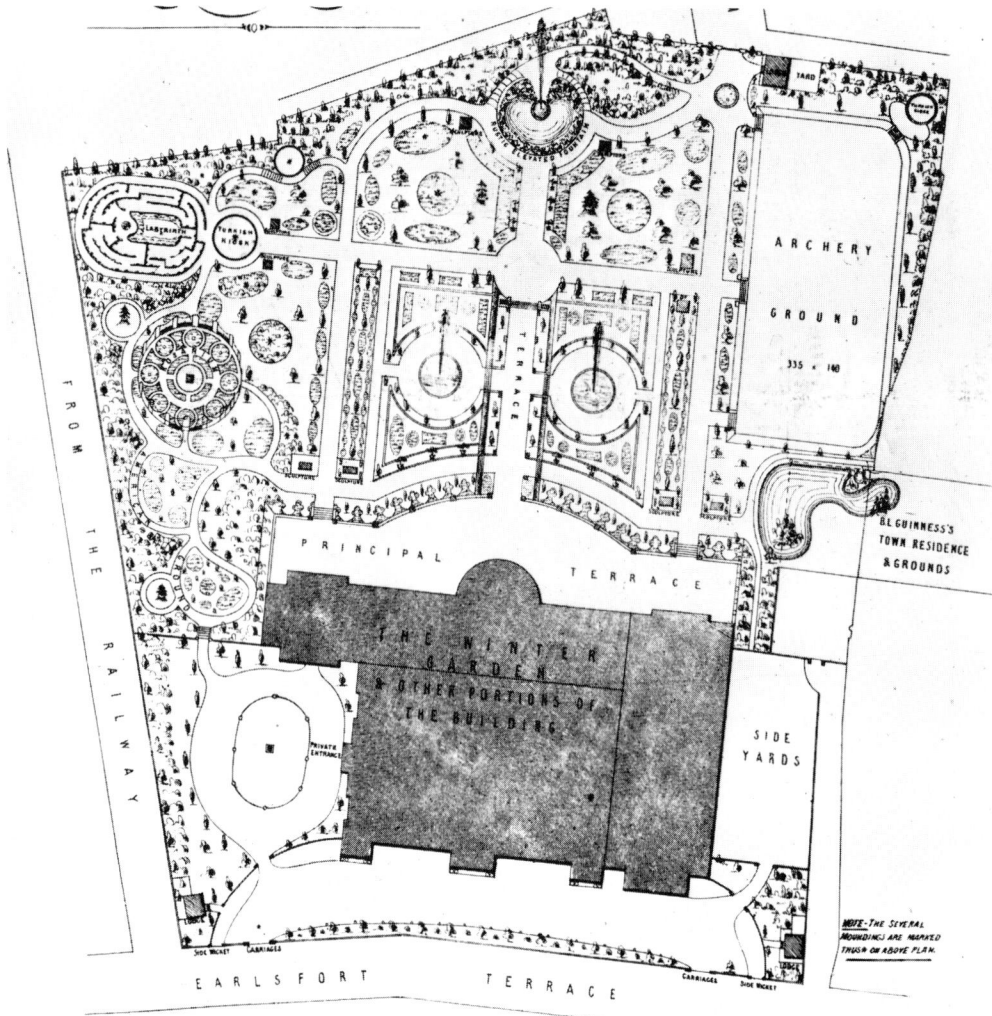

Mr Niven's most prestigious commission of this period was for a parterre before the Viceregal Lodge in the Phoenix Park.[29] Before its porticoed front he designed two sunken panels of lawn, each edged with a decorative line of alternating Irish yews and rectangular flower-beds. Niven thought that a panel of lawn in Ireland with its wonderful green should not be broken up by being dotted with flower-beds. The Viceregal parterre was surrounded by a raised terrace walk, its classical balustrade supporting flower-filled vases at regular intervals, which opened into a formal vista on the portico's axis.

However, like Paxton, Niven's most important work was not for private gardens but for the great industrial exhibitions which were such a feature of Victoria's reign.[30] In 1852 Niven designed the enormous Winter Garden for the Dublin Industrial Exhibition; in 1863, for the bigger International Exhibition, he was asked to lay out in the middle of Dublin a garden on 15 acres of ground, donated for the purpose by Sir Benjamin Lee Guinness Bt. Being in the city, it was the only garden designed by Niven which was not a foreground to a distant view. In fact, he surrounded the site with 'moundings', in which he threw up the earth excavated from the sunken gardens, around the perimeter to break up the flat surface of the site, or to conceal unsightly buildings outside, or to mask the walled boundaries of the garden. (The device was first used by Loudon in his design for the Derby Arboretum in 1839.) For the central portion of the garden the French style was chosen on account of its capacity to accommodate the great crowds thronging to the exhibition. From the gravelled esplanade in front of the Winter Garden, its curving retaining wall studded with ornamental vases on pedestals and figures of the female goddesses, the crowds descended on to a raised central walk which traversed the garden. On either side were sunken panels resplendent with flowers round raised circular basins, at the centre of which the Goddesses of Arts and Industry held aloft torches. From these *jets d'eau* reached skyward but fell in cascading droplets into the basin at the spectators' feet. The vista terminated in a great *rocher*, or rock-work. Modelled on Hubert Robert's Bains d'Apollo at Versailles, river gods disported themselves in a series of rocky niches at various levels, glistening in the cascades of water which fell from the upper levels of the rock-work into the basin below. In Dublin the cascades fell over the rocks and through a series of shady niches in which giant figures of river gods bathed in the falling water. The *rocher* was designed to be illuminated in the evenings in various colours, the water itself flowing in multi-coloured currents, as in Le Nôtre's unexecuted scheme for the *parterre d'eau* at Versailles. From here gravelled *allées*, lined with high cylinders of clipped hollies alternating with spire-like Lombardy poplars, led to the sunken archery green overlooked by Sir Benjamin Lee Guinness's Gothic gazebo at one end. On the other side the formal walks led into a number of meandering paths which passed through a woodland area, or *bosquet*, with a labyrinth, a rosarium and an American garden.

In the following years Niven designed elaborate formal settings for Santry Court[31] and for Templeogue,[32] both seats of Sir Compton Domvile Bt. in Co. Dublin. At Santry he laid down a formal *cour d'entrée* in front of the house and a sunken panel garden, flanked by raised walks with enfilades of Irish yews, leading to an oval terrace with a *jet d'eau* in an oval basin from which the park, its formal vistas and follies could be seen. The plan is similar to the central portion of the plan of Le Nôtre's nephew, Desgots, for Greenwich Park, London. Niven also designed a circular sunken garden round the 'Trianon' or cottage of Sir Compton's wife in the park. At Templeogue he recreated a formal setting in the French manner for a late seventeenth-century *rivière d'eau*, or cascade, which had long been neglected.

Niven's practice was as wide and varied as was nineteenth-century society. He laid out the grounds of grand hotels, such as those of the Royal Marine Hotel at Kingstown,[33] now much altered, and the pleasure-grounds of wealthy milling families like the Reeves at Athgarvan, Co. Kildare.[34]

At his own house, Garden Farm, Niven ran a market-gardening enterprise, a fashionable nursery, and a horticultural school where the students were imbued with the strict moral principles of 'self-denial, self-control, self-instruction and thorough fidelity', and practical horticulture in equal measure. In later life Niven took to

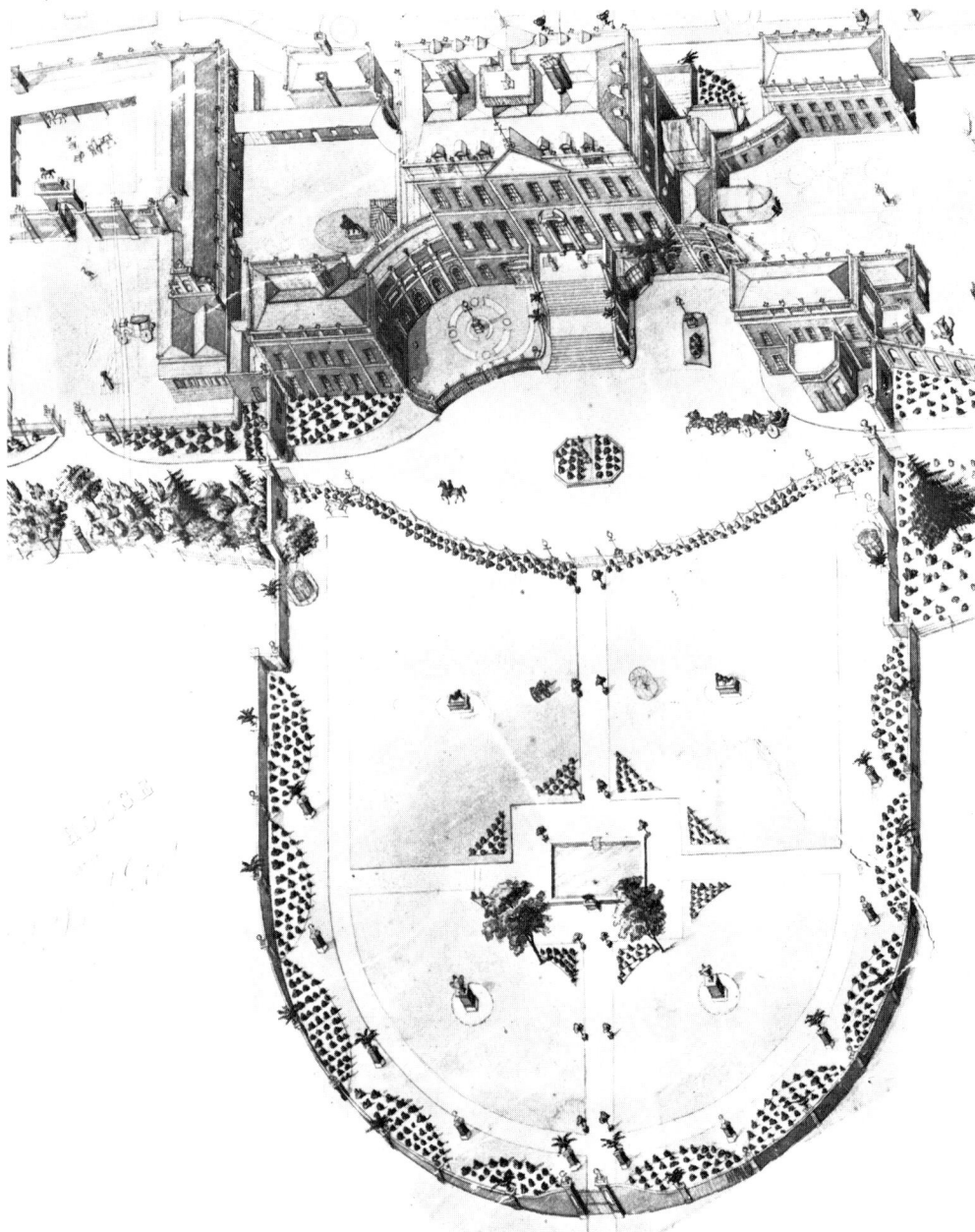

publishing evangelical tracts.[35] In his energies and interests he was a Victorian *par excellence*. He died at Garden Farm in February 1879.

That other more famous Victorian, Joseph Paxton (1803–65), unfortunately undertook only one major garden work in Ireland, that at Narrow Water Castle, Co. Down, but in 1848 he enlarged Lismore Castle, Co. Waterford, for his friend and patron, the Duke of Devonshire.[36] It stands in battlemented splendour on a rock overlooking the wooded valley of the Blackwater, with the spire of Lismore Cathedral and the five-arched bridge over the river completing the picturesque composition. Its walled garden with towers, terraces and battlements is the earliest garden extant in Ireland, dating from 1626. The fortified towers on the high terrace were converted into castellated summer-houses, affording splendid views of the Knockmealdown and Comeragh Mountains. A flight of steps, which leads to a centre walk between herbaceous borders backed by yew hedges, was laid out in dramatic alignment on the spire of the cathedral. This walk is romantically connected with the pleasure-grounds, below the castle by a first-floor level passage in the gate-house spanning the avenue, which were later laid out in Robinsonian style round an old avenue of English yews, still standing, planted in 1717. They boasted a unique floral parterre, whose pattern was based on an illuminated page of an ancient Celtic breviary which was one of the treasures of the castle.[37]

Some of Paxton's pupils worked in Ireland, including his assistant Edward Milner, who designed the parterre beds at Powerscourt (see p. 83) and, for the Gerrard family, an extensive terraced garden at Gibbstown Park, Co. Meath. This consisted of a series of massive raised beds, framed in cut stone, round a fountain with a remarkable bronze vase, with symbolical figures representing Night and Day (after Thorwaldsen) which had been exhibited at the International Exhibition in Dublin in 1852.[38] Another of Paxton's pupils, Mr Chapman, started to practise here in 1863[39], and James Howe (see p. 86) laid down a brick and gravel panel garden in front of the new 'château' at Straffan, Co. Kildare, of Mr Barton, the Bordeaux wine merchant.[40]

Other landscape gardeners were supplying plans for new parterres during the 1870s: a Mr Armour of Dublin created the parterres in front of Mr Cosby's new house at Stradbally Hall, Co. Leix;[41] a Mr Hockley designed a panelled garden at Leyrath, Co. Kilkenny.[42] Many such gardens were designed by architects rather than landscape gardeners, a fashion severely criticized by William Robinson later in the century. William Burn designed the terraces which connected his Elizabethan Revival mansion to the lake at Dartrey Co. Monaghan;[43] P. C. Hardwick designed

STRAFFAN HOUSE, CO. KILDARE. *The parterre, designed by James Howe, c. 1900.*

DARTREY CASTLE, CO. MONAGHAN. *The lake and terraces, c. 1900.*

ADARE MANOR, CO.
LIMERICK. *The parterre,
designed by P. C. Hardwick,
c. 1900.*
KILKENNY CASTLE,
CO. KILKENNY. *View
from the castle of the
parterre, c. 1900.*

GARDENMORRIS, CO.
WATERFORD. *The*
manoir *and formal
garden, c. 1890.*

KILKEA CASTLE, CO.
KILDARE. *The parterre
with its surrounding*
galerie, *c. 1900.*

a parterre in front of his façade at Adare Manor, Co. Limerick;[44] and Hungerford Pollen supplied a colour scheme for a parterre at Kilkenny Castle for the Marquess of Ormonde at the same time as he was decorating the Great Hall there.[45]

After the republication in 1865 of Du Cerceau's famous book on early French gardening and architecture, *Les Plus Excellents Bâtiments de France* (1576), there was a renewal of interest in the earlier sixteenth-century French style, which flourished in the reign of François I. Indeed, a number of houses, such as Gardenmorris, Co. Waterford, and Ramsfort, Co. Wexford, were rebuilt in the early asymmetrical style of French architecture. The gardens were characterized by the simplicity of their geometrical patterns and the arcaded galleries, derived from medieval cloisters, by which they were surrounded. The garden of Kilkea Castle, Co. Kildare, a seat of the Duke of Leinster, was of this character, as was the garden behind Bantry House, Co. Cork, although it had a gallery on one side only. On another it was overlooked by a glazed gallery like that designed by Richard Turner for Marlfield, Co. Tipperary. Further parterres in this simple geometric style (but without their surrounding galleries) were laid out by the Vicomte de Rohan Chabot at Thomastown Castle, Co. Tipperary, now sadly gone, and by Captain Hall at Narrow Water Castle, Co. Down.

BANTRY HOUSE, CO. CORK. *The conservatory, parterre and* galerie, *c. 1895.*

NARROW WATER CASTLE, CO. DOWN. *View of the parterre from the castle. c. 1900.*

SHELTON ABBEY, CO. WICKLOW. *The fan parterre, c. 1935.*

BARONSCOURT, CO. TYRONE. *The lake and ramped parterres, c. 1895.*

HILLSBOROUGH, CO. DOWN. *The ramped* allée, *c. 1895.*

HILLSBOROUGH, CO. DOWN. *The rotunda, c. 1895.*

More baroque compositions, however, like the fan parterre at Shelton Abbey, Co. Wicklow, continued to be carried out, and at Baronscourt, Co. Tyrone, the seat of the Duke of Abercorn, a great parterre was designed by Broderick Thomas, and, later, another by Ninian Niven to connect the first to the lakeside terrace. A ramped *allée* lined with Irish yews leads from the portico at Hillsborough, Co. Down, to a balustraded terrace by the lake, from which one can look over at a domed rotunda on the opposite bank. At Ramsfort, Co. Wexford, Stephen Ram returned from France in 1846 to recreate his family seat in the French style.[46] Below the newly extended house he cut a series of shallow grass terraces, linked by flights of steps. (The balustrade of one of these had been the altar rail of the church of Santo Stephano in Venice.) At the head of the river, which bisected the garden, there was a cascade with a single-arch bridge, forming the base for an elegent Italian temple. From the rustic seat therein the most glorious view up the length of the river, which had been widened to form a lake in front of the house, was obtained. On one of the islands, which was reached by a handsome bridge, was a small chapel with a campanile in the Romanesque style. A further campanile rose over the domestic chapel in the house, and yet a third from a convent which Ram had founded in the park and which must have assumed a monastic air, pleasing to this convert to Roman Catholicism. On an eminence north of the lake he raised an Italianate summer-house, over the entrance of which he had inscribed the words of Sir Francis Bacon: 'God Almighty first planted a garden; and, indeed it is the purest of human pleasures.' Today the Ramsfort gardens are being swallowed by an encroaching sea of laurel. The chapels, the temples, the bridges are gone; the margins of the lake are now blurred by reeds; the gate at the end of the vista is unpainted; and the shell in the fountain is cracked and broken.

A garden created in a similar mixture of French and Italian styles was St Anne's, Co. Dublin, begun in 1824 by Sir Benjamin Lee Guinness Bt. His first major work in the demesne was the construction of a sham ruin over the entrance drive to commemorate the birth of his eldest daughter, Annie Lee, in 1838. Sir Benjamin was an antiquary, interested not only in the ancient monuments of Ireland but also in those of classical Rome. St Anne's stood on a natural platform overlooking Dublin Bay, and behind it was the panorama of the Dublin and Wicklow Mountains, with the volcanic cones of the Great and Little Sugar Loaf Mountains silhouetted by the setting sun. The similarity to the Bay of Naples with Vesuvius in the background may have suggested to him the construction, in a walled garden next to the house, of a replica of a Herculanean house and garden,[47] and also a water-temple, based on a Pompeian model, on the artificial lake below the house. The walled garden was entered through a *claire-voie* screen of bronze which was painted yew green and

RAMSFORT, CO. WEXFORD. *The* manoir *and its terraces, c. 1895.*

ST ANNE'S, CO.
DUBLIN. *The house and its
conservatory designed by
Richard Turner, c. 1900.*

ST ANNE'S, DUBLIN.
The Yew Walk, c. 1900.

elaborately gilded. The centre walk was made into an outdoor sculpture gallery for a collection of marble statuary bought on Sir Benjamin's travels in Italy. As a background, a castellated yew hedge was made on either side, and the walk terminated in a nymphaeum, flanked by obelisks sculpted in yew, which contained in 1864 a sculpted group of Jupiter and Thetis, reputedly the work of G. L. Bernini.[48]

The rest of the garden at St Anne's was divided into quarters. In one was an aviary with golden pheasants; in another a floral temple of arches and chains in cast iron. Yet another was enclosed by a circular yew hedge with alcoves and arches in which stood allegorical Italian statues representing the five continents, all of which were reflected in the great circular marble basin which occupied the centre.[49] In the last was a perfect replica of a Herculanean dwelling, its courtyard and interior paved with tiles copied from a design found in the excavations. At the centre of the courtyard was a bronze figure of a Roman soldier, also discovered during the excavations at Herculaneum. The interior was entered through a wide, pillared doorway, and its windows, filled with stained glass, overlooked a romantic valley below.

From the walled garden a path led down through a rustic grotto, with the Hill of Howth framed in the principal arch, to the sheet of water in the valley. This was fed by the holy well of St Anne, from which the estate derived its name. Here the Pompeian water-temple, with its marble pillars, stood on a single arch of sea-worn boulders from the beach, and here shoals of carp swam to be fed. A path led up the

ST ANNE'S, DUBLIN.
*The Temple of the Julii,
c. 1900.*

48

ST ANNE'S, DUBLIN.
The Round Garden, c. 1900.

ST ANNE'S, DUBLIN.
*The Pompeian water-
temple, c. 1900.*
ST ANNE'S, DUBLIN.
*View from the temple over
the lake, c. 1900.*

valley, watered by a stream with many falls, both natural and artificial, and enriched with grottoes and bowers, a Gothic bridge, a secluded hermitage, and a Druidic circle of basaltic rocks taken from the Giant's Causeway.[50] At the top, one left the valley through another rustic archway and reached the clock-tower over the gates into the walled garden. From this point one could look back on the great façade of the house and, later, a splendid pile of red brick stables to the west. On the opposite side of the house a *grande terrasse* stretched away above the sea-shore, enclosed on the landward side by a tall yew hedge with alcoves for statuary and with arched openings into a chain of flower-gardens behind. At the end, a flight of steps led down to a similar terrace which revealed spectacular sea views along its length, until the walk terminated at a sham ruin.[51]

When the property was inherited by Sir Benjamin's son and daughter-in-law, Lord and Lady Ardilaun, in 1873, they enlarged the house to the designs of J. F. Fuller. Their lavish *palazzo* included a Palm Court with a domed conservatory designed by Richard Turner at one end.[52] During the reconstruction Lord and Lady Ardilaun removed the replica of the Roman Tomb of the Julii at St Remy, which Sir Benjamin had mounted in a dramatic way on the roof of his house, and rebuilt it on a wooded bluff overlooking the lake. They also erected the Georgian door-case of the original house as an entrance to a French lavender garden. Lord and Lady Ardilaun were Francophiles, and the house contained a remarkable collection of Napoleonic *objets d'art*. They laid out grand *allées*, mainly of evergreen oaks, Lord Ardilaun's favourite tree, thousands of which he raised from acorns each year. The *allées* radiated from the house, one aligned on the house itself, another on the spire of All Saints' Church at the north-east corner of the demesne, and another on a gate which was never constructed! A pair of pavilions erected in the grounds were absurdly called Café Blanc and Café Brun, in imitation of Parisian cafés, and they had an arcade of tall elms framing the view from the house.[53] St Anne's was subsequently acquired by Dublin Corporation. In its care the house was vandalized and eventually demolished. The grounds are now a public park, but the old temples and follies still lie neglected.

Ashford Castle, Cong, Co. Galway, was another Guinness seat with an eclectic mixture of styles. Bought by Sir Benjamin Lee Guinness as a shooting-lodge in 1852, it was enlarged, in château style, with a great circular stone basin in front to reflect its new roofline. Sir Benjamin's son, Lord Ardilaun, had it entirely altered, to the designs of Fuller, into the battlemented castle we see today. Around it he constructed embattled outworks, towers, a castellated bridge and gate-house, which give the castle the appearance of an island fortress reflected in the still waters of Lough Corrib. It still retains, however, many of the formal gardens and vistas, which were also laid out by the Ardilauns.[54] Lady Ardilaun later recounted a visit to Ashford by Oscar Wilde, aged eighteen. After lunch, they went out to look at the recently completed gardens. Thinking Oscar might feel shy, she turned to him:

"Do you like my garden?"

"No," he said clearly, "it is very dull." Quite taken aback, I exclaimed, "What do you mean?"

"I mean that it is very dull. Don't you think so?"

"Don't you think my initials are well done?"

"Yes, but I don't care for them done in bedding plants, even if they are your initials."

"The gardener wanted to do the family crest, but as it's a pig, I wouldn't let him." I told him.

"Oh, you should have; it would have been the perfect culmination of absurdity," he replied.

Oscar got quite excited picturing how the picture could be done, suggesting flesh-coloured begonias for the body and a houseleek, round and prickly for the eye, and love-lies bleeding pegged down in twiddles for the tail.[55]

ASHFORD CASTLE, CO. MAYO. *The Round Pond.*

KYLEMORE CASTLE, CO. GALWAY. *The castle and church designed by J. F. Fuller, c. 1895.*

KYLEMORE CASTLE, CO. GALWAY. *The conservatories with parterre designed by Mr Garnier on Cranstons' Patent, c. 1895.*

Lady Ardilaun strangely attributed her later deep interest in gardening to the shock that Oscar had given her on that occasion.

Kylemore Castle near by was also erected (1864–68) to the designs of J. F. Fuller for the Manchester industrialist Mitchell Henry. This granite castle, situated on a terrace overlooking Lough Pollecoppal, is surrounded by an amphitheatre of mountains sloping to the water's edge. During the creation of the gardens by his gardener, Mr Garnier, the public road had to be moved to the opposite shore of the lake at Mr Mitchell's expense. Mr Garnier planted acres of trees on the mountain sides, planted a pinetum in 1875, and designed, *c.* 1890, a huge Gothic conservatory on Cranston's Patent.[56]

One of the great gardens of the day was at Woodstock, Co. Kilkenny, the seat of W. F. Tighe and his wife, Lady Louisa, who as a girl had spent some time in France and in Belgium, where her mother, the Duchess of Richmond and Gordon, had given the famous ball on the evening before the battle of Waterloo. Woodstock had a remarkable setting on a high plateau above the deep gorge of the river Nore and below a high hill known as Mount Alto. In 1860 a Scotsman, Charles Macdonald, came there as head gardener, having been previously employed at Dalkeith, near Perth, under Charles MacIntosh, author of *The Book of the Garden* (1850), then at Trentham Hall, Staffordshire, and Dunrobin Castle, Scotland, where he had designed a formal parterre round the dairy. Both Trentham and Dunrobin have French parterres laid out in front of them by the great Victorian partners Sir Charles Barry and W. A. Nesfield. Macdonald's early years were therefore spent in the shadow of these great Victorian gardeners and designers.[57]

WOODSTOCK, CO. KILKENNY. *The parterre designed by Charles Macdonald, c. 1895.*

WOODSTOCK, CO. KILKENNY. *The terrace garden leading to the conservatory designed by Richard Turner, c. 1895.*

On his arrival at Woodstock Macdonald started to construct a formal parterre of four sunken panels in front of the house. The levelling required the removal of 200,000 cubic yards of earth and retention by a cut granite wall of stone, quarried on the estate and ornamented by local masons with granite vases, balls and finials. A delicately detailed iron staircase, flanked by a pair of Warwick vases,[58] was designed by Richard Turner to join the drawing-room of the house to the parterre below.[59] The two nearer panels, in an embroidered design in box with a red gravel background, were in the style of a *parterre des pièces coupées*. It appropriately incorporated a shamrock motif and a variety of colour in the design – cotton lavender, Japanese laurel, Alexandrian laurel, butcher's broom, as well as the greens of Portugal laurel, laurustinus, box and yew. The scroll-work was then filled with a variety of coloured gravels obtained on the estate. The further pair of sunken panels was designed as a St Andrew's cross, with one pair of the resultant triangles filled with scroll-work in a Grecian honeysuckle design, and the other pair filled with flowers.[60]

From the raised parterre the eye ran over ten miles of undulating country. Through the trees three distinct openings were made: one a vista to the river, another to a ruined tower, and a third to a neighbouring house. Below was a formal croquet lawn, and at a lower level still was a formal canal. On the upper level a walk led up through an arboretum, whose principal feature was an avenue of 130 monkey-puzzles, *Araucaria araucana*, one tree rivalling a tree at Dropmore, Buckinghamshire, as the biggest in cultivation.[61] The walk then led through a rockery, formed in the quarry from which the stone for the terraces had been obtained. The boulders were arranged in broken mimic cliffs, in low scattered masses on the ground, as miniature islands in pools.

Through a circular bulb garden and an egg-shaped rosarium one finally reached the terrace garden, planned before Mr Macdonald's arrival by Lady Louisa herself. The main terrace led to a circular, domed conservatory, one of Richard Turner's finest works. The dome's glass was light blue, and the walls light grey, inset with beautiful specimens of stained glass on which the family armorial bearings and quarterings were emblazoned. A vista in the other direction was terminated by a superb semicircular iron seat, with a honeysuckle motif, painted in blue and gold, probably also the work of Turner. The terrace itself had a rope design of box-edged beds filled with red and white gravels quarried on the estate. A long drive by the river below led to a picturesque glen, where a resort for public picnics, dancing and Irish fiddling was laid out. It was centred round the Red House, a Swiss Cottage overlooking a tangled 100-ft ravine, over which a cascade tumbled into the rocky depths below. Above it was Lady Louisa's private summer-house in rustic style, decorated with bones and antlers.[62]

53

The floral parterre, or the *parterre des fleurs*, was also born in France at the Grand Trianon of Versailles, where the garden attributed to Michel Le Bouteux (gardener to the Duc de Vendôme) had an abundance of flowers. In this particular garden the Soirées de Trianon were conducted on a magnificent scale, the flowers in the parterre being changed each evening. On one evening Louis XIV and his court were obliged to leave the gardens as his more sensitive courtiers fainted, on account of the over-powering scent of the tuberoses. In the nineteenth century bedding was normally changed three times a year, in spring, summer and autumn – sometimes more frequently. At Castle Leslie, Co. Monaghan, the colour scheme of the parterre was changed for each day of a house party.[63] Gardeners would quietly remove the flowers of the previous day and replant in a new colour scheme, tidying up the previous days' growth of the box edging and spraying it with an appropriate scent before the guests came down to breakfast. It was expected in most gardens that the bedding-out design would be different each year, so at the end of each season, vast quantities of tulip bulbs, begonia tubers and the like were sold off, and a new lot of a new colour or a recently raised cultivar brought in. The head gardeners of the great Victorian gardens were therefore besieged by bands of thrusting nursery salesmen, wanting to sell them their firm's latest calceolaria or pelargonium for next year's bedding scheme. The new plants were of varying quality and, not unnaturally, many head gardeners became confused with this new-found abundance and variety. Some cautiously tried them out in trial beds in the walled garden before placing them in a position of importance in the parterre the following year.

W. E. Gumbleton (1840–1911) of Belgrove, Great Island, Co. Cork, took on the task of independently testing the new plants as they came on the market and conveying his results in a public-spirited way to the horticultural world through the columns of the gardening press.[64] In order to acquire as many species and varieties as possible he corresponded with the heads of botanical institutions all over the world, frequently visiting England and the Continent, in particular France, to view the latest varieties growing in their nurseries. In 1870 he was testing a new hybrid gladiolus series from M. Lemoine of Nancy; in 1875 he was growing Souchet's gladiolus series from France, a *Hydrangea serrata* 'Rosalba' from Van Houtte's in Holland, and a collection of bedding-plants from Herr Max Leichtlin's famous garden at Baden-Baden. Some years later he had spotted zonal pelargoniums, of various degrees of marking, from M. Brouant of Poitiers, dahlias from M. Roebel of Zurich and M. Thibaut of Sceaux, deutzias from M. Lemoine, browallias in the conservatory from Sanders, calceolarias from the great English nurseries of Veitch and Carwells, and verbascum varieties from Mr Smith of Newry, Co. Down.

In 1876, still not to be outdone, Gumbleton was testing cannas from Sprenger, Lemoine and Bruant, gazanias from Lemoine and Pfitzer of Stuttgart, *Feijowa sellowiana* from M. Monet of Lyons, begonias from Rev. Edwin Lascelles of Newton St Loe, Bath, and a host of Mexican plants from the Montarioso Nursery in Santa Barbara, California. *Buddleia colvilei*, grown under the shelter of a high wall, flowered for the first time in cultivation at Belgrove in 1891; *Azara microphylla* 'Variegata' originated there; and the garden still possesses one of the largest *Magnolia campbellii* in existence. An insatiable and thorough collector, Gumbleton possessed one of the best botanical libraries in these islands and this he left to the National Botanic Garden at Glasnevin. Yet such was the horticultural glut in his garden that a visitor in 1891 was obliged to finish his account in *The Gardeners' Chronicle* thus:

It will be understood from the above that Belgrove is stocked with objects of interest, and one follows another with rapid succession, and Mr. Gumbleton has the history of each ready for you, that it is with a certain sense of relief that you at last hear him say: "And that is all I have to show you; good morning."

Since Gumbleton's death, the garden has sadly deteriorated, but it still possesses a remarkable collection of rare trees and shrubs of unusual size.

In Ireland almost every house of consequence or public park of any size had a floral parterre. There were noteworthy ones at Castle Bernard, Co. Cork, and at

BELGROVE, CO. CORK. *Mr W. E. Gumbleton in his garden, c. 1905.*

Kilruddery, Co. Wicklow, in front of William Burn's Great Conservatory, but the genre seems to have reached its zenith at the neighbouring demesnes of St Helen's, the seat of Viscount Gough,[65] and Mount Merrion, Co. Dublin, the seat of the Earl of Pembroke.[66] Their proximity sharpened their rivalry. At St Helen's 72,000 plants a year were required for the parterre, which extended over four shallow terraces and overlooked Dublin Bay to the north. The fifty species of succulent which made up the winter bedding and the swell of the floral diapason in spring and summer were intermingled with the trophies of Field-Marshal Gough. The design of some of the beds, we are told, was based on the medals which hung on his breast; the Bell Terrace was named after the bell he had taken from the Temple of Heaven in Peking; and the conservatory was hung with grim relics of the Afghan War.

More orthodox and attractive was the bedding scheme at Mount Merrion. In a walled garden, not round the house because of the elevation of the site, Lady Pembroke laid out an elaborate floral system of harmonizing, contrasting and toning colours, interplanted with foliage plants to cool the glare of the floral colours. A floral parterre was usually ornamented with a central sculpted vase or statuary. Often it was of groups of playful children in the Versailles tradition – in Louis XIV's words, there was childhood everywhere. This was copied in the parterres of Castle Blayney, Headfort, Johnstown Castle, and in front of the Earl of Mayo's 'château' built at Palmerstown, Co. Kildare, in 1872. The great industrial and craft exhibitions provided sculpted groups for many Victorian gardens, such as the bronze group of the shepherd attacked by the tiger which Mr Adair bought for his gardens at Bellegrove, Co. Leix, at the Great Dublin Exhibition of 1863.[67] Many ornaments, such as the terracotta pots in the parterre at Dunsany Castle, were made and supplied by Mr Lavender of Grafton Street, Dublin.[68]

The most striking ornaments of the Irish Victorian garden were the glasshouses of Richard Turner of the Hammersmith Iron Foundry, Dublin. He designed and manufactured a curvilinear glasshouse which, with its domes, barrel-vaulted galleries and apses of light and elegant cast-iron, resembled *treillage* pavilions of eighteenth-century France or the *galeries de charpenterie* of a sixteenth-century garden. The great glasshouses at the botanical gardens at Kew, Belfast and Glasnevin were either partly or wholly designed by him, as was the house in the Royal Horticultural Society's former garden in Regent's Park. His smaller ones are more exquisite in their detail – be they free-standing circular ones as at Woodstock, Co. Kilkenny, attached to the house as at Marlfield, Co. Tipperary,[69] or like the pair formerly at Gracedieu, Co. Waterford.[70] The most beautiful of all is the elegant glasshouse at Ballyfin, Co. Leix. Turner also produced cheaper and more modest houses, as at

MARLFIELD, CO.
TIPPERARY. *The
conservatory designed by
Richard Turner, 1978.*
BALLYFIN, CO. LEIX.
*The conservatory designed by
Richard Turner, 1975.*

CAHIR PARK, CO.
TIPPERARY. *The river,
Swiss Cottage, and the bridge
designed by Richard
Turner.*

Roebuck Castle, Co. Dublin,[71] and a number of demesne bridges of unusual structure such as the one at Cahir Park, Co. Tipperary, which has now, unfortunately, been taken down.[72]

Conservatories in Ireland appeared in a number of different styles. For example, one at Bellegrove, Co. Leix, was designed by Sir Thomas Deane with pairs of terracotta pillars, cast from models of those in San Giovanni Laterano in Rome;[73] another, designed by William Burn at Kilruddery, was in the Early English style and had a pierced balustrade like that at Dalkeith Palace in Scotland; and a third, at Glenmaroon, Co. Dublin, was in the Gothic style.[74] Built in 1862, it had a floor of Minton tiles in blue and white, and the planting within it and around it was always in the same blue and white colour scheme, a discipline which had previously been adopted round the Trianon de Porcelaine at Versailles.

Many glasshouses had ferneries attached to them, as the Victorian fern craze had many adherents in Ireland, particularly among the wealthy professional and

BELLEGROVE, CO.
LEIX. *The ruins of the
conservatory, designed by
Sir Thomas Deane.
Drawing by Jeremy
Williams, c. 1975.*
KILRUDDERY, CO.
WICKLOW. *The parterre
and conservatory designed by
William Burn, c. 1910.*

KILRUDDERY, CO.
WICKLOW. *The interior of
the conservatory, c. 1910.*

merchant classes of the suburbs of Dublin and Belfast. The most elaborate was that
of Edward Westby of Roebuck Castle, Co. Dublin.[75] Built by Kennans of Dublin in
1876 to the designs of Moncur and MacKenzie, it was divided into two areas by an
elaborate curtain of rockery, one for temperate ferns, the other for tropical ferns,
designed by a specialist, Mr Biggs of Chester. Various picturesque features were
incorporated in this rock-work, such as a stalactite cavern whose dome was mirrored
in the waters of a shallow pool, fed by a tiny rivulet that wound its way through the
fernery. A path led up to the summit of a mass of rock, whose cavernous pockets,
deep fissures and apparently time-worn hollows were fringed and draped with the
most elegant ferns, and the peaks, breaks and spurs were very well contrived. Just
before a visitor left the fernery his attention was unpleasantly arrested by an overhanging crag which seemed poised at a dangerously threatening angle, and his
apprehension was not lessened by the apparent severance of a supporting span of
rock. Such a structure was of course feigned, a further illustration of Mr Biggs's

curious skill. After the rock-work had been completed, Mr Bracken, a garden artist, was employed to paint and tint it to give an appearance of age!

The ferneries of Mrs White at Killakee[76] and Mr Valentine, a mining and railway magnate at Glenavna, near Belfast, were similar in that each was composed of a central enfilade of rustic arches, studded with shells and clothed with ferns, mosses and begonias, flanked by aisles of smaller arches similarly clothed. The central perspective at Killakee had a suite of oval basins with *jets d'eau*, and was terminated at one end in a rustic alcove sheltering a marble statue and at the other by a cascade falling into a goldfish pool, decorated along the edge with petrified wood from the Scottish mines. The glass roofs were covered with tacsonias (Banana Passion Fruit) and *Ficus repens* forming an exquisite drapery all over the house. The central aisle at Glenavna had a cascade shaded by 6-ft-long fronds of *Woodwardia radicans*, and opposite was a rock-work ascent, from the summit of which one could look across at the cascade and down into the crests of the ferns growing below. The centrepiece was a great pile of rocks liberally planted with dracaenas, yuccas, begonias, todeas, and above all, a *Monstera deliciosa*, the very name of which is redolent of the jungle-like ambience of a fernery.

The fernery imparts a kind of superstitious awe, especially to those who have ever imbibed a taste for fairy lore, as you might reasonably expect to see one start from amongst the ferns, or a water-sprite from out a cavernous well, darkly shaded by rich plants and creeping foliage.[77]

The Victorian fancy for fairy lore, fed by such poems as Christina Rossetti's *Goblin Market*, and the fairy paintings of Richard Doyle and Richard Dadd, grew alongside an appreciation for the fernery landscape.

ROCKVILLE, CO. DUBLIN. *A side aisle of the fernery, c. 1910.*

58

The most elaborate series of greenhouses belonged to Thomas Bewley (1810–75), a remarkable Dublin businessman, at Rockville,[78] in Blackrock, another suburb. Its construction and the gorgeousness of its decoration were unsurpassed in Ireland at that time. It was composed of three arched aisles with shingle floors leading to a great rock mass at the end. The arches were formed in slate stone from the lead mines of Co. Wicklow and sprang from a variety of rugged pillars and pedestals, ornamented with linings of red granite. The joints in the rustic work were left open to simulate age or decay. Hanging in leafy profusion, ferns, lycopods, begonias and *Ficus repens* drooped so abundantly that it was necessary to push them aside to get through. The walls were composed of petrified limestone (tufa), niches in them being planted with great groups of ferns, as if lining a cave. The plate-glass roof was covered with climbing plants which also hung down into the aisles round an enormous *Chamaerops humilis* in the centre. The rock-work was of so many materials that it would have furnished matter for a geological study: Ballycorus clay slate, red granite, grey granite, quartz, red sandstone, conglomerate, tufa and petrified moss. There were numerous niches and recesses, and a winding path through a tunnel led to the summit. From here one could look down into the crests of the finest tree ferns in Europe – one a *Dicksonia antarctica*, 20 ft across. Begonias drooped naturally from high ledges, one 'Queen Victoria' begonia draping itself over nearly 5 ft of a perpendicular mass of red granite, its roots clinging to the stone like ivy. Elsewhere, an *Alsophila macarthuri*, one of the most elegant of tree ferns, sprang from a mass of purple conglomerate, and near it was a fine *Alsophila australis*, canopied over a moss-covered heap of old red sandstone from which it was easy to raise young ferns from spores. The sloping sides of the rock-work were hung with exotic vines, hoyas, bignonias, Bourbon palms, cinnamons and cassias. One visitor thought this fernery was gloomy, catacomb-like, unnatural and funereal – 'It bristled all over with art' – but to William Robinson it was reminiscent of Darwin's impressions of the quiet gloom of the Brazilian rain forest. In truth, in these ferneries a rich and cultivated European might enjoy on home ground some of the excitements of this tropical jungle described by Darwin in *The Voyage of the Beagle*. Another visitor thought he had come 'on the ruins of a once sacred fane, over which, now deserted alike by priest and devotee, vegetation is gradually but surely exercising dominion'. For another the wreathed buttresses, the draped arches and the luxuriant atmosphere conjured up the ruins of the buildings of a forgotten race such as are found in Central America, where vegetation in wild, melancholy grandeur is obliterating the evidence of any previous civilization.

The Victorians thought there was a strong moral force behind the passion for ferns, that their dull greenery was a desirable reflection of the quiet and even tenor of Victorian family life! Brilliant displays of bedding-plants were said to engage the attention only of 'the inobservant or the careless'. However, such high-mindedness was not the source of the contemporary cult of the orchid, for their *louche* beauty and sexual mores were the subject of intense interest, once Darwin had published his remarkable book on *The Fertilization of Orchids* (1862). J. C. Lyons of Ladeston, Co. Meath, had previously written an excellent handbook on their cultivation,[79] and Mr Pope of Glasnevin had supplied Darwin with many orchid species for his research, but Mr Bewley's collection was undoubtedly the finest, including some specimens from the famous Mrs Lawrence's collection, others from Mr Reed's, and a *Cattleya superba* which was said to be a match for the famous plant at La Mortola.[80]

At Rockville grew lycopodiums imported from Ceylon, ferns from Burma, and scores of West Indian orchids, collected by Bewley's own private explorer-botanist, now unknown to us. Many were bought at Stevens's orchid auctions in London, where the hammer often fell at a hundred guineas for some of the great forest orchids. These treasures were grown not in pots but in landscaped settings inside the glass-houses simulating their tropical habitats exactly, ferns and fine-leaved plants native to the orchids' region making green backgrounds for the bright violets, purples and oranges of the orchids' flowers. Climbing plants were trained to suspend gracefully from the roofs, as, for example, from the roof of the East Indian house, *Cissus discolor*, which fell in long streaming sheets 'in regulated wild abandon and grandeur'. So powerful was the effect on one visitor that he imagined that by the spell of a magician he had been carried in a mesmeric sleep over continent and ocean only to open his eyes to gaze upon a tropical forest scene.

At one end through a curtain of rock-work one entered the Killarney fern house, a charming cave-like structure, with hundreds of Killarney ferns planted over the rugged slopes, arches and fissures, the only light being admitted through tiny stained-glass windows set deep into the walls. William Robinson wrote in *The Gardeners' Chronicle* that the collection was sufficient to make the fame of a ducal garden, an oblique reference to that of the Duke of Devonshire at Chatsworth, whose only rival at that time was a friend of the Queen, the redoubtable Mrs Lawrence of Ealing Park, where half the crowned heads of Europe were said to have come to watch her rarities in flower. Mr Bewley's visitors from all over the world were so numerous that he was obliged to build a special area for their reception and also to construct special paths behind the array of plants in each house, so that his gardeners could tend them while visitors filed down the centre aisle.

A further delightful conceit was to bring exotic desserts on the tree or bush to the table, so that guests might perhaps have orange trees behind them in full fruit, or decorative pots of strawberries standing in the centre of the table with fruit ripe for the picking. In Mr Bewley's light and airy orchard house grew oranges and lemons, limes, peaches, nectarines and myrtleberries. Young vines clambered on the roof, and the beds were edged with a rich and tempting margin of strawberries! William Robinson wrote that Mr Rivers of Sawbridgeworth, the popularizer of this conceit, had no such Orchard House, but that Mr Bewley's was landscaped to combine 'the comforts and advantages of a winter garden with those of a Persian fruit grove'. The visitor was led back to reality through a long glazed arcade, from which he looked through Gothic arches of tufa into the garden outside. Of all this nothing remains, as the garden has been razed to the ground for a housing estate. *Sic transit gloria mundi.*

GLENART, CO. WICKLOW. *The garden, designed by William Shepherd, c. 1900.*

It was such romantic conceptions as these, with begonias growing naturally over rock-work rather than in rows of pots, with orchids growing in landscaped settings rather than on shelves, and with tree ferns grown in old red sandstone to encourage natural regeneration, that led eventually to the decline of the formal French influence on Irish gardening in the late nineteenth century. In the first place Ninian Niven's assistant and pupil William Sheppard reverted to Niven's earlier intermediate style for his garden for the Earl of Carysfort at Glenart Castle, Co. Wicklow,[81] where the main vista curves up the hill to the conservatory and tower, designed by John McGurdy, as the unexecuted design by Niven for Monkstown Castle (see p. 38) was to curve similarly up a hill to an observatory at the summit. The same easy blend of the French and English styles is evident in Sheppard's series of designs for Dublin parks – St Stephen's Green, Palmerston Park and Harold's Cross Park.[82] In his design for Glencormac, Co. Wicklow,[83] for W. R. Jameson, the distiller, however, he abandoned the formal style altogether. Begun in 1881, it consists of a superb collection of trees planted in a park-like manner among undulating hills, with streams and dripping cliffs providing naturalistic focal points, and a scenic backdrop provided by the looming shadows of the Great and Little Sugar Loaf Mountains. William Sheppard, who began his career with Niven in the design of gardens in the formal French taste, had succumbed to the increasing influence of William Robinson and his theory of the 'wild garden'.

3 Arboreta and Pineta: Collectors' Paradises

An arboretum or pinetum is usually thought of as a collection of trees, arranged either at random or botanically, with paths, rides and vistas cutting through it. Despite the beauty of individual trees, this format can be of interest only as arboriculture or dendrology, which according to Sir Ilay Campbell, the famous dendrologist of Crarae, 'is the science of the cultivation of trees and shrubs for decorative purposes'.[1] Science in this respect should clearly become the handmaid of art, and unless this relationship is upheld in the design of an arboretum, interest in specimens can only be botanical or out of admiration for the thoroughness of the collector. The finest arboreta in the world, such as at Westonbirt, Gloucestershire, and the Huntington Botanical Gardens, California, are planted in a form which is pictorial. A beauty of form makes them superior to any mere collection of trees, however rare or fine individual specimens may be.

In the past arboreta have often been planted as separate areas in parkland or pleasure-grounds, yet in the best the plantsman has always been aware of the relationship of one to the other. At first they were planted quite formally in relation to the other pleasure-grounds – an arc of trees as at Coolattin, or an avenue from the house as at Hamwood, and even separate avenues of monkey-puzzles as at Powerscourt. Sometimes the formality of planting went further, as at Mount Shannon, Co. Limerick, where the 1st Earl of Clare planted a pinetum, from seed which he had collected on diplomatic missions, within a circle of Irish yews. Similarly, Hans Hamilton planted his pinetum at Abbotstown, Co. Dublin, in the 1860s within a circle of Deodar cedars. Today mixed arboreta informally arranged are the fashion, as at Kildangan, and conifers have to fit into general planting schemes with deciduous trees.

Loudon in his remarks on the pleasure-ground recommended there should be walks to an arboretum or fruticetum passing wood-houses, moss-houses, root-houses, rock-houses, Swiss cottages, covered seats of wood or stone, temples, ruins, grottoes or caverns. Gertrude Jekyll summarized this in far less elaborate terms: 'It is upon the right relationship of the garden to the house that its value and the enjoyment that is to be derived from it will largely depend. The connection must be intimate and the access not only convenient, but inviting.' Nevertheless, an arboretum is not just a woodland garden after the pattern of William Robinson, however rare the planting; if it were, Mount Usher would be included in this chapter. The many rare and fine trees there are planted primarily as shelter for tender shrubs such as eucryphias, crinodendrons, olearias and others. If an arboretum or pinetum seems to have been, or still is, the chief feature of an estate, we include it in this chapter; although the arboreta at Powerscourt and Birr Castle are among the finest in Ireland, for reasons which we hope will be evident these have been included in Chapters 4 and 7.

The only indigeneous British gymnosperms are *Pinus sylvestris* (Scots Pine), *Juniperus Communis* and *Taxus baccata* (English Yew), though picea and abies species were present in inter-glacial times. Foreign conifers fascinated the nineteenth-century traveller, a reader of Darwin and Hooker, as much as details of Greek architecture had intrigued his classically educated predecessor in the eighteenth century. Just as a young man on the grand tour journeyed to see the caryatid porticoes of the Erechtheion, the structure of the Choragic Monument of Lysicrates, or the sculptured metopes of the Parthenon, so a hundred years later his successor would gaze at the whorling blue-green needles of *Cedrus atlantica* or the sprays of *Thuja plicata* or the drooping branches of *Picea breweriana*. Typical is Sir Victor

Brooke, friend of Lords Annesley and Powerscourt, who in 1894 writes to his wife from California:

You will remember my mania for pines long ago at Powerscourt, and my great studies of old P———'s books. Well fancy my joy driving for days through the homes of these noble trees, gazing right and left at trees, rearing their heads on mighty columns 20 and 25 feet in circumference on all sides of us. Then the great interest of making out what they were, for I can assure you the difference between an infant pine in a pleasure ground of twenty or thirty years old and a veteran of the same tree in his native home, five hundred years old and 250 feet high, is very great.

And again, when he is in the Yosemite Valley:

Crossing the river, close to the hotel, we saw our first *Abies douglasii* [Pseudotsuga menziesii] . . . Forest chiefly *Picea ponderosa* [Picea asperata] which certainly gets bigger the higher you go. Some grand sugar pines. [*Pinus lambertiana*.] One fallen tree measured 20′ circumference, and the trunk 60 yards: allowing 20′ for the top, which is missing, cut off, would make it 200′ high. Distinguished the difference between *Picea grandis* and Nordmann's fir [Abies nordmanniana]. The former is slightly darker, and has the needles much more distinctly compressed from above downwards. Ditto the entire branch. It is found at higher elevation. Both trees attain about the same size as very large silver firs.[2]

Many Irish arboreta were started in Victorian times but on the whole these are later than their English or Scottish counterparts, from which seeds often came to Irish planters. Conifers or taxads, conic, columnar and symmetrical, furnished neatly to the ground, as compared with wantonly branched broad-leaved trees, were the equivalent of the Victorian parterre, appealing to the Victorians' sense of formality and neatness in gardening. Many of these exotic conifers (i.e., belonging naturally or originally to another part of the world) grew well in the Irish climate on the eastern seaboard as well as in the south-west, and this undoubtedly encouraged collectors. For example, a *Picea brewerana* planted in 1924 at Castlewellan from seeds from the Scottish arboretum at Dawyck was 35 ft by 5 ft 2 in in 1970, whereas the original Dawyck trees planted in 1908 were only 42 ft by 3 ft 5 in at the same date.[3] Likewise at Fota a *Cedrus atlantica glauca* planted in 1850 was 108 ft by 10 ft 11 in in 1966, whereas the original planted at Eastnor Castle ten years earlier was only 110 ft by 16 ft 9 in in 1961.

Although some of the newly made forest parks today have sections of arboreta left from the eighteenth century, their overall layout is primarily designed as block planting. For instance, the first stop on the Exotic Tree Trail at Avondale Forest Park, Co. Wicklow, is at a plantation of giant eucalypts. These have been planted because their hard, heavy, wood is used for construction work, not because their pink bark, grey spear-shaped leaves, growth and form contrast so beautifully with native trees. This plan was the result of a collaboration between A. C. Forbes, the Director of Forestry, and Augustine Henry, the great Irish botanist-explorer. Widely travelled, Henry had been on the medical staff of the Chinese Imperial Maritime Customs Service at Shanghai. After travels into the interior of China he sent 16,000 specimens of dried plants and seeds to Kew – in 1896 alone some 500 species and 25 genera of flora from the gorges and mountains along the Yangtse Kiang, 1,000 miles from the sea. The beauty of some of these trees and shrubs later induced Messrs Veitch to send out E. H. Wilson to obtain them in a living state. After returning to Ireland from Asia, Henry started his great and now rare work, *The Trees of Great Britain and Ireland*, with Henry John Elwes, a landowner of Colesbourne, Gloucestershire, and eventually Henry became Professor of Forestry at the Royal College of Science, Dublin. Forbes and Henry planted a series of 1-acre plots at Avondale, after the pattern of Continental forestry. A grove of trees and a memorial stone there recognizes Henry's pioneering work as a tree breeder and foreseer of scientifically produced forests.

Such forest parks belonging to departments of agriculture are necessary for all interested in arboriculture and sylviculture. Yet despite their being superbly sited,

as at Avondale, Shelton Abbey,[4] and Tollymore where there was much eighteenth-century planting, the present layout is by forest plots, each section containing species belonging to the same natural order or genus, 'the object being that of combining the planting of these with a forestry school for working foresters and woodmen'.[5] Indeed, the success or failure of different species in this planting is of vital interest to owners of arboreta, but unless the trees are planted 'for decorative purposes' they cannot be considered as gardening or landscaping.

One of the best-known estates with a fine arboretum in mid-Victorian times was Earl Annesley's at Castlewellan,[6] near Newcastle, Co. Down. A Scottish baronial castle of blue-grey local granite, built to the design of William Burn between 1856 and 1860, it stands high on two long terraces with garlanded urns (by the same architect) and looks down to a lake, with views from the windows to Slieve Donard and the deep-toned range of the Mourne Mountains. From the towers of the castle and the highest points of the garden a panorama spreads out across the Bay of Dundrum to the Isle of Man. Many generations have appreciated the spot scenically, and in order to build the present castle a 'beautiful Gothic Temple, for rest and pleasure, lifting its spheric cone among the mountains with great grandeur' was demolished.[7] Castlewellan is only three miles from the sea and therefore has few frosts; facing east and south, it is well sheltered from the prevailing wind by trees in the deer park (Slieve na Slat) at the back. The average rainfall is 35 in, and the

CASTLEWELLAN, CO.
DOWN. *The walled
garden, c. 1920.*

soil is light, acid gravel (Silurian shale) in which anything will grow with a little phosphate added.

The garden was started by William Annesley, before he was raised to the peerage, as early as 1740 – the high brick walls of the kitchen-garden are his – but the present castle and gardens were the work of William Richard, 4th Earl Annesley, about 100 years later. Many writers, including R. C. Jenkinson, have stated that it was 'his brother Hugh, who succeeded him, who started to lay out the gardens and extensive woodlands'.[8] But this cannot have been so because the correspondent of *The Gardeners' Chronicle* of 1872, two years before the 5th Earl succeeded, lists many trees planted and growing, as well as the main vista of the pleasure-grounds. Ten wellingtonias were already 27 ft high, a *Rhododendron ponticum* was 207 ft in circumference and 18 ft high, many *Araucaria araucana* (Monkey-Puzzles) were 30 ft, and the double-tiered Italian basin and fountain were already in position on the sloping central axis of the garden, where they could be seen from nearly every part of the grounds. The glasshouses, vineries and conservatories also contained many plants, among them *Dicksonia antarctica, Cordyline indivisa,* and *Phormium tenax* (New Zealand Flax) which Hugh, 5th Earl Annesley, afterwards grew out-of-doors in sheltered and frostless positions. There must have been some studied regularity in the midst of this planting, for the Portugal laurels, some 200 of them in avenues and single trees, all clipped into domed heads, were interplanted throughout the arboretum as in a French

65

formal garden. Solid masses of golden colour were distributed throughout by planting many *Chamaecyparis pisifera* 'Plumosa Aurea', which had been introduced from Japan in the 1860s. The purple of many cut-leaf maples contrasted with conifers in the autumn, and at the same time of year *Cryptomeria japonica* 'Elegans' turned a bronze red. Irish yews provided contrasts.

The gardeners seem to have been as well treated as the plants. The head gardener's house was built to face south and 'was supplied with every convenience requisite for the health and well-being of the inhabitants: a capital lavatory is placed in the interior, and is a nice addition not often thought of'.[9] The same correspondent remarks on the method of planting bays, Portugal laurels, *Crytomeria japonica*, silver hollies, *Cupressus lawsoniana*, *C. macrocarpa* and hemlock spruce. There is no doubt that these gardens became famous through the energy and enthusiasm of Thomas Ryan, head gardener, and Hugh, 5th Earl Annesley, born in 1831, who succeeded to about 70,000 acres in 1874 and realized that although he lived 300 miles further north than Cornwall he might yet be able to grow many plants from subtropical climes. 'Hardy' for him meant 'without winter protection', and his successful planting proved he was right. He also extended the grounds and planted fully: a drive three miles round the lakeside was constructed, and to the east Ballymaginalty Wood was planted in the 1890s, rising from the shores of the lake. Huge trees in this wood today are witness to the success of planting at this time, among them *Picea spinulosa*, from seed sent from Sir George King, Director of the Calcutta Botanical Garden, and which is now the oldest specimen in the British Isles.

Lord Annesley also built 'summer houses galore' in which he and his friends rested when walking, shooting or fishing. One of these, named the Moorish Tower, a gazebo built *c.* 1860, stood on a rocky ledge high above the lake and was furnished with a convenient lift for serving tea and drinks. It is now in ruins but was apparently 'about 20 feet in diameter inside and hexagonal in shape . . . first floor of smooth Victorian brick . . . Moorish key-hole shaped windows . . . Photograph circa 1900 shows the gazebo clad outside in vertical split logs . . . with shallow roof with heavy Russian-looking barge boards'.[10]

In 1895 F. W. Burbidge, then Curator of the Trinity College Botanic Garden notes that the monkey-puzzles were dense, healthy and green, with their lower branches sweeping the lawns, and he marvelled at the largest weeping ash he had ever seen.[11] He also goes into raptures about *Vitis coignetiae*, a now common climber in our gardens, which was given by Lord Annesley to gardening friends. By that date Castlewellan was essentially a tree and shrub garden: Japanese maples by the dozen, *Cryptomeria japonica* 'Elegans' by the hundred, many *Desfontainea spinosa*, and a *Rhododendron ponticum*, now 330 ft in circumference and in those times believed to be the largest in the British Isles. Just after Burbidge comments on these plants the appalling winter of 1895–6, a winter so severe that common laurels were killed in England, also struck Ireland. The losses at Castlewellan, with 15° Fahrenheit of frost for a prolonged period, were widespread, especially among plants which had recently been moved. Eleven hundred species and varieties of rare plants were killed; but many survived to be witnesses of a period which must have been the apogee of the Castlewellan gardens. Unaffected by the cold were the heated glasshouses, nineteen in all, including five for orchids, stove and foliage plants, vineries for muscat and black Hamburg grapes and houses for peaches and nectarines, gardenias and azaleas.

These vineries and conservatories at Castlewellan had been erected by Gray of Chelsea prior to 1872.[12] In one of them a fountain shooting water 35 ft high must have emulated its predecessor, Osler's Crystal Fountain in the Great Exhibition in Hyde Park (1851). A photograph of Lady Annesley in her conservatory illustrates some of this magnificence.[13] One of the most beautiful women of her day, she lightly poses, leaning on a polished granite table; behind her rise bamboos and tree ferns, while round the corner, three-tailed Japanese fish brought from the East struggle to survive in their bowl. The perfume of a water-lily from Zanzibar in the tropical aquatic house in the gardens might aptly encircle her.

In Earl Annesley's list at the turn of the century the majority of plants had been sent to him by Veitch's from Japan, and many of them had colourful names as well

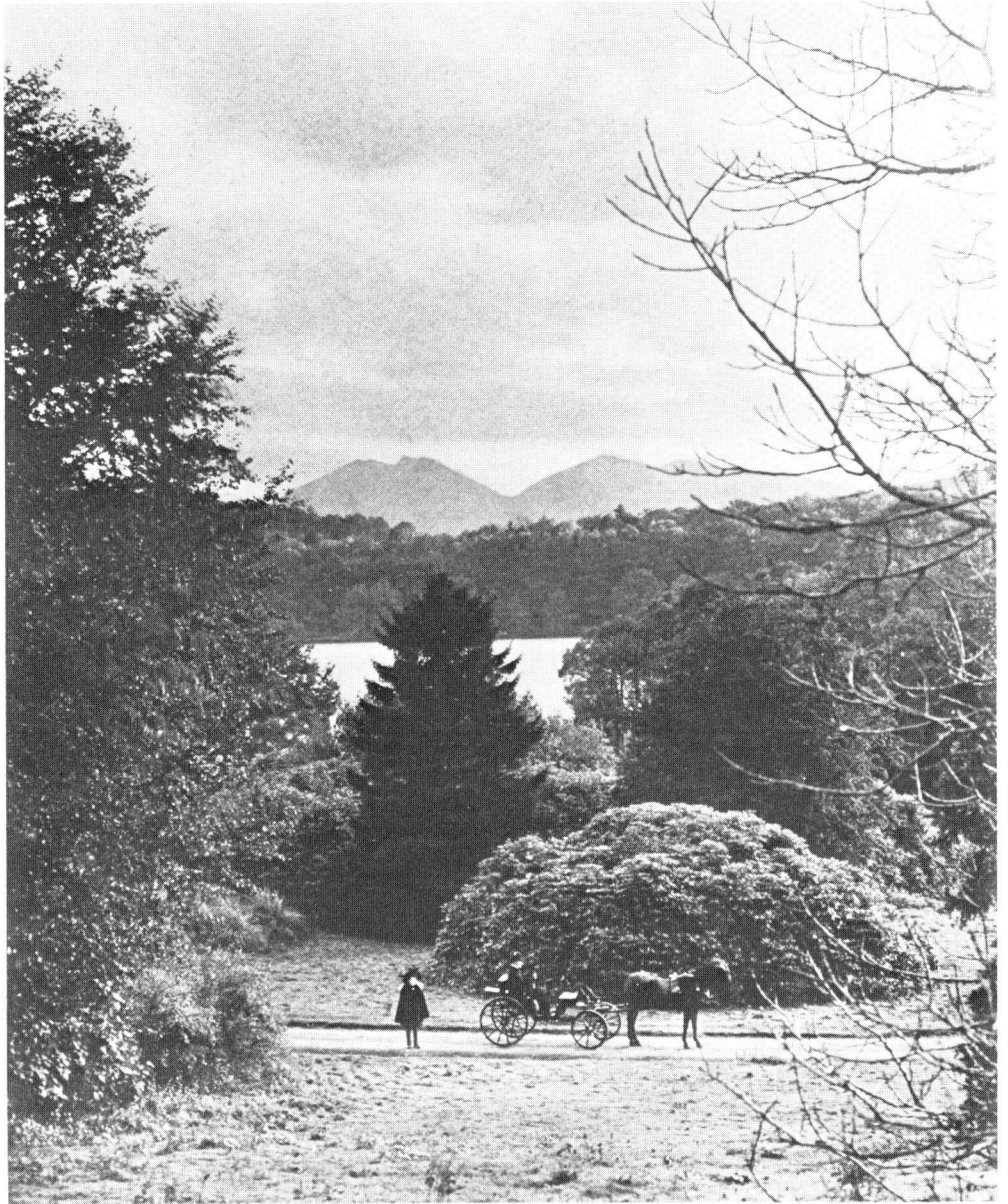

as brilliant flowers. *Acer japonicum polymorphum atropurpureum* (Red Maple) had been sent direct from Messrs L. Boehmer of Yokohama. By 1902 these had a graceful foliage and vigorous habit, being about 8 ft high and 50 ft in circumference, with colour, just before dropping leaves, as bright as a guardsman's coat. In the previous spring these trees had been savaged by eight Japanese deer which escaped into the Spring Garden and devoured fifteen of them as far as they could reach.[14] The next largest group of trees was from Australasia and New Zealand. Lord Annesley said he had little success with eucalypts, which grew so fast that they were blown over in storms, yet there are many growing happily in the grounds today. Nineteen plants were listed from China, including the hardy *Glyptostrobus lineatus* with bright green foliage, then said to be the rarest conifer in Britain; and lastly ten from the Himalayas and Nepal.

Photographs of some of the best of these trees can be seen in Lord Annesley's *Beautiful and Rare Trees and Plants* (1903): a rare (in 1903) *Eucryphia pinnatifolia* (p. 26) with its large white flowers and golden anthers, heavily composted with peat, loam and manure so that it produced flowers for three weeks in August; the tallest-known *Dacrydium franklinii* (p. 27), the Tasmania Huon Pine, half-hardy elsewhere, with its unique habit, dull green leaves and pendulous branches; *Pinus montezumae* (p. 45), 11 ft only, *c.* 1903, the first to be planted there but dead by 1961; *Pittosporum mayii* (p. 16), planted *c.* 1873, a fast grower with small, honey-scented purple flowers at

67

CASTLEWELLAN, CO. DOWN. Abies concolor, *with the mountains in the background, c. 1903.*

CASTLEWELLAN, CO. DOWN. Araucaria imbricata (*now* araucana), *c. 1903.*

CASTLEWELLAN, CO. DOWN. *Lady Annesley and* Vitis coignetiae, *c. 1903.*

the end of April; *Abies veitchii* (p. 11), the Silver Fir, discovered by Veitch on Fujiyama and introduced in 1879, planted at Castlewellan in 1898 and 66 ft by 6 ft 5 in in 1970. Even *Rhus toxicodendron*, Poison Oak, was photographed – that frightful shrub which causes acute irritation to skin, eyelids and glands. Indeed, a German governess, who picked this plant to decorate the church for Harvest Festival, became ill with a temperature and was in bed for a week.

After the death of Earl Annesley, from 1908 until the 1940s not much work was carried out in the gardens. During the First World War Lady Mabel Annesley, the 5th Earl's daughter, who had inherited and had resumed her maiden name after her husband had been killed while serving in the forces, tried with much courage, patience and endurance to keep the estate going during those difficult years which struck fatal blows at many similar estates. Her sister Constance describes Castlewellan at this time:

Gone were the trim grass edges to the avenue. . . . Rushes were growing in the low-lying swamp by the Town Lake. Trees had been felled and their severed stumps stuck abruptly out of the earth. Others lay fallen on the ground. There were ragged gaps in the rhododendron plantation. . . . But it had a wild and lamentable loveliness more dear to me than the trim pomp of the past.[15]

Mabel Annesley was not a specialist gardener, though she loved the place, and after emigrating to New Zealand, from where so many of the plants had come, she wrote back to her granddaughter nostalgically in August, 1950: 'I am so glad the *Sino-Grande* has flowered. Your father told me about the 560 flowers on the *Falconeri* (because it was the one I'd planted).'[16] These two rhododendrons are still a magnificent sight when in flower, especially the fragrant *R. falconeri* which is at the top of a bank, and as one looks up from below on a bright day the sky is patterned with clusters of pale-yellow flowers and leaves like rust-coloured felt.

Not until the 1950s when Gerald Annesley and his gardener took over did real expertise begin to show again. In the late 1960s a development plan for the whole park was drawn up by the Government. The working of it was put in the hands of an arboretum committee to include a Head Forester, Mr Gerald Annesley and others, all of whom had a background of forestry or horticulture. Perhaps because the committee was not yoked to any Civil Service department, it has worked speedily and efficiently. The arboretum has been kept as a separate entity in the midst of a forest park which has been treated with landscape as a foremost interest; that is to say, the whole area has not been blocked off with rows of Sitka spruce but has been left with open spaces as landscaping in the midst of the planting, respecting the contours of the land in a manner well known to eighteenth-century planners yet still not used by many modern forest park planners. There are now 1,200 acres in all, with a caravan park and special areas for fishing, walking, pony trekking and shooting.

A full-time forester, with four assistants, is in charge of the arboretum, now a total of 115 acres. During the years 1967–9 an unemployment relief scheme, in a tradition long known in Ireland, brought in 117 men, many of them skilled masons, who were of much value. Since then a propagating unit, a day-to-day recording system and extensive cataloguing mean that the arboretum is better looked after than it has ever been. Much of the initial work involved the clearing of repetitive planting of cypresses in the 1890s: trees had been planted in such numbers that it would seem the owner and his gardeners overstocked, and even overcrowded, the area in order to possess an arboretum which would impress their rivals. The flower-garden with its twin borders of herbaceous plants along the central vista to the fountain is virtually unchanged. Many of the plants have remained for years, and only a few are rare. It is obvious that the chief energies of the committee are concerned with the arboretum. It might even be possible for them in future to provide a commercial nursery for the public, which with an information centre, maps and brochures of natural history could provide a unique service.

Castlewellan is thus a resplendent example of the adaptation of a large Victorian estate to modern conditions. No longer is the owner absent from his garden in the most enjoyable season of the year, when the plants are at their best, as Lord Annesley said, 'owing to the abominable custom of going to London in the summer'; but hundreds of thousands of visitors are welcome and have ample space in which to enjoy a perfectly kept arboretum, garden and forest park.

The sheltered shores of Queenstown harbour were famous throughout the eighteenth century for the successful planting of many subtropical plants, and keen horticulturalists during the nineteenth century continued to create gardens in this area. The most famous of these was at Fota Island, eight miles from Cork, in the tidal estuary of the river Lee as it enters the great harbour of Cobh. From the moment one travels along the causeway at Fota up the green drive to the broad stretch of gravel flanked by huge holm-oaks near the house, it is thrilling to look across the lawn to the many fine old trees.

69

FOTA, CO. CORK. *The house, parterre and terraces, c. 1895.*

When Hugh Smith Barry (1816–57) was a boy, he would have watched a sturdy square tower designed by John Hargrave being built as an eye-catcher from the house.[17] During his lifetime as owner of Fota Island he reclaimed land from the sea, sheltered the 1,100 acres with belts of firs, built a high-walled, 4-acre fruit garden, constructed terraces behind the house, dug out a lake and made a sunken Italian garden, with charming walls and statuary, and, above all, planted a 15-acre arboretum on light sandy soil. In this planning for the arboretum he showed sensitivity, for the trees are widely spaced in a park-like setting, and the arboretum is an integral part of the whole garden.

James Smith Barry's son and heir, later Lord Barrymore, was only fourteen years old when he succeeded to Fota, and for forty years he was lucky to have the services of a great gardener, William Osborne; like Lord Powerscourt and Alexander Robertson, it was a splendid partnership in which each was essential to the other. From the age of seven, when he planted an *Abies nordmanniana*, the young Lord Barrymore's knowledge of horticulture grew, as did this tree which was one of the first planted after its introduction from the Caucasus in 1838. It is lime-tolerant and therefore thrives on the water-supply at Fota which is full of lime. The Fota Catalogue sent to Kew in 1912 gives details of trees planted before that date, and it is interesting to see, on the ground at Fota, how the tradition of planting by James Smith Barry and his successor Lord Barrymore was carried on by his daughter, the Hon. Mrs William Bell, and her husband from 1915 until her death in 1975. During Lord Barrymore's time many exotic plants were exchanged with his friends Lord Annesley, Lord Headfort and Sir Frederick Moore, and his neighbour Mr Gumbleton.

A rare *Arbutus menziesii*, planted by Major and Mrs Bell in 1935, is now nearly 50 ft high and in May is a mass of crimson fruiting spray, with shining cinnamon bark. This is a tree which C. L. Jepson, when in northern California, believed 'held the traveller, forester, hunter, artist and botanist . . . by the spell of its crown of flowers and masses of red fruits, its terra-cotta bark and burnished foliage'. Unfortunately, it is now dying and likely to need removing soon. A huge and tall *Magnolia campbellii*, the finest of all magnolias, growing on a wall at the back of the house, was planted in 1872 after being obtained from Van Geert St Armand. A splendid *Pinus montezumae*, a slightly different tree from the one at Mount Usher, seems healthier and fresher than any round Lake Maggiore, where they flourish. A *Cornus capitata* (Bentham's Cornel or *Benthamia fragifera*), a tree which never flowers at Kew but which here at Fota is luxuriant, has cruciform petals of white blossom in June and July, branches trailing to the ground, and a pretty strawberry-like fruit, better than those produced in Cornwall. W. J. Bean writes that this tree is 'the finest

FOTA, CO. CORK. *The Montezuma Pine, c. 1910.*

FOTA, CO. CORK. Cryptomeria japonica '*Elegans*', *c. 1970.*

FOTA, CO. CORK. *The Algerian Cedar, c. 1910.*

FOTA, CO. CORK. *The Mexican Fir, c. 1910.*

71

he has seen' and dates it from the original introduction in 1825.[18] 'Although', he adds, 'it is a Himalayan species it stands exposure to sea winds very well in the coastal areas of the west . . .' A fine *Drimys winteri*, exceptionally slender and upright, is, according to the Fota catalogue, one of two trees raised from seed by Gerald Loder at Wakehurst Place, Sussex, and then planted at Fota in 1903.[19] Lastly, a rare *Cupressus torulosa* var. *corneyana* rises in columnar fashion to a height of 73 ft.

Other interesting plants were obtained from sources all over the world until recent times; among them, a *Platanus orientalis* from seed collected by Major and Mrs Bell from the Seraglio Palace Garden, Istanbul, and a *Parrotia persica* from the botanical gardens at Edinburgh in 1902. Between such a garden as Fota and botanical gardens throughout the world there was an interchange of seeds and plants, many of which from Glasnevin are noted in the account books. The peak at Fota was the period 1910–11, but the Bells were continually adding to the garden until 1961 when camellias were planted which came from the Companhía Hortículo Agrícola Portuense, Oporto.

FOTA, CO. CORK. *The gate, erected in 1890, to the walled garden, 1960s.*

Gardening has not always been easy at Fota, however. In January 1870 huge springtides and south-west gales broke the sea-wall for 300 yards and covered the pleasure-grounds to a height of 7 ft for nearly a week, killing laurels and welling-tonias, and stripping lakeside bamboos of every leaf. Thirty years later F. W. Burbidge remarks on the healthiness of the plants: bamboos, with graceful feathery foliage in clumps of 400–500 canes, and *Phormium tenax* (Powerscourt variety) growing on the island in the lake on stiff mud or slob mixed with sea shells; callas (trumpet lilies) round the water had as many as fifty blooms; and gunnera, New Zealand flax and other waterside plants all seemed to have recovered from the salt flood. Again in 1922 high winds felled some of the shelter-belts, and the garden suffered much.

In its heyday Fota must have been incomparable: in the 4-acre walled garden twenty New Zealand tree ferns, with 12-ft fronds, surrounded, sheltered and totally overshadowed by forest trees, all seemed to be flourishing, and *Chamaerops humilis* (Dwarf Fan Palm) grew as if in its native forest.[20] As early as 1867, long before it was thought of at Battersea for outside planting, this palm at Fota was 12 ft high, and aloes, phormium, bamboos and pampas grass had all been planted outside by this date. From the pleasure-ground a fine wrought-iron gate, erected in 1890 in memory of Lady Mary Smith Barry,[21] led to a small garden enclosed by yew hedges with mixed borders in front of them.[22] In the formal garden in 1897 it took 100,000 plants annually to fill the borders, past which a vista led to a semicircular stone seat similar to those on which seductive maidens lounge in Alma Tadema's paintings. In addition, there were two more gardens: a rose garden and a sunken Italian garden with paved paths and a fine Foscarini *quattrocento* well-head, brought from Italy by Lady Barrymore in 1910.

Today at Fota the epoch of melon house, peach house and vineries has gone; the era of begonias, fuchsias and pelargoniums in the greenhouse has finished; the time for crotons, gardenias and caladiums in the stove house has departed; the walled garden is derelict. Yet it is cheering to know that the world-famous arboretum has been taken over by the Department of Dairy Husbandry of University College, Cork. At least our descendants may have a chance to marvel at the wonderful and dedicated planting of our ancestors.

A long, austere, mid-eighteenth-century range of grey Ardbraccan stone, Headfort House dominates its demesne from a ridge twenty miles west of Drogheda, Co. Meath, between the placid rivers Moynalty and Blackwater. The ancestral seat of the Marquesses of Headfort, it must be the largest estate in Ireland to remain in

HEADFORT, CO. MEATH. *Aerial view of the house, park and island arboreta, c. 1960.*

73

private ownership intact and unspoiled. The smooth golf-course in the far distance to the south-east and the roofs and Round Tower of Kells, rising above the trees to the south-west, enhance the prospect from the house. On this open side lies a semi-circular parterre (1879), with uniformly unimaginative topiary yews and castellated hedge, no longer formally planted with bright Victorian bedding. Below this, rich parkland drops to the river Blackwater, which curves through, sometimes hidden, sometimes divided, but eventually appearing as a silver strip below Kells. A huge arc, from the handsome stone bridge carrying the main road to the tall obelisk piercing the distant skyline, is still a majestic landscape in its own right.

But Headfort's claim to fame today, however, is for the pinetum laid out by Geoffrey Thomas, 4th Marquess of Headfort (1878–1943). Like his fellow peers, Lords Annesley and Powerscourt, he acquired the knowledge of a forester, employed and kept excellent head gardeners, had ample funds, and knew what he wanted. On Great Island, a 10-acre island in the Blackwater, connected to the parkland by a handsome bridge of Headfort oak, he started a pinetum in 1913, advised by Sir Frederick Moore of Glasnevin and W. J. Bean of Kew who planted the first tree, a *Tsuga heterophylla* (Western Hemlock), which today is more than 96 ft by 23 ft 2 in. His head gardener from 1912 to 1929 was William Trevethick, a Cornishman who became famous for raising rhododendrons in other parts of the gardens and for propagating nothofagus, eucryphia and viburnum.

Two wide rides were pegged out on Great Island, the main one 22 yards wide, and the other, a crossing ride, planned as a long vista in a straight line from the distant bridge on the Kells–Drogheda road near the entrance gates – landscaping on a grand eighteenth-century scale but with trees and shrubs which an eighteenth-century planter had never heard of. The arboretum is botanically devised, Kew nomenclature is used throughout (but many of the trees are unlabelled today), and each family has its own area: pines on a high gravel ridge, and spruces lower, on moister ground, with shelter provided by hundreds of Sitka spruce and *Thuja plicata*. Nevertheless, Headfort lies inland, and Great Island is at the lowest point in the park, so spring frosts are sometimes severe, like the 12° Fahrenheit of frost in March, 1928, after many plants had started growth. A rich and deep alluvial soil, slightly acid of neutral, to a depth of 8 ft in places, and a rainfall of 36–50 in, has produced remarkable growth throughout the years all over this estate. For example, a *Cupressus cashmeriana*, a beautiful but tender tree with pendulous grey sprays, is, according to Bean, the 'tallest example known' in Britain. Today the arboretum extends to Little Island on the river also, and has grown to 250 species and varieties: huge Douglas firs, wellingtonias and redwoods are particularly fine, especially when relieved by masses of *Rosa moyesii*, banks of azaleas and other flowering shrubs.

74

The finest hour for Lord Headfort and Mr Boyle, his Scottish gardener who succeeded Mr Trevethick, was in 1931 when he received the award of a RHS gold medal for his collection of conifers, very few of which were more than eighteen years old. Shortly after this award, Lord Headfort planted to the east of the house a small memorial garden to his friend George Forrest, the great botanist-explorer who had introduced hundreds of rhododendrons ranging from *R. giganteum*, an 80-ft tree, to *R. forrestii* var. *repens*, a creeping plant a few inches high; from *R. sinogrande* with leaves 2 ft long and 1 ft wide, to *R. radicans*, with leaves less than half an inch. Forrest died in 1932 in Burma aged forty, 'for love of duty in search of rare plants', on his seventh and what was planned to be his final expedition for the Royal Horti-cultural Society. All growers of rhododendrons are indebted to him for his discoveries. In this memorial garden at Headfort grow many dwarf rhododendrons found by Forrest in the eastern Himalayas, all hardy and flourishing, though grown too large.

On the other end of this front of the house to the south-west stands a large thicket of *Thuja plicata* (Western Red Cedar), planted in 1881, a huge conical self-layered mass of green stems from rooted layers, with a passage cut through which, when one enters, has the powerful fruity aroma of pineapple from the thuja but which, unfortunately, leads on the other side to a rubbish dump. It will not be long before many conifers naturalize themselves in our landscape just as *Rhododendron ponticum* has done already. Sitka spruce, *Thuja plicata*, *Abies grandis* and Lawson's cypresses seed naturally with local regeneration. Further off at Headfort to the north-west, amidst woods with 40-ft rhododendrons, is an American garden enclosed by walls on two sides. Here grow many treasures, including splendid specimens of *Prunus serrula*, *Magnolia grandiflora*, *M. veitchii*, *Nothofagus dombeyi* and *Liriodendron chinensis*. Leading directly out of this stand rows of Irish yews and wellingtonias, and two huge parallel hedges of yew, 250 years old, but healthy with clean, red stems, clipped but arched and bulging like static elephants – an efficient wind-break and excellent back-ground, leading to extensive greenhouses and a little garden house containing records.

HEADFORT, CO. MEATH. *The Yew Arcades, c. 1895.*

Although damage by storms is visible throughout the estate, especially on Little Island, fortunately many of the species were planted in twos and threes so that gaps are not too evident. Arboreta require little weeding and no ploughing, they manure

themselves, and provide shade and shelter, but it is essential to preserve shelter-belts; otherwise visiting hurricanes from North America (like the infamous 107-knot 'Debbie') penetrate, shearing off trees and shrubs. There is, therefore, a minimum standard of maintenance below which deterioration sets in rapidly, and some smaller estates are currently neglected. In high Victorian times these were well managed, but that management has steadily been withdrawn because of financial pressures and lack of skilled labour. Today, therefore, these arboreta are underthinned, unpruned, wind-blown, diseased, and damaged by livestock or ill-conceived felling. The final stage is decay and dereliction; pests and diseases abound; ash, sycamore, hazel and wych-elm coppices alone regenerate. Many trees are dead and dying, and the only advantageous result is that dense ground flora and shrub layer develop into valuable wildlife habitats – yet that can also be said of well-managed hardwood plantations. Conifers are of less value for wildlife, but the Victorians in general planted mixed arboreta which, even on a small scale, were a very important visual feature in the landscape of Ireland, where the total acreage of woodland today is less than 9 per cent compared with 20 per cent throughout the EEC area.

Hamwood, a mile beyond Dunboyne from Dublin, is a typical example of reduced management in the last fifty years. When a party of the Royal Scottish Arboricultural Society went there in 1897, they found an elegant house, built in 1768 by Charles Hamilton, agent to the Duke of Leinster at Carton, sheltered and set in 'a beautifully undulating and well-wooded country'. Fine conifers had been planted in the 1840s by Charles Hamilton's father, and the whole estate was admirably looked after. Among the trees which these Scottish excursionists admired and which are still growing today are a fine *Betula alba laciniata*, a fern-leaved birch from the 1840s which has thrived well in the fertile limestone soil. Originally the main feature of the arboretum, but now much overgrown in an avenue stretching away from the house, some magnificent conifers have also survived: *Cedrus deodara*, 95 ft by 12 ft; *Pinus monticola* (Western White Pine), (planted in 1847 and according to Alan Mitchell the only one surviving of thirteen mentioned by Elwes and Henry in *The Trees of Great Britain and Ireland*, 1904–8), now 95 ft by 10 ft 7 in, but a little thin; a *Pinus radiata*, 85 ft by 19 ft, and a *Cupressus macrocarpa* (1844), 85 ft by 21 ft 7 in. What was a 'charming flower garden' at the turn of this century is now a wilderness. The Duke of Leinster no longer owns Carton, but Mr Hamilton continues in the family tradition as agent to the Carton estate. The current problems of labour and upkeep seem as insuperable in the smaller estate as they are evident in the larger. As nineteen gardeners at Powerscourt a hundred years ago were altogether paid a total of £10 12s for a six-day week,[23] it is not surprising that with modern wages the work is not done.

The arboretum at Woburn Lodge, Co. Down, adjoining Mount Stewart, has also suffered from economic difficulties in its upkeep but has survived because the family has moved to a smaller house on the estate, surrendering the large house to a Borstal institution. George Dunbar started to plant exotic trees there in 1866 first providing them with a shelter-belt to the north-east. His work was continued by his daughter, Mrs Dunbar Buller, who made a walled garden near the house, and her gardening activity was continued by Mr and Mrs Reyell Pack Beresford who planted griselinias as shelter (now grown huge) and *Magnolia salicifolia* and *Olearia frostii* (then known as *Aster frostii*), both of which have grown to tree dimensions. The family then seems to have suffered financial crises, and many trees were felled. But Mr Arthur Pack Beresford inherited and resurrected Dunbar's garden by thinning and planting. He is also said to have brought back seed from New Zealand, including *Cornus capitata* which is a native of Himalaya or China.

The extensive lawns round the house at Fenagh, Co. Carlow, are still kept short, but the wooded areas beyond are sadly neglected through lack of labour. The nineteenth-century house was built by the Pack Beresford family which still lives there; it stands about 350 ft above sea-level on a light soil with a granite subsoil, which makes the tree growth surprising. In high Victorian times there were areas which were entitled the South and North Pineta, the Japanese Water Garden, the

Rock Garden, designed by Thomas Smith of Newry, the Lower Pinetum and the Pleasure-grounds, including the drive lined with rhododendrons. Alan Mitchell in his article 'Noteworthy Collections of Conifers in Ireland' (*Forestry Report*, London 1972, pp. 225–6) lists 62 trees at Fenagh as noteworthy – a figure exceeded only by Headfort (80), Powerscourt (75) and Fota (63). Most of the trees at Fenagh are about 125 years old; many are abies, and others include a Douglas fir (1855), 126 ft by 13 ft 10 in, and a *Thuja plicata* (1880), 103 ft by 12 ft 2 in. The difficulties in upkeep of grounds such as these seem insuperable without much labour. At Blandsfort, Co. Leix, the seat of the Bland family, there is a collection of conifers contemporaneous with that at Fenagh. Alan Mitchell finds sixty conifers worthy of note here in his paper to the pine conference in 1961, yet much of the arboretum is now inaccessible as a result of damage caused by a series of storms.

Exceptions to this lack of maintenance are two smaller estates within nine miles of each other as the crow flies across the border: Kildrum, Co. Donegal, and Brook Hall, Co. Derry.[24] Both have been owned by the Gilliland family since the mid-eighteenth century. Kildrum, a Victorianized Georgian house, is the older arboretum and today ranks primarily as a tree garden, with shelter-belts on the west of Sitka spruce and *Cupressus macrocarpa* (many of which were blown down by hurricane 'Debbie'). Rhododendrons do well, dog-tooth violets are naturalized, a bog garden is rich in primulas, astilbes and evergreen azaleas; healthy conifers grow in natural association with broad-leaved trees. In 1932 Commander Gilliland inherited the estate, and twenty-five years later Mr David Gilliland took over. The microclimate of Lough Foyle by Brook Hall, which he also owns, is frostless, and the growth of trees is therefore speedy. A *Cupressocyparis leylandii* planted in 1937 is now 68 ft, and there are many rare trees, such as *Abies pindrow* var. *intermedia*, which came from Sir John Ross at Rostrevor, and which was given an award of merit at the RHS in 1944. This tree is one of only two in Ireland, the other being at Kildrum, but according to Mr Gilliland it is 'becoming progressively more ugly with age'.[25] Broad-leaved trees like *Nyssa sylvatica* (Tupelo), autumnally brilliant, and many rare beech trees mix with a tall *Eucalyptus gunnii* (Cider Gum), the hardiest of the eucalypts, and *Picea orientalis*, that handsome large-coned spruce. Among others are a hardy *Podocarpus macrophyllus chinensis* discovered by Augustine Henry in China and fragrantly flowering in late summer, a metasequoia, a native of China from the original seed distributed by the Arnold Arboretum in 1948, but no larger than those in Kent and Surrey, and a *Davidia involucrata*, now common in gardens, which is very beautiful with its exceptionally large white bracts above each flower head. Brook Hall is full of horticultural interest, though it possesses no long vistas or formal planning, except that the arboretum borders the drive to the house from the Derry road and drops to Lough Foyle, beside which is a large walled garden with rare shrubs. This is now a wilderness almost beyond recall.

Some smaller arboreta started by the rich nobility in early Victorian times are still in splendid condition. At Abbey Leix, Co. Leix, terraces, garden, pleasure-grounds, parkland and arboretum lead out of each other to form a very agreeable unit. Once again it is the 25-acre arboretum and woodlands which have survived the best of these areas. The handsome house, built to the designs of James Wyatt in 1773, is set perfectly with terraced garden directly overlooking parkland and lily pond. These terraces, so letters in the house relate, are modelled on those of the famous Villa Aloupka near Yalta on the shores of the Black Sea. This seems an unlikely connection, but it appears that Emma Herbert, daughter of the 11th Earl of Pembroke, in 1839 married the 3rd Viscount de Vesci, the owner of Abbey Leix. Her mother, a Woronzov, came from Aloupka and had designed an Italian garden at Wilton, the first of its kind in England. With its central fountain and steps down it must have been the prototype for Abbey Leix. However, an examination of a series of water-colours in the house shows that the scale of Aloupka was different: large terraces and flights of steps at Aloupka lead down to the sea; more modest ones at Abbey Leix look out on to the lily pond in the parkland.

As early as 1825 Brewer's *The Beauties of Ireland* describes Abbey Leix as 'very extensive and greatly enriched with woods of a fine and venerable growth', and so it

is still. Extensive woodland on the far side of the river Nore contains oaks from primeval forest, which still regenerate at Abbey Leix – indeed this may be the only place in Ireland where this is happening to any extent. A *Quercus petraea* is said to be 1,000 years old. The woods are rightly famous in May for a carpet of bluebells interwoven among countless ferns for as far as the eye can see. On the near side of the river and sloping gently down to it the arboretum, with many fine broad-leaved trees interplanted with conifers, is intersected with paths meandering through it. The rarest of conifers is the large Sitka spruce, planted from seed introduced by David Douglas *c.* 1835. Today it stands at more than 125 ft by 15 ft 4 in. John, 4th Viscount de Vesci, who succeeded in 1875, planted extensively and was in touch with botanist-explorers as is borne out by the 1892 account book, p. 19, at Glasnevin, which details some 73 packets of rhododendron seeds from the Sikkim Himalayas (east of Nepal, north of Darjeeling) received from him. In what is now called the pinetum one can see a *Populus canescens* (Grey Poplar), 115 ft by 10 ft 3 in in 1969, which makes it as tall as the 'most notable specimen in the British Isles' which is at Birr Castle. Alan Mitchell has listed all the rare trees. The rainfall averages between 30 and 33 in, and the soil is pH5–6 but with a limeless subsoil. In 'Noteworthy Collections of Conifers in Ireland' Alan Mitchell lists Abbey Leix as having 28 notable trees, as compared, for example, with 75 at Powerscourt. Numbers, however, are by no means a criterion, and Abbey Leix has a delightful mixed arboretum with fine trees in a lovely setting.

The woodland at Ballywalter Park, Co. Down, is very typical of planting near a house by a rich Victorian industrialist, and it has survived 130 years – longer than the rest of the pleasure-grounds. Andrew Mulholland, owner of the largest linen mill in Belfast, on retiring after his mayoralty in 1846 decided he would build a house and estate worthy of his wealth and influence. He therefore employed his friend Charles Lanyon to design a house at Ballywalter, a strange site, on the dull, flat, eastern side of the Ards Peninsula, eight miles south of Donaghadee and looking over the beach in the distance. Lanyon partly knocked down and partly enclosed a previous house on a piece of gently rising ground, and built an Italianate *palazzo*, a large pile with an enormous 60 ft central hall resembling a bank or club.

The clothing of Ballywalter Park in park trees and shrubs was on a commensurate scale, yet suitable, as salt gales without shelter-belts to stop them would have made life unpleasant for man, beast and vegetation. A beech bastion on the seaward perimeter was therefore planted, then, by October 1847, more than 40,000 trees and shrubs, chiefly hardwoods such as oak, elm, beech, and sycamore, with some mixed fir, and then another 50,000 in the next year. Many have grown well in the arboretum in the deep, acid loam with prevailing low rainfall; yet huge trees are still felled by gales, including majestic *Quercus ilex*, planted by Andrew Mulholland.

In 1863, a year or two before his death, Mulholland also completed a handsome domed and bay-fronted conservatory of stone and glass at the end of the terrace in front of the house. His great-grandson, the present Lord Dunleath, has had it repaired with a fibreglass dome, a solution which has made its preservation possible. John Mulholland, who succeeded his father and was ennobled in 1892, was more interested in ocean yacht-racing and politics than gardening – two far more expensive hobbies – but he was responsible for more than 300 rhododendron hybrids which now thrive along the west drive or are underplanted in the woodland. Such frills as a private golf course, the planting of a walled rose garden (laid out by John Robinson of Belfast in 1852) and the dressing with flowers and shrubs of a stream brought into the pleasure-ground have now been removed by time and economics. However, the woodland in which kindly conditions have produced natural growth in *Eucalyptus globulus*, embothrium, eucryphia, nothofagus and cornus species, as well as many other fine trees and shrubs, is being maintained with limited labour.

The Tollymore Forest Park, opened in 1955 in the foothills of the Mourne Mountains, Co. Down, stretches for about 1,100 acres, of which 900 are impenetrable 'compartments' of conifers to be used for pit props or other commercial purposes. Although the species of tree in each compartment is named, the dark linear planting of the area does not make it worthy of consideration as a form of landscaping. The remainder is a delightful arboretum which occupies approximately the area of the pleasure-grounds begun by James Hamilton, 1st Earl of Clanbrassil, in the 1750s. Some effort has recently been made to provide contrasts in colour, form and texture of individual trees: cherries and conifers, golden variegated cypresses, *Embothrium Coccinea* (Chilean Fire Bush), American red oaks and Japanese maples are planted in conjunction with darker conifers or under forest trees. An azalea walk lined with *Chamaecyparis lawsoniana* has to be seen in May as one walks along it to the banks of the river Shimna, with its numerous picturesque one-arched bridges from the Clanbrassil days. Close by one of these, the Old Bridge, stands a splendid Spanish chestnut which must be 75 ft high. Among other old trees are a huge *Pinus radiata* (Monterey Pine) and a *Sequoiadendron giganteum*, 89 ft high. A Portuguese *Quercus suber* (Cork Oak) suffers from the knives of souvenir hunters; a very gnarled *Picea abies* 'Clanbrassiliana' (Dwarf Norway Spruce), now 38 ft at the circumference of the crown and 16 ft 8 in high, was found by Lord Clanbrassil when hunting. Banks of bluebells and snowdrops in season delight the townsfolk of Newcastle as well as many thousand others who annually visit the arboretum of this forest park.

The modern trend in arboreta is exemplified by Mr More O'Ferrall's planting since 1946 in the 400 acres of pleasure-grounds which surround his house, racing stables and kitchen gardens at Kildangan, Co. Kildare. Fortunately, mature oaks, limes, beeches and sycamores provide a background for his widely spaced and colourful planting. From the windows of the house the most striking feature is a broad, open vista across dead flat country to the east – as far as the eye can see to the distant horizon. On either side clumps of prunus, sorbus, malus and *Photinia villosa*, ringed by red belts of *Berberis dictophylla*, direct and punctuate the vista. How many people today can consider planting on a distant horizon? All the area between the house and stables is planted with choice ornamental trees, and in the paddocks themselves avenues and hedges of prunus, sorbus, cotoneaster and crataegus provide shelter and shade. At the arched entrance to the stables stand two tight

columns of Kilmacurragh cypresses, and as the original has disappeared from Kilmacurragh these must be from cuttings taken by Sir Frederick Moore. The grey house and brick stables are themselves covered in innumerable climbing roses, intertwined with clematis and schizophragma. The limy soil has provided strong horses as well as splendid shrubs for Mr More O'Ferrall.

KILDANGAN, CO. KILDARE. *The house in its setting of trees and lawn.*

The newest arboretum in Ireland is the John F. Kennedy Park at New Ross, Co. Wexford. This was initiated in response to the wish of many US citizens of Irish origin, and supported by the Irish Government, in memory of the President after his tragic death in November, 1963. How much more beneficial a memorial than just a slab of inscribed stone! Ever since the foundation of the National Botanic Garden at Glasnevin by the Dublin Society in 1796, the area there has been insufficient for a comprehensive collection of trees and shrubs. In 1964 by a fortunate coincidence a farm of 390 acres on the lower slopes of Slieve Coilte, in the very parish where previous generations of the Kennedys had farmed, became available for acquisition. The soil was largely Brown Earth and suitable; but the position, about nine miles from the sea, was open and subjected to roaring winds which dry out the vegetation. The average rainfall is 39 in. Frost is recorded for 100 days a year, but the topographical gradient and southern aspect nullify its effects.

The planning was masterly, and a rare combination in committee of government departments: Agriculture and Fisheries, Forestry and Wildlife and the Office of Public Works. Two hundred and seventy acres were allotted for specimen trees, shrubs and amenity areas, and 140 acres for forest plots, each planted with a particular species. The detailed allocation of space to different genera was the work of Mr Aidan Brady, the Director of the National Botanic Garden, Glasnevin, and Mr Tony Hanan, the Director of the Arboretum, who died in 1972. In a collection which aims at 6,000 species (about 4,800 shrubs and 1,200 trees) a conflict is bound to arise between botanical planting and aesthetic placing. Can a strip of acers with every possible variation in bright colours be satisfactory when massed? The relationship of polychromatic acers to forest trees towering over them provides a very necessary contrast between the hot colours and a cool background. Can the placing of all varieties of eucalypts be pleasing when they are planted *en masse*?

The contrast in habit, bark texture and grey leaves of the eucalypts requires a native tree to show it off best. In fact, how can the botanist and landscape artist be happily united in one arboretum? These are questions which time in this arboretum alone can answer. Throughout the arboretum three specimens of each plant are spaced together, with room as the Director says for 'a full, free and unhindered canopy' and to allow for mutual support. It seems that some attempt has been made to equate the work of botanist and landscaper in that gymnosperms (including conifers, taxads and ginkgos) are interwoven on the circuit of the arboretum with angiosperms (non-coniferous trees as varied as oak and magnolia).

On arrival one is immediately aware of the excellent design and use of materials in the complex one-storeyed building called the visitor centre. Western red cedar timber and grey bedding stone from Co. Clare are floored with Connemara marble slabs both inside and out, and one looks through huge windows at the distant arboretum. Near the buildings stands the Kennedy memorial stone, and the surrounding planting has been left from the old estate. This is a felicitous link with the past: large clumps of *Rhododendron ponticum* and *R. arboreum* glow in the afternoon sun, and a pair of *Araucaria imbricata* (Monkey-Puzzle) symbolizes the growth of trees from other climes, a tradition being carried on in the arboretum itself. The view from the office complex stretches out across an extensive expanse of Wexford landscape to the low skyline. Shelter-belts and screens throughout the arboretum have been placed about 30 yards apart in places where the winds rage through, and these, with internal blocks of trees, have reduced the wind-run by 50 per cent in ten years. These trees provide a welcome contrast to the planting by genera: *Larix kaemferi* (Japanese Larch), *Quercus rubra*, Lawson cypress, *Picea abies* (Norway Spruce), *Alnus rubra* (Oregon Alder), and even *Eucalyptus gunnii* (Cider Gum), which is unusual in a perimeter screen despite its speedy growth. *Alnus cordata* (Italian Alder), handsome and uncommon, has grown 34 ft in nine years. Streams have been re-aligned to form cascades, ponds and a charming small lake with waterfowl.

With its absence of cars, except to visit a panoramic viewpoint on Slieve Coilte, the whole arboretum is much appreciated by about 80,000 visitors annually,[26] and in the words of Dr John Durand 'gives much promise of future riches'. A forest garden with separate plots and a scientifically laid-out arboretum have been grafted to form a park in which people may enjoy their leisure and increase their knowledge of trees and shrubs. What better memorial to a much-loved President than a place where trees will always endure?

4 Italy in Ireland: Powerscourt, Ilnacullin and Mount Stewart

During the opulence of High Victorian times the making of Italianate 'gravel gardens', designed by Sir Charles Barry (1795–1860) and William Nesfield (1835–1888), with their huge mass-produced statues and urns, water-temples and basins, terraces and balustrades, was endlessly copied in smaller gardens. The rigidity of the formal parterre of flowers, the twice-yearly carpet bedding and bedding-out, and the indiscriminate use of showy colour schemes soon produced a reaction. It was the fiery-tempered Irish gardener, William Robinson (1838–1935), who roared out his opposition in his magazine *The Garden* and *Gardening*, and in his books *The Wild Garden* (1870) and *The English Flower Garden* (1883). Natural, loose planting, 'wild gardening in meadow-grass', the cottage garden enlarged, ramblers and creepers on the house – all were recommended and advocated. Unfortunately, Robinson's bigoted intolerance of any possible form of gardening other than his own runs like a polluted stream throughout his writing. No sculpture should be permitted: 'a garden is a thing of life, and beauty does not arise from any stonework'. Carpet bedding was forbidden, and the extensive use of 'glass sheds staring at us' was abhorred. The fight between Robinson and his opponents was as bitter and uncompromising as that between Payne Knight and Price, exponents of the Picturesque, nearly a century earlier. Shelley had thought they were like 'two ill-trained beagles . . . snarling at each other when they could not catch the hare'.[1] In Robinson's time the hare (his opponent) was successfully caught by him; and the fashion to lay out Robinsonian woodland gardens (not just arboreta or pineta) could not be resisted in Ireland, where the climate was kind and the growth of trees speedy. The country is full of examples of Robinson's type of planting, many of them more fascinating than he would have dreamt of, as the entry of exotic plants from all over the world increased with the twentieth century. However, neither the stone discipline of Nesfield and later of Reginald Blomfield, nor the riotous freedom of Robinson can form a first-rate garden. Architect and plantsman must go hand in hand, the one complementing the other. Even in the planting of woodland areas there should be a sense of natural architectural form: leaf designs, structure of trees and hedges, colour contrasts, textural variety – a combination of what Christopher Hussey called 'mass with texture, architectural sense with horticultural science'. The Italian Renaissance found the key to this perfect garden in which art and nature went hand in hand, and we believe that the three gardens we have chosen in this chapter illustrate these ideas.

The first garden, chronologically, is at Powerscourt. It shows, more than the others, the influence of the formal Victorian school of Barry and Nesfield, yet, like each of the others, it has an axis which holds it together structurally, and the transition to the wild garden is perfectly managed. From the charred shell of the once-magnificent house a cadence of broad and noble terraces, gracefully curved at the sides, forms a vast amphitheatre, with a large round pond and central fountain as its arena. Bisecting this on a north–south axis descends the perron, a flight of steps twice balustraded laterally in black and gold wrought-iron railings. But one's eye is first carried across the middle distance of the wooded, unspoiled demesne of Charleville to the backdrop of the sky and the Wicklow Hills. The whole perfect site is an example of the advice given on garden construction by Leon Battista Alberti, the Italian Renaissance author and architect: 'Familiar mountains' should be seen 'beyond the delicacy of gardens'.[2] Here at Powerscourt this delicacy is achieved by a rare unity between man's planting of trees, shrubs and flowers, and the use of sculpture and water in a formal terraced garden – the one leading into the other, so that art and nature are joined, as in many of the great Italian gardens.

POWERSCOURT, CO.
WICKLOW. *Lord
Powerscourt in his completed
garden, c. 1895.*

POWERSCOURT, CO.
WICKLOW. *Terraces and
parterre, c. 1895.*

Victorian photographs show clearly that there were only two straight terraces before 1860, and this is borne out by Mervyn, 7th Viscount Powerscourt's account, *A Description and History of Powerscourt* (1903) and the three volumes of the 'Powerscourt Plans' (1893),[3] which show details of each stage in the making of the gardens. Although John Rocque's map (1760)[4] shows a central path leading from the house door to a circular pond, it is but the skeleton of a body clothed by the 7th Viscount Powerscourt. He could well remember the start of the construction of the terraces by the architect Daniel Robertson,[5] commissioned by his father, for on his seventh birthday, a cold October morning in 1843, he was dragged from his schoolroom to lay the first stone. To substantiate this an inscription on a brass plate on the perron records the construction of buildings and terraces of local granite from the quarry at Glencree, four miles west of Enniskerry. Daniel Robertson's many plans for terraces, gardens and stone-work are dated between 1841 and 1843. There are baroque

features in his design for the central 40-ft-wide steps and balustrade from the first to the second terrace. The ground then gradually slopes down to an informal pond, before which is another flight of steps. Yet the lawns on either side and the banks to the east and west are informally planted with trees and shrubs. The effect, therefore, is a strange mixture of styles, but it remains the important next step in the construction of the terraces from their appearance in Rocque's plan of 1760. Robertson also designed a round bed for an American Garden.[6] Kalmias, fuchsias and azaleas were to be planted in segmental beds round a central statue, with standard roses in baskets (as at Blenheim Palace) decorating the circumference; but this was never constructed.[7] The making of the terrace was not without difficulties. Lord Powerscourt, in his notes to 'Powerscourt Plans', relates one of them with regard to Daniel Robertson:

At the time he was drawing these plans . . . he was always in debt, and the Sheriff's officers were after him. Warning being given of their approach to arrest him, he used to hide in the domes on the roof of the House. He was much given to drink and was never able to design or draw so well as when his brain was excited by sherry. He suffered from gout and used to be wheeled out on the Terrace in a wheelbarrow, with a bottle of sherry, and as long as that lasted he was able to design and direct the workmen, but when the sherry was finished he collapsed and was incapable of working till the drunken fit evaporated.

84

In 1844 Richard, 6th Viscount Powerscourt, died on his way home from Italy, and the work was stopped for fourteen years, by which time the 7th Viscount Powerscourt had come of age and had decided to continue the work, although Daniel Robertson had also died.

From 1854 for six years Lord Powerscourt had the services of a fine Scottish gardener, Alexander Robertson (no relation to Daniel Robertson), who came from the large estate of the Duncans at Camperdown, near Dundee. Like many of his countrymen Alexander Robertson was no ordinary gardener and in 1858 was appointed Steward as well as Head Gardener, thus undertaking the management of the whole demesne. Together Lord Powerscourt and Robertson worked out the sets of plans before them. In a relationship which must have been very similar to those between Humphry Repton and many of his patrons earlier in that century Lord Powerscourt clearly shows his admiration for Robertson and his determination to carry out his plans after his premature death in 1860:

I worked out with him the ideas which we both formed, and the Terraces were laid out and arranged as they have since remained, by him. He was at work at the semicircular Terraces on the lower part next Juggy's pond, and had just completed the east side of these, when he got an anthrax in his neck, which was cut (he was a very full-blooded man) and the exhaustion caused by the issue pulled him down so much that he died. His grave is in the old churchyard at the east end of the Terrace, near where his work was ended.[8]

From this account it can easily be seen that the designs of Alexander Robertson, based on those of Daniel Robertson, even to the semi-circular terraces on the lower part of the slope, were never fundamentally altered, though certain refinements were incorporated.

In the meantime Lord Powerscourt made trips to Versailles, to the great gardens of Schönbrunn, near Vienna, to Schwetzingen, near Mannheim and 'other places'. In each of these he recorded features which he adapted for use at home; but it is curious he did not visit any Italian gardens, for the original plan of Daniel Robertson is essentially Italian in origin, being based, so he said, on the steeply terraced gardens at the Sicilian Villa Butera (now the Villa Trabia) in Bagheria, then a place of *villeggiatura* for the Palermitan nobility. How did Daniel Robertson find out about the terraced gardens of this Villa? As far as we know neither he nor Lord Powerscourt visited Sicily, and there are no previous accounts published in Britain of these gardens. But John Butler, 2nd Marquess of Ormonde, in his *Autumn in Sicily* (Dublin, 1852) briefly describes the Villa Butera where, in 1830, 'nothing can be more beautiful than the view from the gardens, and the disorder in which they were allowed to remain looked worse from the contrast of the lovely scenery round them'. Living at Kilkenny Castle, a friend of Lord Powerscourt, could he not have given him a first-hand account of these gardens? Both Versailles and Schwetzingen are plateau gardens after the French manner, though at Schwetzingen there are a flight of steps and an exquisite wrought-iron balustrade which Lord Powerscourt must have noticed, as the Powerscourt one is similar. Also, he would have seen that Schwetzingen is one of the few Continental gardens which had not been deformalized in the English manner. A wide parterre in front of the *Schloss*, with a central axis punctuated by a round pond with fountain, and lined by formally planted trees, leads to a distant small lake. But, unlike Powerscourt, the terrain is flat. The pair of stags facing each other at Schwetzingen must have given Lord Powerscourt the idea for the pair of winged horses in a similar position at Powerscourt. Not far from Schwetzingen is the garden at Veitschöchheim, near Würzburg, which must be included under his 'other places', for there he would have seen a *pegasus* cavorting near water. The clothing of the Powerscourt garden came, therefore, from the wardrobe of ideas collected from many formal gardens which he saw in France and Germany and subsequently redesigned to suit his own Italianate setting.

It was fortunate for Lord Powerscourt that in 1858 there was a great number of workmen seeking employment from the Glencree area of his 36,000-acre Wicklow estate. About 100 men with carts and horses shifted soil by means of a roadway on an inclined plain from the house to Juggy's pond. At the bottom the soil was dumped into the pond which had been drained first. As a result, the depth of the pond was reduced from 14 ft to 6 ft, but it still leaked on the south-east side and had to be built up. After distributing marl over the area and making a further reduction in the depth, it was made watertight. The terrace on the extreme eastern side of the axis was also built up to match its counterpart, and then an amphitheatre was formed round the pond with four successive terraces below the top one. The work went on until 1867.[9] Lord Powerscourt described some of the difficulties:

When we were forming these terraces, we discovered that the surface of the water came out of the face of the slopes and threatened to carry them away and destroy our work. We found on examination that the land we were working on had in ancient times been part of a glacier moraine, and the ice, having carried down the gravel, had lain probably for centuries at certain levels, which were marked by thin coats of marl, which were impervious to water and did not correspond with our terraces.

Robertson suggested, as the only way of getting rid of this difficulty, that before we formed the terraces we should tap these marly deposits and dig holes through them, behind where our terraces were to be, so that the water inside, on coming out on these marly levels, should fall down through the holes into the next stratum and disappear. This was done, and we had no more trouble.[10]

The ground then being cleared at the water's edge, a boat-house was built of tufa taken from the banks of the Dargle river near the lower road from Enniskerry to the Dargle bridge.

Prior to 1875 at least three more designs were drawn for Lord Powerscourt, who accepted certain features from each. From the 1866 design of James Howe, a landscape gardener, some scroll-work beds on the terraces were adapted, but Howe died less than a year after his Powerscourt plan in circumstances which cannot have been very different from those of Daniel Robertson:

Mr Howe died shortly after this plan was completed, of drink. He had been at Glaslough, Co. Monaghan, laying out improvements for Colonel Charles Lesley and was taken with delirium tremens, and left and only got home . . . in time to die there.[11]

The more sober designs of Mr Broderick Thomas followed in the next year. He rightly pointed out a hummock in the centre of the sloping lawn. This 'stomach', as he called it, hid half the pond in the view from the windows of the drawing-room. 'His idea was to formalize the pond and make it more a rectangular, baroque fountain basin and his design would have been simple but it was considered better to have the pond in its natural state.' The hummock was removed, but the pond was left in its natural state. A neighbour of Lord Powerscourt's, Sir George Hodson Bt. of Hollybrook (see p. 152), also drew up very formal designs in 1873, and these formed the basis for the subsequent plans of Francis Penrose, as Hodson had drawn lateral flights of steps to meet the central perron on the large terrace.

After this, the four flights of granite steps were constructed to complete the whole central axis. Here Lord Powerscourt showed his unerring sense of scale, for in Daniel Robertson's original plans a flight of steps the same size as the upper ones was drawn; but Lord Powerscourt sensed that two such masses of steps would be too large for the house and would also be monotonous. To avoid this he employed Francis Penrose,[12] first to reduce the width of the steps, then to carry out pebble or rough pavement work in incline planes similar to those in Italian towns, 'where the ascent and descent is made by mules with burthens as well as by foot passengers'. These lateral inclines and the central floor of the platform are paved in formal patterns designed by Francis Penrose; the material comprises black and white pebbles, brought from the beach at Bray, four miles off, which were then embedded in concrete in the Italian manner. All that then remained to complete was the wrought-iron railings which Lord Powerscourt used to surmount the perron. He had found these lying disused and broken in a courtyard in Homberg in Hesse, where they had been balcony railings to the central windows of an old castle before being replaced by modern cast-iron work. Further curved sections were added by a Birmingham firm, so that it is now impossible to tell where the old ends and the new begins.

There is a similar terrace at the foot of the perron along the top of a wall to an alcove where stand two splendid bronze seventeenth-century baroque statues of the god Aeolus. These were bought by Lord Powerscourt after they had been saved from Prince Jérôme Napoléon's Parisian possessions which the communards destroyed by setting fire to the Palais Royal at the end of the Franco-Prussian War. Prince Jérôme Napoléon, the nephew of Napoléon III, and somewhat of a political embarrassment to him, relates the history of the statues and makes recommendations for their new site at Powerscourt, which show his aesthetic taste, however inept his political judgement may have been:

les deux statues viennent de chez le Duc de Litta de Milan où ils étaient placées à sa campaigne de Lainate . . . les figures doivent être placées contre un mur . . . Au Palais Royal, les Éoles jettaient du gaz par les bouches et de l'eau entre leur jambes, c'était original et jolie.[13]

Lord Powerscourt followed the Prince's suggestions, and the statues were placed at the foot of the perron against a wall and surmounted by a pediment in an alcove, in the arch of which is the head of Apollo as the sun god, similar to that at the top of the Powerscourt coat of arms. The builder was George Moyers of Dublin, the material is Cornish granite, and it is copied from one at Herculaneum. Directly below Apollo's head a bronze sundial is fixed in the wall, with the motto above it: *Horas non numero nisi serenas,*[14] a motto that applies to visits to all great gardens which cannot be seen and enjoyed in about half an hour including tea. As Prince Napoléon said, the two splendid baroque statues of Aeolus were from the Duke of Litta's garden in the Villa Arese at Lainate, where the pavilion is decorated with pebble mosaic of natural stone similar to the perron at Powerscourt, although there is no evidence that Lord Powerscourt saw this garden. The statues are no longer connected, as in Paris, to a gas main and so do not breathe fire, but they cheerfully spout water '*entre leur jambes*'.

The statuary at Powerscourt forms a major part of the whole composition, as it does in similar gardens in Italy. All the statues on the upper terrace are marble, and those on the second are in bronze. The copies of the Apollo Belvedere and Diana the Huntress, nearest the central axis on the upper terrace, were brought from Italy by the 6th Viscount Powerscourt, who also commissioned the near-by panels in the pedestals with the coats of arms. He likewise brought back the copy of the Laocoön, which is now placed on a plinth against the ivied wall opposite the long western walk looking south. This plinth, a single block of granite quarried in Glencree, caused some problems before it reached its final position supporting Laocoön and his struggling sons. Lord Powerscourt writes:

It was such a weight that when it got on to the road, the subsoil being soft and boggy, it sunk through the road and buried itself in the soft earth. We had to dig it out again, and laid planks upon the road to support it. Then, in order to get it down to the terrace, we had to make a platform of planks, rolling it a few yards, and bringing the planks forward again from behind, and so gradually rolling it all the way, some four miles . . . It took more than a week to bring it from its bed to the terrace, and when we got it nearly to its position, and it was on the walk in front of the conservatory, it again slipped off the planks, and buried itself in the soil. But when we had got it as far as that we were not going to be beat with it! It was placed in its position, and then the rough surface cut off it, and the stone made into a smooth rectangular block.[15]

Among the statues on the upper terrace are two winged figures of Fame and Victory, commissioned in 1866 by Lord Powerscourt from Professor Hagen, a sculptor in Berlin. Seeing them in the sculptor's studio, the King of Prussia said he wished to buy them to celebrate the decisive victory of Prussia over Austria at Sadowa in that year. At the risk of royal disapproval he was persuaded to accept bronze copies, and the originals came to Powerscourt. Neither is especially fine work, and from a distance they remind one of figures of angels common in cemeteries. The same sculptor was commissioned to execute the *pegasi* now on top of the boat-house at the pool's edge. Painted to look like bronze, although they are made of

POWERSCOURT, CO. WICKLOW. *One of the pegasi, c. 1970.*

zinc, they have a place of honour in the garden, as they are taken from the Powerscourt coat of arms. Heraldically, they are 'two pegasi argent, maned, hoofed and wings addorsed'; and they are correctly placed near the pool, as Pegasus is symbolically the Steed of the Water, whose wings connote the wind of the freedom of the imagination. When seen from the top of the perron, terminating the long vista and with their shadows reflected in the water, they are well in scale with the Triton fountain in the centre.

This fountain was designed by Lawrence Macdonald, a sculptor who lived in the Piazza Barberini in Rome, and it was made in cement by Sir Thomas Farrell, a Dublin craftsman. Modelled on Bernini's Triton Fountain (1642) in the Piazza Barberini, it lacks one of the best features of the original – the Triton's startling elevation in the open hinge of a large scallop shell, like a huge irregular saucer over which water pours. Nor has it the handsome central shaft made up of a quartet of dolphins' bodies, which combine to give height to the sea-god and merge with the shell into an organic whole. However, like Bernini's original, the Triton's head is thrown back as he drinks water from the conch held above his lips; and the jet at Powerscourt, which is said to reach 100 ft, far exceeds that in the Piazza.[16]

Two large plaster groups designed in the heroic style by Alexander MacDonald had been brought from Rome by the 6th Viscount Powerscourt: the first, Hector and Andromache, and the second, Ajax with the body of Patroclus, were then modelled in Portland stone by Mr Kirk, a Dublin sculptor. The former stands by the old churchyard near the east end of the upper terrace; the latter terminates the fine avenue of *Araucaria araucana* and *Abies douglasii*, which extend the upper terrace to more than 800 yards. Also at the east end of the upper terrace stand two bronze copies of the 'Sitting Mercury' and the 'Sleeping Faun' bought in Naples in 1883, the originals from Herculaneum being now in the Museo Nazionale in Naples. On each side of the upper central platform are two granite pedestals on each of which is a group of *putti* in bronze by Joseph Marin, a contemporary of Louis XV. Many of the urns and vases on the side flights are copies of those at Versailles, which had previously been seen only at Bagatelle, the house in Paris of Sir Richard Wallace, the founder of the Wallace Collection in London, until Lord Hertford obtained permission from King Louis-Philippe to have them copied for his own garden in Paris, and from these stem the ones at Powerscourt.

In a summer-house at the end of the walk on the west side of the terrace were placed two Hindu idols elaborately carved in soap stone (now in the Victoria and Albert Museum, London). These are two aspects of Parvati, the consort of Shiva, the destroyer: in the first, where she has eight arms, one of which disembowels a victim while another beheads a warrior, she certainly personifies the destructive aspect; in the other she is Rambha (or Annapurna) the food-giver, who benefits mankind, symbolized by her carrying a mango in each hand. Both statues came from outside a temple in Mysore, and as the brahmin in charge would not accept money for them, Lord Powerscourt sent him an illustrated copy of Shakespeare.[17] Since the days of the British Raj, neither shekels nor Shakespeare can enable a foreigner to remove relics from their shrines in India.

Another of Lord Powerscourt's acquisitions, which fortunately would also not be possible today, was the handsome pair of Roman sarcophagi that he found in a monastery garden near the Colosseum. One, which is in Parian marble, was being used as a drinking-trough, while the other stored chicken food. Around one of these the 8th Viscountess laid out a garden of roses and sweet-scented herbs, entered under a pergola. Near by was a finely carved head of one of the O'Tooles, former proprietors of Powerscourt, which was rescued from the ruins of an old church on the estate.[18] In addition, on the top platform there are two Carrara marble *tazze*, each 9 ft in diameter, which hold flowers in sunken beds designed by Edward Milner;[19] also four lions couchant modelled by Francis Penrose on those at the foot of the steps leading up to the Capitol in Rome; four large busts, now in Julia's Garden, of Italian artists: Michelangelo, Leonardo da Vinci, Benvenuto Cellini and Raphael, copies (1878) of those in the Vatican; and four large seats of polished granite from Newry, Co. Down.

POWERSCOURT, CO.
WICKLOW. *The
perspective gate from
Bamberg cathedral, c. 1900.*

The walled garden, which is older than any part we have been considering, runs on the western side and is entered by a gate at the western end of the walk at the far end of the top terrace. This gate of wrought iron, painted in black and gold, is the finest in the gardens and originally came from Bamberg Cathedral, although it was bought in London. It has a charming *trompe-l'oeil* perspective design in delicate scroll-work and is topped by a graceful vase in wrought-iron. On one occasion when he was travelling Lord Powerscourt 'found the iron railings on either side of the high altar with the empty space where this gate had formerly stood'. These eighteenth-century perspective gates and screens can be seen in a number of churches in Germany: there are especially fine ones at St Ulric's church at Augsburg, and a rood screen, *c.* 1735, in the Benedictine Abbey church at Weingarten. Presumably they were placed in a church to add another dimension to the building, and therefore when removed from their setting may have lost their meaning. Opposite the glass-houses and leading to the kitchen garden, with its small leaden eighteenth-century fountain of a female figure, is a double gate, called the Venetian Gate, on account of its being made in Venice for Lord Powerscourt at the beginning of the nineteenth century. The vine work is similar to German and Austrian work of the previous century, and the vases on the granite piers that hold this gate were made by the same firm of Capo d'Istria stone. On the eastern side of the walled garden is a copy of an old German gate, called 'The Chorus Gate', made by a London firm. The original has not been traced, but the detail is like that of a German gate of the late seventeenth century at Goerlitz in Germany.

The four glasshouses, in excellent repair today, two 50 ft and two 100 ft long, still stand on the north wall at the western end of the top terrace. Constructed by Ormson of Cheslea, they used to be kept at different temperatures. The hottest, the Stove House, contained plants, many of which we should now call house plants, as modern methods of cultivation have made them suitable for room temperatures: *Maranta zebrina, Dracaena hookerana, Philodendron* × *corsinianum,* caladiums and many begonias.

In 1870 Mr Malcolm Dunn was Head Gardener, and his planting of the platform on the second terrace was typical of that period. The side beds contained blue lobelia edged with grey *Cerastium tomentosum*; the centre beds were carpeted in summer with pelargoniums and calceolarias.[20] Often each bed contained one species, the most visually attractive to contemporary taste at that time being beds of massed gladioli. Modern taste, influenced by the herbaceous planting of William Robinson, does not approve of such formal planting, yet in a formal garden plants can and should be used as a background and foil to the sculpture and architecture of the garden, as the French and the Italians well know. 'Municipal' planting and topiary work which one sees at Powerscourt today, is similar to Victorian bedding and is wholly correct in formal beds. Malcolm Dunn also had to deal at Powerscourt with *Phylloxera vastatrix*, the vine pest, which subsequently wiped out most of the vines in France and Europe. It was caused by a genus of plant lice which killed the native vines, and only by grafting healthy native vines on to immune stock from California could the pest be cured. However, Malcolm Dunn used drastic measures between July 1867 and December 1869, resulting in complete success. All young wood was pruned close in, the roots of all infected vines were lifted and cut, and the rest were washed, scrubbed and dusted with lime.[21]

At the southern end of the walled garden is the Green Pond with its water-lilies and central fountain (1859) from which dolphins spout water. Then one finds oneself in the American Garden, or Pleasure-grounds, an area of superb ornamental trees which thrive in the lime-free soil as well as anywhere in Ireland. Alongside the Green Pond is a splendid *Euonymous incidus* of brilliant red foliage with jagged double-toothed leaves. At the end of the pond is a huge *Eucalyptus globulus* (Tasmanian Blue Gum), the largest in Ireland, where they grow better than anywhere else in the British Isles. On the right, down the slope, stands an Arizona cypress, not unlike those tender cypresses one sees in Italian gardens. Near this is a rare *Juniperus cedrus*, a native of the Canary Islands, where there are few specimens left. Correctly planted, at the bottom of a slope, as it likes moisture, is a huge Sitka spruce (151 ft by 17 ft 8 in). Near the Tower a *Picea likiangensis* (16 ft by 6 ft 2 in in 1966) is described by Alan Mitchell as 'superb, very blue'. On the right, at the bottom of the slope, is a fine *Abies cephalonica* (Greek Fir), most distinctive of all the silver firs, planted in 1906 (75 ft by 15 ft 2 in in 1966), with a huge growth. Some handsome *Abies nordmanniana* (Causasian Fir) were planted in 1867, and after 100 years the largest on the River Drive is more than 135 ft with a girth of more than 14 ft. Near by stands one of the most beautiful trees in these gardens, *Nothofagus betuloides* (52 ft in 1966), a hardy evergreen beech from the southern hemisphere. Although this specimen is smaller than one at Mount Usher, it is a fine tree of dense habit with closely crowded dark-green leaves. Next to it is its relative *N. dombeyi*, a rich, pale, evergreen pyramid of more open habit. This tree was 58 ft in 1966, and once again the climate at Mount Usher seems to suit the growth of *N. dombeyi*, as a larger specimen there of the same age proves. From the furthest bank of the Triton Pool (Juggy's Pond), one can look up the stepped vista to the house, with an unequalled *Cupressus macrocarpa* on one side, with a multiple bole 118 ft by 15 ft 5 in in 1966.

On the way down to the waterfall in the Dargle Valley one passes the Tinnehinch Gates, which were bought at the Paris Exhibition of 1867 and have since acquired the name of the Golden Gates. Near them is a superb *Sequoia sempervirens*, planted in 1866 and now, at more than 130 ft by 13 ft 11 in, the finest in Ireland. The Gate-lodge had been built in 1854 to the designs of Sir George Hodson, and he also planned the road from these gates through the Deer Park to the river. All the work was carried out by Alexander Robertson (1867–9); four bridges were built and the course of the river altered. Conifers and ornamental trees line the three-mile route: araucaria, *Abies douglasii*, *Thuya gigantea*, *Picea nobilis* and *P. nordmanniana*, *Cupressus macrocarpa*, *Cedrus atlantica*. On the right-hand side, on the way down, stands a splendid *Abies procera* (Noble Fir), more than 130 ft high, which is obviously enjoying the moist climate and deep soil, as it produces many huge rich-coloured cones. On the left in the same alluvial soil a grove of about 100 *Araucaria araucana* was planted, *c.* 1870 – according to Lord Powerscourt, with his 'own hand, as well as some pines along the road' – and today they look remarkably healthy. Monkey-puzzles, the first conifers grown in Europe from south of the Equator, have a fine sculptural form very different from any other tree, and they are often best in a grove where they withstand sea wind, exposure and draughts excellently.

Edmund Murphy, editor of *The Irish Farmers' and Gardeners' Magazine* (1842, p. 201), writes that 'the deer park at the Waterfall was planted under our superintendence about twelve years ago'. This is a surprisingly early date. He also says that a Mr Sullivan advised on the planting of the Dargle river from Bray to the Dargle Glen. We know nothing of Mr Sullivan, but Edmund Murphy, according to Loudon's *An Encyclopaedia of Gardening* (1822), was accounted 'with Hely Dutton and James Fraser', one of the three principal landscape gardeners in Ireland at that time.

The formation of a new lake high in the Deer Park was started in 1834 by the 6th Viscount Powerscourt to designs drawn by Henry Thomas Provis, but it was not a success. The dam was badly made of porous gravelly soil from the site, and a bank was constructed, enclosing a spring of water on the north side. Consequently, a short time after it had been erected the bank burst, and the water in the newly formed lake rushed down the valley all the way to Bray, tearing down bridges and flooding what was at that time a common at Bray. In 1858 a further attempt was made under the supervision of Alexander Robertson; this was successful, and the whole space up to the paddock was occupied by two lakes, held by two dams.

At the time of the Great Famine (1847) two precipitous drives through the Deer Park, the Earl's Drive and the Lady's Drive, and the Tinnehinch Avenue were constructed as famine relief schemes. In addition, Lord Powerscourt gave instructions that almost all the deer should be shot to provide food for the workers and their families. The plans for the roads were those of Thomas Parnell, who had been trained as an engineer. He was uncle of Charles Stewart Parnell and one of the old-established family at Avondale, Co. Wicklow, the fine estate which Charles Stewart Parnell eventually inherited.

Throughout the estate all Lord Powerscourt's planting was from seed purchased at Stevens's Auction Room, Covent Garden, and propagated in his own nursery. The extent of his planting on both sides of Glencree cannot be appreciated until one reads the figures: 400,000 trees annually for ten years (1870–80) in the 700-acre Ballyreagh plantations. Details were given by him in a lecture in London:[22] larch, Scots pine, *Pinus radiata, chamaecyparis lawsoniana*, wellingtonias, *Araucaria araucana* and Corsican pine in exposed places where, as at Ilnacullin later, they proved better than Douglas firs, which lost leaders in high wind. The greatest set-back to his planting occurred during the ice and snow of the night of 11/12 January, 1895, when 10 in of snow fell in the night, making 26 in in all. Thujas and cypresses lost top and side branches, Scots pines were stripped bare as telegraph poles, holm-oaks were mangled, and specimens of arbutus had to be pruned to the ground. In his lecture Lord Powerscourt does not mention Sitka spruce. 'These trees', wrote a visitor on a Royal Scottish Arboricultural excursion in 1898, 'have thriven remarkably well, and are now fast assuming timber proportions, the larch being perfectly free from the "blister" which proves such a scourge to it in many parts of Great Britain.' Planting on this scale to some extent counteracted the wholesale denudation of the countryside by working-tenants, when they became new owners of land after the Land Act (1903). Of great interest to foresters, at a time when forestry received small attention from the public, was Lord Powerscourt's use of promising species of newer conifers. 'Nobody can say that I have not left my mark on the country', he wrote. We are indebted to him for a foresight shown by few landowners in Ireland.

On returning to the main garden one sees in a hollow on the eastern side of the main vista what the 8th Viscount Powerscourt called the Japanese garden. Begun

POWERSCOURT, CO. WICKLOW. *The Japanese Garden, c. 1970.*

in 1908 after extensive drainage, it has few Japanese trees, shrubs or features. There is a stone lantern, traditionally used to light the way to the tea-house, which here is replaced by a blue open pagoda. There is also an eighteenth-century grotto in the hillside, which one feels was incorporated more by accident than good management into the Japanese garden layout. Once again the petrified moss from the banks of the Dargle provided the necessary material for the grotto, and very charming it is with its ferns, mosses and small cascades among the tufa. On the islands in the ponds, formed by the stream, were Japanese tortoises and bronze cranes, now gone.[23] The inevitable red wooden bridge is also a Japanese feature, yet here possessing none of the symbolism of the bridge in a real Japanese garden, where it is traditionally placed on the path of life. The planting of *Callistemon rigidus* (Australian Scarlet Bottle Brushes) in clumps, and such trees as balsam fir and black spruce from North America, does not seem to be especially Japanese either.

The only other feature of interest is a picturesque folly tower like a pepper-pot, beyond the walled garden, built from the stones of part of the Protestant church by the 8th Viscount Powerscourt in 1910. Sheila Wingfield (Viscountess Powerscourt) describes the building and setting of this tower, built by her father-in-law:

Here all was privacy, quiet and a closeness of rare trees. And here with a couple of estate workmen and his own hands he had achieved a long ambition by building himself a mediae-val tower . . . now it stood filled with mortars and ancient arms up to the crenellations, covered with lanterns hung from brackets and surrounded by historic cannon, carronades, cannon-balls, old chain shot, gyves and cressets which alternated with an astrolabe and a clepsydra, a water-clock used by the ancients . . .[24]

The tower was so convincingly medieval that a garden boy showing tourists round was once heard to say, 'Now this is terrible old. Didn't the lady of the castle watch the hunt from the top while she worked at her embroidery?'[25] Barbara Jones in *Follies and Grottoes* (1974) accurately describes the tower: 'round, neat, castellated, splay-footed. Steps curve down to a massive door and the tower is protected by a bastion embellished with guns from the Armada and the Battle of the Boyne, cressets, a large mortar, decapitation irons and a stone phallus.' A folly *par excellence*.

In these gardens the most criticized feature is the unashamedly eclectic collection of sculpture – fountains, basins, busts, statues, seats, vases, urns and coffins – originals and copies, in marble, cement and granite, bronze and zinc, ancient and modern, baroque and neo-classical. An unpalatable glut for some, a worthy feast for others. Yet there is a *bravura* about it all which typifies the characteristic taste of a collector in the last quarter of the nineteenth century. Fortunately, the garden is spacious and

ILNACULLIN, CO. CORK. *Aerial view of the garden and Glengarriff Bay.*

is able to absorb this prodigal display of detail, though with the roofless house at its back the statuary appears more prominent than it did with the fine Palladian house as a living entity. We should be grateful to the foresters for the state of the arboretum, as we are indebted to Mr and Mrs Ralph Slazenger for the upkeep of the gardens. An unforgettable time to visit is on a summer's evening after the bus-loads have departed, when the long shadows of the statues and the conifers stretch across the perron and the Triton Pool, and when the horizon of the Sugar Loaf Mountain is bathed in lymphatic Irish light.[26]

Fra Francesco Colonna of Treviso, the Dominican monk, reputed to be the author of *Hypnerotomachia Poliphili* (1499), a most unreadable romance, well illustrated by woodcuts showing pergolas, fountains, pillared *loggie*, clipped box and sunken parterres of Italian Renaissance gardens, minutely describes the place of his heart's desire, the perfect garden. It is an island garden, where the contrast between art and nature is more evident than inland. Man's order created in the garden of such a Blessed Isle is cut off by the water from the wildness of Nature. Nevertheless, as Elizabeth McDougall points out, not everything was entirely formal in the garden of the Italian Renaissance:

The existence of groves and irregular or naturalistic areas in Renaissance gardens is often ignored. The Renaissance garden is usually thought to be entirely architectural and formal, an attitude that goes back to the eighteenth century . . . and which is typified by Pope. Yet it is possible to show that there were indeed informal or naturalistic areas of importance to the garden design. They were not, as Pope said, planted symmetrically in regard to each other, nor were they part of a farm, as distinct from the garden of the villa.[27]

Isola Madre on Lake Maggiore, Schloss Mainau on Lake Constance and Oilean NaCuileann (Ilnacullin) in Glengarriff Bay, Co. Cork, today illustrate these characteristics of perfect island gardens. The first two have the advantage of over 150 years of planting, and at Mainau the climate is defeated by temporary greenhouses which, when removed in spring, reveal banana trees and date palms. But the azure blue sea or lake (always thus – even on Irish postcards) circumscribes each of the gardens, and the encircling mountains knit sea or lake with sky.

For some years from 1896 John Annan Bryce (1874–1924), the Belfast-born East India merchant and Scottish M.P., brother of Lord Bryce, one-time Chief Secretary to Ireland, and Ambassador to the United States, had rented Glengarriff Castle on the mainland and had become progressively fonder of the neighbourhood and keen to start a garden there. After unsuccessful attempts to buy land, he was eventually

ILNACULLIN, CO. CORK. *The barren island on which the garden was begun, c. 1900.*

95

ILNACULLIN, CO.
CORK. *The same view,
1977.*

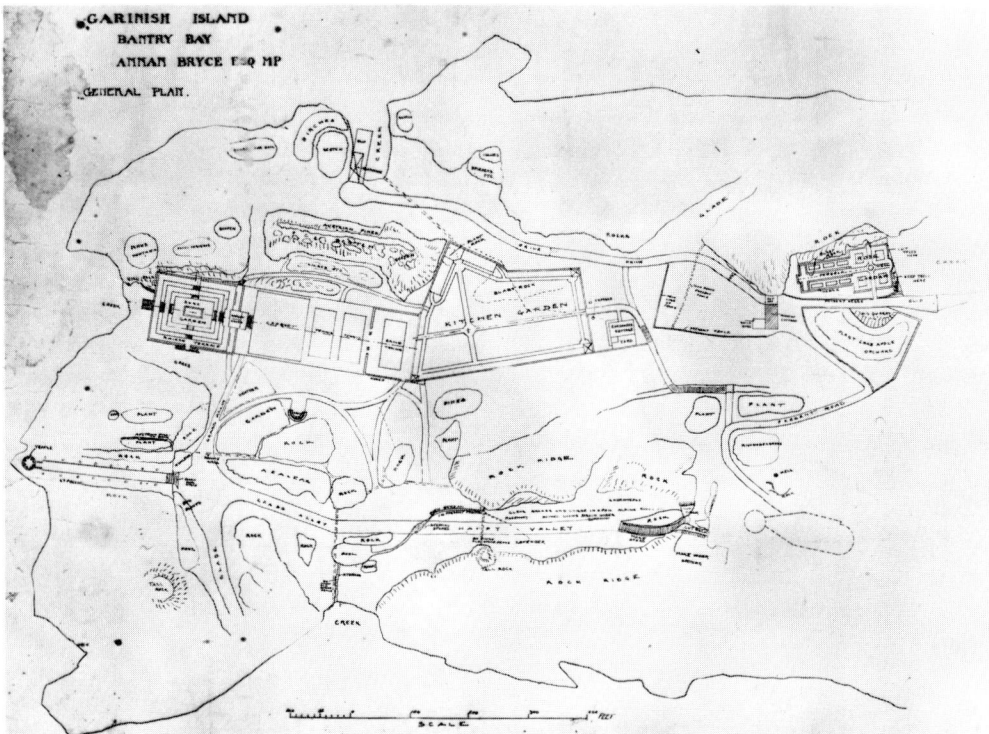

ILNACULLIN, CO.
CORK. *Harold Peto's plan
for the house and gardens.*

ILNACULLIN, CO.
CORK. *The hexagonal
pavilion, 1975.*

I   JOHNSTOWN CASTLE. *The Castle and the Upper Lake.*

R I V E R

V   MOUNT USHER.
River with bridges.

VI   DARGLE GLEN.
Water Garden with sculpture by Ian Stuart.

VII JAPANESE GARDEN, TULLY. *The Tea House.*

VIII DRUMLECK. *Doorcase at the end of the vista.*

IX BIRR CASTLE.
View from the river terrace.

X MALAHIDE CASTLE.
The Shrubbery.

XI GLENVEAGH CASTLE.
Formal paved garden.

XII MOUNT CONGREVE.
The Greenhouse.

XIII POWERSCOURT.
The Triton Fountain.

XIV ST ANNE'S.
*Watercolour drawing by
M. Waterfield,* c. *1910.*

persuaded by his wife to buy Ilnacullin (Garinish) island from the British Government. His contemporaries thought him foolhardy when in 1910 he started to work on this rocky, goat-ridden reef, with no natural springs of water. Heather and gorse alone flourished on the sphagnum peat and blue shale, while two or three small potato patches were the sole cultivation. First, therefore, the transport of some soil and humus from the mainland was necessary; after that the blasting of rock to find a spot to plant; then the planting of shelter belts of *Cupressus macrocarpa*, *Pinus laricio* and *P. radiata*; and finally, the designs of Harold Peto (1854–1933), the English garden architect, well known for his work at Iford Manor, Wiltshire, and in the south of France. From the first moment he looked down from the hill on Ilnacullin he was convinced he could design an Italian-style garden appropriate to that setting. Peto forcefully expressed his ideas about garden design in his privately printed work *The Book of Iford* (1917), when writing of Italian baroque gardens:

The entirely subordinate place in the scheme which flowers occupy gives a breadth and quietude to the whole which is sympathetic, the picture being painted with cypress hedges, canals and water-tanks, broad walks with seats and statues and tall cypresses.
    If more of our English Gardens could have an increase of this influence it would be well, instead of their running riot in masses of colour irrespective of form.

Annan Bryce accepted his designs, but not his horticultural ideas, and his subsequent partnership with Peto was in the great tradition: Bryce, the plantsman and Peto, the architect, both well read in garden history, each understanding the wishes of the other, and willing to compromise to find a suitable solution. Thus was the garden brought to life, by as many as a hundred men in the very early stages, working for three years until the outbreak of the First World War. After the War it was continued, but Bryce died, aged fifty, in 1924 and so saw his garden developing for only fourteen years. In working thus for his son he became one of the last in a tradition of gardeners who have planted for their successors. Had not Ulysses found his aged father planting trees when he had returned home after a ten-year absence, and asked him why he was planting 'that which he was never able to enjoy the fruits of'? The good old man (taking him for a stranger) gently replied, 'I plant against the day my son Ulysses comes home'. Peto also designed a large house for Annan Bruce. It was Romanesque Italian in its fenestration, with semicircular arches, crowning small shafts, and built on three and four storeys, with balconies and a large garden room from which to survey the scene. From an examination of the plans and elevations it would appear that Peto was as distinguished in garden architecture as he was second-rate in designing houses. Fortunately, through shortage of funds, the house was never built, and his son, Rowland Bryce, who succeeded, lived on the island in a cottage which was enlarged. There room was found for summer guests like AE (George Russell) and G. B. Shaw, who was there in 1923 when he was writing *Saint Joan*.
    As the garden was planned, a woodland glade extends the length of the 37-acre island from east to west, from the base of the hill to the sea. At the centre of this axis lies an open lawn, surrounded by trees and shrubs, providing a much-needed interval in the planting, as a resting-place for the eye and as a green nucleus for brighter horticultural colour. On one side the lawn is separated from the hill by mixed borders of flowers bisecting a large walled kitchen garden; on the other the axis leads to an open Italianate temple, the central feature of the whole design, then directly on to a large rectangular water-lily pond edged with paving and with a copy of Giovanni da Bologna's Mercury poised in the centre. This is surrounded on all sides by shrubs and grass walks intersecting the beds, leading to steps up to belvederes and look-outs on garden and sea. Near the pond at the west end of the axis, through the arches of Peto's Italianate pavilion with Ionic columns of Bath stone, appear the islets, headlands and coves of Glengarriff Bay.
    The garden is a perfect example of Robinsonian wild gardening held together by Italian formality in design and buildings. Every walk leads to an architectural feature: colonnades, flights of steps, urns, terraces or clipped hedges and conical

97

cypresses, and, above all, to glorious views across the water. Almost none of the gardens of the Italian Renaissance was set by the sea. On the other hand, many seaside villas were built for the refreshment of the patricians of ancient Rome. It is not surprising, therefore, that Harold Peto should have based his gardens at Ilnacullin on the latter. His own garden at Iford Manor is reminiscent of a garden made within the site of an excavated Roman villa, with a collection of detached columns, bases and capitals set out in an apparently predetermined fashion.

The letters of Pliny the Younger describe these seaside villas – in particular, his own on the Laurentian coast – as being characterized by the large number of pavilions, or *diaetae*, which were placed at the focal points of the garden. In one of these, situated on a point overlooking the sea, he dined on warm summer evenings with his friends, with the warm sea water lapping against the shore below and the view of the Alban Hills beyond. The resemblance of the pavilion at Ilnacullin to this, and others of ancient Rome, is reinforced by the use in it of the richly varying colours of the marbles, the red of *rosso antico* in the column shafts, the balustrades of white Carrara marble, yellow-veined marble from the island of Scyros, and green Connemara marble, done in *scagliola* on the floor. It was the work of Italian craftsmen, brought to the island for this purpose. On the opposite side of the sunken garden, which, in itself, resembles nothing more than a small garden of ancient Pompeii with its pool surrounded by a paved garden, and plants growing in small beds and pots, is a covered gallery, or *cryptoporticus*, like that under which Pliny and his friends walked and took the air in poor weather long ago. The roofless circular temple, high above the sea at one end of a vista, must, like the Temple of Venus and that of the Sybil at Tivoli, have been designed to take a statue of the goddess, which would appear silhouetted against the landscape of the bay, with the rugged Caha Mountains forming a backdrop to the whole scene.[28]

Were this garden to have none of these features, it would be similar to Tresco in the Scillies or Logan in Wigtownshire; but it excels these in having structure and form combined with admirable planting. At the top of the hill stands an intact Martello tower and ruined fort, built originally in 1800 by the British Government to take a garrison of an officer and ten men, who, it was presumed, might help to stem another French invasion similar to that led by Wolfe Tone in 1796, or even to deter Napoleon from landing on this remote island. The garrison remained forgotten until 1825, when it was replaced by herons.

One of the pleasantest qualities of good gardeners is their customary generosity in sharing plants with each other, and here, on Ilnacullin, many of the plants came

ILNACULLIN, CO.
CORK. Dacrydium
cupressinum, *1977*.

from Richard Annesley of Annes Grove, a friend of Rowland l'Estrange Bryce, who lived on the island and managed the property for his widowed mother from 1932 until her death seven years later. He carried on his gardening activities with enthusiasm where his father and mother had left off until his own death in 1953, before which he had bequeathed the island to An Taisce (the Irish National Trust), then an infant organization of which he had been a founder member. But, until An Taisce was able to look after it, he hoped it would be possible for the Irish State to take it over. This is what happened, and An Taisce has never claimed it.

Neither climate nor soil is as favourable as at Powerscourt or at Mount Stewart, the other gardens described in this chapter. The mean average rainfall is about 73 in, and there is a lack of sunshine. However, frosts rarely exceed 6° Fahrenheit and, if heavier, do not last for long. The island gets its fair share of gales, and trees which grow well have to withstand sea salt and wind. Douglas fir, for example, loses leaders and becomes bare on the windward side, whereas *Cupressus macrocarpa* 'Lutea', originally from the cliffs of Monterey, with its deep roots flourishes, gaining over 50 ft in twelve years from planting. *Pinus radiata* (Monterey Pine) and *P. thunbergii* also stand up very well in a maritime position. A specimen of *Pinus radiata* (1912) is the oldest and tallest tree on the island. A 30-ft *Dacrydium cupressinum* (New Zealand Red Pine), with slender hanging branches like combed-out hair, was thought by

99

W. J. Bean to be 'the best specimen recorded', and also mentioned by Bean is an *Acacia melanoxylon* (Blackwood), with its yellow spring flowers, which is more than 55 ft high.[29] There is a very tall and tender *Eucalyptus viminalis* (Ribbon Gum) whose bark peels in strips, and eucryphia, pittosporum, hoheria, grevillea, abutilon and leptospermum grow well in large quantities. There are few walls for climbers, but *Phileostegia viburnoides*, looking somewhat like schizophragma with its shiny leaves and panicles of white flowers, greets one in September from a north wall near the pier where one disembarks from a small boat.

After the death of an owner who personally supervises the making of a garden, followed by the departure of his family, a personal touch is easily lost, and, as is often the case in great houses, the garden becomes a museum or collection of plants. Such has not been the case at Ilnacullin. Since 1953 the loving care and expert knowledge of Mr Sidney Maskell, Assistant Principal Architect to the Commissioners of Public Works,[30] assisted by Mr Murdo Mackenzie, a Scot, who has spent fifty years on the island, have not only provided a continuity and improvement in the planting but, by so doing, in recent years have given more than 50,000 visitors annually a rewarding experience on this island paradise.

In 1915 the 7th Marquess of Londonderry succeeded to the title and inherited seats at Wynard Park, Stockton on Tees; Seaham Hall, Co. Durham; Springfield, Rutland; Mount Stewart, Co. Down; as well as the family's town residence, Londonderry House, in Park Lane, London. It is not surprising that his father and grandfather had lived for but a few weeks of each year at Mount Stewart, when, like the celebrated Lord Castlereagh, the Foreign Secretary, they had played a large part in British politics. Although Lord Londonderry's father had been Lord Lieutenant of Ireland (1886–9), and loyal tenants in 1858 had erected the 135-ft Scrabo Tower[31] on a near-by hill at Newtownards to the memory of the 3rd Marquess, the energies of the family in the nineteenth century had been directed towards the English, rather than the Irish, political scene. In 1871 the estate at Mount Stewart was 'unhappily like many other places in Ireland, too seldom inhabited'.[32] At that time there were eleven glasshouses, 500 ft in length, a vinery with a vine planted in 1769, a conservatory and a walled kitchen garden of $7\frac{1}{2}$ acres. But the head gardener was 'doomed to a life of comparative inactivity . . . owing to the influence of the non-resident principle'.[33] The main flower-garden, as in many large estates in Ireland and Scotland, was more than a mile from the house.

After the First World War, the Amending Act of Lloyd George separated the six counties as a self-governing area with a parliament of its own at Stormont, and Lord Londonderry, at the express wish of King George V, was appointed Minister of Education in this first Northern Ireland Parliament, a position he held for five years. During that time the Londonderrys lived at Mount Stewart, and the present garden was begun. It was a time of high unemployment in Northern Ireland, and the British Government asked landlords to take on as many men as they could. More than twenty additional men worked at Mount Stewart to make a new garden.

In previous years Edith, Lady Londonderry, had found the house and immediate surroundings to be 'the dampest, darkest and saddest place' she had ever stayed in during the winter months. 'Large ilex trees blocked out all light and air.'[34] Not surprisingly, on taking up residence she started on new gardens near the house in the English manner. Plans of the Mount Stewart gardens are in the Library of the University of California, in a file with other plans of Gertrude Jekyll and Edwin Lutyens. In the 1920s Miss Jekyll evidently was asked by Lady Londonderry to show exactly how the garden should be planted, rather than to produce plans for a new garden outlay.[35] Miss Jekyll's plans resemble contemporary gardens, such as those at Hidcote Manor, Gloucestershire, and Sissinghurst Castle, Kent, in having form and structure created by walls and hedges enclosing areas and compartments, each with different planting and character. On the horticultural side Lady Londonderry was advised by Sir John Ross of Bladensburg[36] before he died in 1926. His garden, which he had created at Rostrevor House on the slopes of a sheltered hill overlooking Carlingford Lough, Co. Down, in 1920 possessed the largest private

100

collection of plants in all Ireland. Today it is partly wilderness and partly built over, with one area forming a convent garden.

In 1922 Lady Londonderry visited Sir John Ross to seek his help. Much to his surprise, he saw an armoured car escorting her party, for such were prerequisites in Northern Ireland for politicians and their families in those years. She must have been horticulturally ingenuous, for, by way of complimenting him on his garden, she told him, 'It might have been the gardens at Kew'; to which he aptly replied, 'Dear Lady Londonderry, never mention Kew to me again. I can grow things here that Kew has never heard of.'

The value of such rare collections in private ownership cannot be overestimated. They show what the possibilities are for growth in any particular climate, and they also give valuable help to foresters with regard to new species. Such collections – and Mount Congreve, Co. Waterford, is today a supreme example – are often regarded as ornamental. This is far from the truth. They are national assets, and, if a body such as the National Trust cannot take them over, the State ought to do so. But, fifty years ago, at the death of Sir John Ross, such a State responsibility was unheard of, and, therefore, his unique garden has been allowed to disappear. Fortunately, like so many gardeners, he was always willing to allow inspection of specimens grown, ready to grant information concerning hardiness or rate of growth of his plants, and most generous in his horticultural gifts.

Lady Londonderry's other mentor was Sir Herbert Maxwell of Monreith, Wigtownshire. She could not have been advised by two gardeners with longer experience or knowledge of planting in warm seaside climates with generous acid soil such as they found at Mount Stewart. They 'incited' her, she wrote, to try to grow plants, trees and shrubs usually only grown in greenhouses. She found this strange, as her only previous gardening experience had been at her mother's home, Dunrobin Castle, Sutherland, on the eastern side of the extreme north of Scotland. Nevertheless, a garden had evidently flourished there for some centuries, as Sir Robert Gordon of Straloch, Geographer to Charles I, described it in a letter to the King:

Dunrobin, the Erle of Sutherland, his speciall residence, a house well seated upon a mote by the sea, with fair orchards, where there be pleasant gardens planted with all kinds of fruits, hearbs, and flowrs used in this kingdom, and abundance of good saphorn saffron, tabacco and rosemarie . . .[37]

As we all know, Great Britain is divided climatically not into north and south but east and west, as the Gulf Stream raises the temperature of our western seas in winter but lowers them in summer. Air currents pass over 4,000 miles of water from Florida to Co. Kerry or Land's End, and the moisture is carried east, is chilled on meeting land, lifts and condenses into rain or fog. On the coastline this does not happen immediately, and such landfalls which the Gulf Stream washes remain warm. This includes an enclosed lough like Strangford Lough and the western coastline of Scotland. Lady Londonderry soon discovered that at Mount Stewart, on a peninsula only four miles wide and twenty long, the Gulf Stream keeps the temperature high and the air humid even in hot weather. Nor is the sunshine deficient and the rainfall excessive, as on the west coast of Ireland. The soil is light, overlying marl and gravel. After fifty years in this garden, the growth of *Acacia longifolia* (Mimosa), cordylines, eucalypts, tender olearias and rhododendrons prove the advice given by Sir Herbert Maxwell and Sir John Ross to have been excellent.[38]

A terrace with stone balustrade, made in Victorian times, stretches the full length of the south side of the house which is only two-storeyed and unusually long. Lady Londonderry planned this terrace and the sculpture of the Italian garden immediately below to resemble that at the Villa Gamberaia at Settignano, near Florence,[39] where there is indeed a similar grassy terrace with balustrade punctuated by urns and statues. But the magnificent view from the terrace at Gamberaia over the Tuscan countryside and the domes of Florence does not resemble the vista to the Mourne Mountains over Strangford Lough, which now can be seen only from the first-storey windows of the house. The design of the beds in the centre of the garden was adapted

MOUNT STEWART, CO.
DOWN. Cordyline
indivisa.

MOUNT STEWART, CO.
DOWN. *Statuary, c. 1935.*

on a modified scale from one of the gardens at Dunrobin.[40] The humour, such as in the mural relief of the huntsman and his dog at the Villa Gamberaia, was imitated in the sculpture at Mount Stewart, although the execution is dissimilar. There is an old Irish tradition of animals in sculpture, and these are often seen in gardens, on furniture and plaster work. In fact, it is an ancient Roman tradition. Cicero describes effigies of animals, '*in vicem adversas*', formed in box trees; and in the Medici garden in Rome there were elephants, a wild boar, a ram, a hare and a ship with sails. At Mount Stewart Thomas Beattie, a local craftsman, moulded cement to the designs of Lady Londonderry: gnomes and gryphons, cats and kittens, dogs and dodos, horses and hedgehogs, baboons, rabbits, squirrels, crocodiles, as well as groups like lions behind a basin held up by a dog, a Noah's Ark, and numerous monkey terms.[41] The mythical creatures and the guardian terms, with their sly digs at humanity, irrepressible, solemn, scandal-mongering, backchatting, simpering, etc., are based on those in the delicious *giardino segreto* at the Casino of the Villa Farnese, at Capra-rola, north of Rome, where Cardinal Alessandro Farnese escaped from the pomp and circumstance of the life of a prince of the Church in the sixteenth century. Here, the beauty of the pagan world lived again, so much so that Queen Christina was moved to say, 'I dare not speak the name of Jesus, lest I break the spell'. The same might be said of the gardens of Mount Stewart, whose mythical beasts and creatures recur in many of Lady Londonderry's fairy stories. It is not so much in the crafts-manship of these animals that the fault lies but in the total disregard for the scale of the objects. For example, a horse may be much smaller than a near-by dodo, which, in turn, may be the size of a neighbouring Noah's Ark. Some of the humorously sculpted groups, such as a monkey holding a pot on its head while seated on a term, or a fox turning round to view the bird and the grapes, are more successful, bearing some resemblance to their witty equivalents in Italian gardens. Twin pairs of classical columns supporting mythical beasts are similar to those at the entrance to the *isolotto* of the Boboli Gardens in Florence, except that the heraldic griffons on the columns in the *isolotto* are replaced here by a pair of dragons statant from the Londonderry coat of arms. The balustrade, broken at regular intervals to accom-modate lemon pots, is also a feature of the *isolotto*. The intention was obviously to

MOUNT STEWART, CO. DOWN. *The Italian Garden, 1975.*

give to the gardens a structural form with stone and topiary work as borders to the different areas; but less statuary might have achieved the effect adequately. The cement has not weathered much, and even the abundant growth of plants has not concealed the assertive presence of some of these objects.

As Lady Londonderry admitted, the Spanish Garden (originally called the Pool Garden) below a flight of semicircular steps, was named only on account of the green Spanish roof tiles[42] on the summer-house, up which climbs the tender *Lapegeria rosa* (Chilean Bellflower) with lily-shaped crimson flowers. Arches of *Cupressus macrocarpa* were used as supports to honeysuckle on the borders of the garden but these have recently been replaced by yew. The design of the garden, according to Lady Londonderry, was taken from 'an Adam ceiling at the Mansion House'.[43]

The terraced Sunk Garden on the west side of the house was also bordered by a tall *Cupressus macrocarpa* hedge, framing the pergola by the house. Again there is formality in the planting of four large geometrical beds, divided from the grass by smaller bay and heather hedges. This garden leads into the paved Shamrock Garden, so called on account of its shape. It also was bordered by a *Cupressus macrocarpa* hedge, which must have been chosen on account of its fast growth but, because of its quick die-back from the ground, has had to be replaced by a *Cupressocyparis leylandii*. On top of this hedge there used to be cut a varied series of topiary scenes taken from 'Queen Mary's Psalter', now in the British Museum. In the centre of the garden is a bed cut from the flagstones in the shape of the Red (Bloody) Hand of Ulster, planted in *Irestine herbstii*. Beyond this, in topiary work, a large Irish harp is placed on a circular topiary table. The conifers in the area by the drive provide a rich background to this garden. The most sheltered part of the gardens is situated between the main entrance gates and the house, and in it grow many of the oldest trees: *Sequoia sempervirens*, *Cedrus atlantica glauca*, *Araucaria imbricata*, Douglas firs, *Abies grandis*, as well as many eucryphias, rhododendrons and heaths. They form a majestic collection which make an impressive entrance to the imposing north front of the house. This is obviously the best way to enter the gardens, but, as a tourist, one is brought in on the other side of the house. The Mairi Garden, near this entrance, should be seen in high summer, though there is a huge *Drimys winteri* which in May casts a scent over the whole garden. The trees here are all splendid specimens but have grown too large for this comparatively small garden.

The lake in the grounds is at least 7 acres and beautifully planted at the margins with irises, gunnera and arums. On a walk round one sees fine natural outcrops of rock and objects brought back by various Lords Londonderry on their travels: a cairn of stones from the Giant's Causeway in 1800 and a Japanese lantern and

MOUNT STEWART, CO. DOWN. *The Spanish Garden, c. 1930.*

MOUNT STEWART, CO. DOWN. *The Head Gardener making a frame for topiary work, c. 1930.*

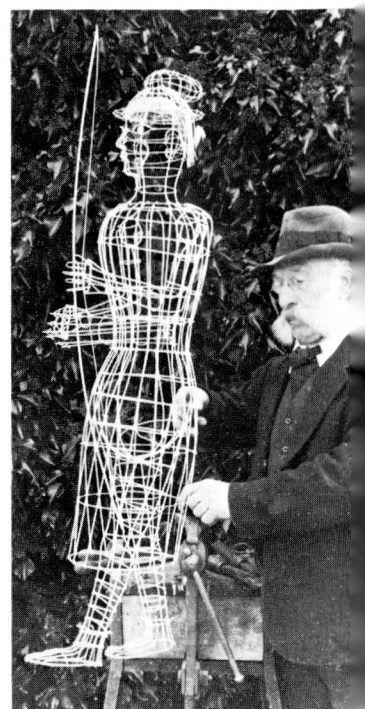

pagoda from Nikko, Japan, about a hundred years later. On the hill to the west, with a fine view over the lough, is Tir na nOg, the family burial ground, flanked at the entrance by statues of St Patrick and St Brigit.[44] The stone 'gateway', like those of ancient Erin, is open to the sky – a welcome change from the gloomy mausolea of many nineteenth-century landowners. It is planted with dark evergreens as a background to rosemary and roses, and many fine trees, such as the southern hemisphere beeches, and bright shrubs like *Cupressus cashmeriana, Pernettya mucronata* prevent the area from ever becoming gloomy. Tir na nOg, the Land of the Young, has an important place in Irish mythology, and W. B. Yeats, inspired by the story of Oisin in Tir na nOg, summed up the imagination of an Irish story-teller as:

always running off to Tir-ña-nog . . . which is as near to the country-people of today as it was to Cuchulain and his companions. His belief in its nearness cherished in its turn the lyrical temper, which is always athirst for an emotion, a beauty which cannot be found in its perfection upon earth, or only for a moment.[45]

There are many paths through the wild garden, all well planted: the Jubilee Avenue Walk (1935), the Rock Walk by the Lake, the Ladies' Walk from the House to the site of the original kitchen garden, the Woodland Walk and the Tennis Court Walk. It is landscaping on the grand scale, designed to give views of the house, the lake and bridge, a stream and a life-size statue of a white stag. Throughout this area there is much fine planting, especially of rhododendrons: fine, pale-yellow lily-like flowers of *R. Nuttallii* growing in the thin woodland; funnel-shaped flowers with red stripes of the tender *R. rhabotum*; fragrant white flowers of *R. taggianum*. Lady Londonderry reveals a strange method of growing some of these rhododendrons: 'some people grow them up their cabbage plants, the draecenas of Australia. I have tried some trained over a balloon with success.'[46]

This area complements the gardens immediately round the house, which are typical of the best of garden design between 1890 and 1925 – that is to say, they are compartmental gardens, modelled on the Italian Renaissance villa plan, which make use of hedges and walls in the layout of small divisions within large areas. With flowers planted freely in the Gertrude Jekyll manner, yet often in formally shaped beds, with pergolas for the support of climbers, with topiary work and local statuary, Mount Stewart is eclectic. The chief glory of the gardens is in the imaginative planting, whether in the wild garden in the William Robinson manner or in the different areas of the gardens close to the house. All bear witness to the skill of Lady Londonderry and her advisers, and to the recent care of the National Trust of Northern Ireland, which has undertaken much replanting, especially of the many *Cupressus macrocarpa* hedges that died off at their bases after fifty years. This is certainly not a lost demesne.

5 The Robinsonian Revolution

In 1822 John Constable reacted against the Claudean style of landscape painting which had flourished in the eighteenth century. As the styles of landscape painting and of landscape gardening were then so closely intertwined, his dislike for one was matched by his loathing for the other. 'I never had a desire to see sights, and a gentleman's park is my aversion', he said on one occasion.[1] Turning away, therefore, from the grand and contrived views of his predecessors, he chose to paint instead the simple rural scene, the wayside cottage rather than the classical temple, the Suffolk cornfield rather than the landscape park, and the functional millpond rather than the Claudean lake. His passion for modest nature was later shared by Crome and the Norwich school of painters, and spread to France through the influence of Corot.[2]

A parallel reaction in landscape gardening was much slower in coming, but when it did, in the latter half of the nineteenth century, it was against the excesses of the Victorian formal garden rather than the contrivance of the eighteenth-century landscape park. In 1870 William Robinson (1838–1937) published *The Wild Garden* in which he advocated a return to a simpler style of landscape gardening, based on a study of the unselfconscious naturalism of the cottage garden and on an attentive study of unadorned nature. He was conscious of the revolution which had already taken place in landscape painting and proposed that the approach to the natural scene should be that which should be adopted by the landscape gardener; for example:

Great landscape painters like Crome, Corot, and Turner seek things not only because they are natural, but also beautiful; selecting views and waiting for the light that suits the chosen subject, best, they gave us pictures, working always from a faithful study of nature and from stores of Knowledge gathered from her, and, that too, is the only true path for the gardener.[3]

His dislike for the formal garden is linked with his advocacy of the landscape painter as the gardener's model when he writes:

It is difficult to imagine Corot sitting down to paint the Grande [sic] Trianon or the terrace patterns of Versailles, though a poor hamlet in the North of France with a few willows near gave him a lovely picture.[4]

He was successful in re-establishing the link between landscape painting and landscape gardening which had been lost among the Victorian revivals of architectural styles of gardening.

William Robinson was born of northern Irish parents at Stradbally, Co. Leix. As a young boy, he entered the service of the Rev. Sir Hunt Johnson-Walsh on the neighbouring estate of Ballykilcavan, and rose over the years to become his trusted head gardener. In the winter of 1861 a violent row is said to have occurred between employer and head gardener. Robinson, extremely upset, left for Dublin one night, but not without having first drawn all the fires in the greenhouses and opened every window, so that by dawn the whole of the baronet's collection of tropical plants was dead or dying. This was a deplorable example of Robinson's lifelong pugnacity.[5]

In Dublin Robinson sought the help of David Moore, the great Director of the National Botanic Garden at Glasnevin, who sent him to the Botanic Society's garden at Regent's Park with an introduction to his friend, Robert Marnock. There he was given employment in building up the garden's collection of native British plants – a task ideal for him. It meant frequent visits to the countryside, 'to the orchid-flecked meadows of Bucks., and the tumbledown undercliffs of the Essex coast'. There he could escape the suffocation of the Victorian flower-garden and see with new eyes the beauty of wild flowers and trees, and wonder how this beauty could again be introduced into our gardens. His arrival in London coincided with the erection of Paxton's Crystal Palace Garden, an extravaganza for which the resources of the world's plant life and entire vocabulary of landscape gardening had been summoned to create a modern Versailles for the jaded appetite of the Victorian public. His fresh eye saw the empty bombast beneath it all. The Crystal Palace and Paxton's garden at Chatsworth, he said, were 'designed as they might be by a theatrical super, who had suddenly inherited a millionaire's fortune'.[6] As Repton had done earlier in the century, he brought from Ireland an eye for natural beauty, picturesque, often wild, which was to have a resuscitating effect on the over-tailored gardens of England. There had never been a parterre at Ballykilcavan, and *jardins à la mode* were few in Ireland, confined to the very grand houses only.

Irish gardening fashions tend to be conservative; to compensate for this, however, there has always been a keen eye for the garden in its natural landscape setting. Robinson reminds us, in *The English Flower Garden*, of Plato's belief that 'The greatest and fairest things are done by Nature, and the lesser by Art'. At a similar moment in the early eighteenth century Pope had warned his fellows: 'In all, let Nature never be forgot', and his equally memorable advice 'Consult the genius of the place in all' is echoed less elegantly by Robinson when he writes: 'The best kind of garden should arise out of its site as happily as a primrose out of a cold bank.' There were remarkable differences between the return to Nature in eighteenth-century landscaping and that which was to occur a century later. The eighteenth-century landscapist believed that Nature had her defects which might be improved by judicious landscaping: marshes might be drained and unsightly outcrops of rock removed from higher ground. Indeed, rock blasting was a commonplace of eighteenth-century improvement. (Its dangers and attendant comedies are wittily described in Thomas Love Peacock's *Headlong Hall*.) Robinson on the other hand felt Nature had no such faults. Outcrops of rock were seen by him as God-given opportunities for natural rock-gardening, a marsh as a chance not to be lightly thrown away for a bog-garden. However, Robinson's apparent respect for Nature did not prevent his ignoring her in another way – for he was prepared to advocate the naturalization of exotic plants from one corner of the globe in the gardens of another. In fact, it was this very aspect of man's intervention in the natural order of things that was to become the chief characteristic of the Robinsonian garden. By the importation of a host of exotic plants into the natural circumstances of a garden's site he hoped to realize an ideal notion of Nature, just as the eighteenth-century landscapist had done. This idea of another Eden was promulgated in a series of lengthy and popular books which struck sweet music in the late Victorian ear. *The Wild Garden* (1870) and *The English Flower Garden* (1883) ran into countless editions and were supplemented by a barrage of articles in the many periodicals and books which Robinson either edited or contributed to between 1870 and 1937. He retired in 1890 to his house and garden at Gravetye Manor, Sussex, there to put into practice his published ideas. In 1911 he produced the sumptuous *Gravetye Manor, or Twenty Years Work round an Old Manor*, which formed an apotheosis of his ideas. He died in 1937, a rich and successful old man, leaving his house and estate to the Charity Commissioners.

By that time the Robinsonian style had truly emerged as that of the era. It took the form of a house standing on a spreading lawn, which was conceived of as an 'improved' meadow, planted with groups of naturalized bulbs and field flowers. This lawn was enclosed by mixed borders of trees, shrubs and flowers, conceived in its turn as an 'improved' country hedgerow or natural shrubbery. An occasional errant tree would break the general shrub line, and colonies of herbaceous plants grow up in summer at its feet. Beyond that was a piece of woodland or water, each again treated as an 'improved' natural copse or stream. The woodland canopy sheltered layers of shade-loving vegetation, and an occasional climber scaled a tree-trunk to reach up to the light. The stream was colonized by water buttercups and lilies in a natural way, and its damp margins were planted with flag irises, exotic primulae and other waterside plants. The temple or folly was replaced as the garden's focal point by the open vista to the surrounding countryside, to river or valley, to mountain or lough. These vistas, he felt, would provide sufficient contrast to the cultivation within. Such gardens are now common in every land, for they are founded, as was the 'International Style' of architecture, on a simple, honest and natural approach to design, and a striking fidelity to the materials. A garden to Robinson was not an outdoor room, nor a decorative promenade, nor a museum of architectural ornament. He might well have paraphrased his contemporary Gertrude Stein, and said: 'A garden is a garden is a garden.'

William Robinson frequently visited the garden at Garinish Island, Lord Dunraven's subtropical paradise off the coast of Kerry at Parknasilla. Near this, two other great Robinsonian gardens were being developed at that time: Derreen, the property of Lord Lansdowne, and Rossdohan, another island, the property of Surgeon-Major Samuel Heard. Derreen lies by a quiet inlet of a deep bay and is enclosed on the inland side by a blue wall of mountain. Its wooded promontory had been in the Petty-Fitzmaurice family since the thirteenth century, though they never lived there, preferring the more civilized country round Lixnaw and Kenmare.[7] In the early nineteenth century the 3rd Marquess of Lansdowne set out to afforest these mountains by planting thousands of sycamore, ash and beech trees, and some hundreds of evergreen Scots and maritime pine, so that by 1860 when his successor, the 4th Marquess, decided to make Derreen his Irish home, the promontory and its surroundings had lost their forbidding aspect.[8] His son, the 5th Marquess (1845–1923), enlarged his father's house there and created to the designs of the architect J. F. Fuller the Victorian villa we see today.[9] It was set down in a woodland clearing on the highest part of the promontory and surrounded by an undulating Robinsonian lawn, which in turn was bordered by the hoary limbs of a woodland of native oak. The 5th Marquess loved Derreen, preferring it to the splendours of Bowood, Wiltshire, or Lansdowne House in London, and every year of his life, with the exception of those when he was Governor-General of Canada and Viceroy of India, spent many months there, supervising the planting of fine trees and rare shrubs. The garden today remains substantially as he left it.[10]

The lawn about the house is spreadeagled with groups of Scots pines, whose branches cast long shadows delightfully distorted by the undulations of the ground. Shade was thus provided for leisurely Victorian tea parties when King

DERREEN, CO. KERRY.
A view of the garden.
DERREEN, CO. KERRY.
Lord Lansdowne (aged 80) in the garden, 1925.

Edward VII and Queen Alexandra, Prime Ministers and Lords Lieutenant made the long journey to Derreen. J. A. Froude, the historian, who wrote there *The English in Ireland in the Eighteenth Century* (3 vols, 1872–4) and gathered local colour for his historical novel *The Two Chiefs of Dunboy*, recalled one such house party:

In another minute we were on the broad walk that leads to the house. The night was hot, my friend's party were on the lawn, some of them had been dining on board a yacht which lay at anchor a mile from the windows. The house stood in the middle of a lawn shut in on all sides by woods, through which however openings had been cut in various places, letting in the view of the water and a landscape of wooded promontories and long creeks. The rest was as nature made it, the primeval forest untouched save for the laurels and rhododendrons which were scattered under the trees . . . all around us rose the wall of mountain.[11]

Froude goes on to describe the intoxicating atmosphere of his first night there, when the party lingered on the lawn, reluctant to go in as the air was so warm, gazing at the moonlight, the mountains silhouetted against the bright night sky, the bridge reflected in the harbour below; and listening to the cries of seals offshore, the voices of fishermen laying out their nets and the call of a heron by the boat-house. From this lawn in front of the house rises a huge dome-shaped outcrop of rock, worn smooth by aeons of time, and now made into a natural rock-garden, of which Robinson would have approved, with self-sown young plants of native ferns growing among saxifrages. The lawn is surrounded by swirling patches of mown grass and curving borders of hardy trees and shrubs, and then drifts off into a series of long vistas which eventually fan out on to the rocky shores, with their spectacular sea views beyond. These long undulating rides float above their rocky substratum and are flanked by loosely arranged borders of flowering shrubs, set against backgrounds formed by pools of rich, dark-green conifers, which are in turn set against the oak-wood. The glossy leaves of huge old rhododendron hybrids reflect the light up into the sombre shadows of the old conifers, behind their hanging domes of close-knit rosettes of leaves, contrasting with the upright habits of Chilean embothriums and myrtles. The sombre myrtles and bays are flecked with the light of adjacent hydrangeas, hoherias and grey-leaved buddleias. Colonies of foliage plants front the glade-sides at intervals, their line broken by the occasional clusters of cordoline palms or phormiums. At the end of one vista a twin-arched bridge crosses a pool of light which is the river falling into the harbour. At the end of another is a simple boat-house, alongside which a long zig-zagging timber foot-bridge leads out to an islet thickly clothed with *Phormium tenax*, *Rhododendron ponticum* and furze under a canopy of Scots pine. The wind sweeps up these vistas, so that only wind-resistant species can be planted along these borders, but backwaters of lawn are tucked in among the woodland to give sheltered glades where more tender plants are grown in the long grass. These little pockets are completely shut off from the sea and the mountains, and have only the sky for reference, but they make one's emergence into the open vistas all the more dramatic. Here tall wattles from New Zealand and crinodendrons from Chile grow, and, most spectacular of all, the wands of tall tree ferns, which have taken control of some parts of the garden, spread themselves by self-distributed spores, which grow best in the drainage channels dug in the dark peaty soil. Myrtles like the soil here, and arbutus thrives better than on the sunny shores of Calabria.

A labyrinth of winding paths leads off from these areas to cross and recross the woodland. The banks on either side are clothed with wild strawberries and whortleberries. Old oaks emerge from huge boulders draped with fern which grows luxuriantly wild; masses of heather are waist deep on the Old Red Sandstone; curtains of Irish ivy drape the vertical faces; the rare Killarney fern is cosseted in quiet pockets; and open banks of rock are gardened with stonecrops and young plants of fern, their rainpools reflecting the Atlantic skies above. A canopy of aged oak is darkened occasionally by a huge specimen conifer – a *Cryptomeria japonica* 'Elegans', for example, which is said to be the biggest in our islands, the tallest of western red cedars (botanically not a cedar). This tree, which was planted by Lord

Lansdowne in 1880, towers over a path charmingly named The King's Oozy. Other trees planted by him in that year are *Abies nordmanniana* and *Pinus radiata*. A huge *Cupressus macrocarpa* had been planted by his father in 1856.[12] The bright trunks of occasional eucalyptus (some of the *Eucalyptus globulus* are, according to Bean, among the largest recorded in cultivation, and were planted in 1870), and groves of silver birch light up the darker areas of woodland. Damp hollows are hidden by waving bamboo groves.

The late nineteenth and early twentieth centuries saw the rise of the great rhododendron mania, which was similar to the tulipomania that swept through Holland in the seventeenth century. Lord Lansdowne, not to be outdone, planted over 100 *R. arboreum* hybrids, mainly Waterer's, one of which was named after his wife. As Viceroy of India, he brought back rare species from the east, and many grew so rapidly in the favourable climate that they had to be cleared to allow others light and room. He was later a subscriber to the Cox and Kingdon-Ward plant-hunting expeditions to the Far East. He also obtained seed from E. H. Wilson's expeditions to China, from Sir Frederick Moore of the National Botanic Garden at Glasnevin, and bought many new and exotic plants from the great nursery firm of Veitch.[13] *Rhododendron sinogrande*, *R. delavayi*, *R. falconeri*, and *R. niveum* from the Bhutan, Sikkim and Tibet are now enormously tall by the woodland paths. Another popular feature of woodland in Victorian times was 'laurel lawns', long vistas opening on to trees over an undergrowth of clipped laurels. Except for one in the garden of Fernhill, Co. Dublin, they have now all gone – victims of rising maintenance costs (see p. 123).

In *The Wild Garden* Robinson proposed the naturalization in our gardens, fields and woods of beautiful, hardy plants from other countries. In gardens in cold climates this usually means planting them out in locations where they can look after themselves, but at Derreen, and other such gardens in mild climates, it means true naturalization: so once planted, they will not only look after themselves but will

ROSSDOHAN, CO. KERRY. *The house designed by J. P. Seddon, c. 1885.*

settle down and propagate as they do in their native habitats, so that the original plant spreads itself into a picturesque group. We have mentioned already how this happens with tree ferns, and many other plants – pernettyas, gaultherias and myrtles – also spread themselves naturally into huge colonies on the edges of rides.

The mild climate and mountain setting by the sea, which Lord Lansdowne compared to Homer's Ithaca, make Derreen one of the finest achievements of Irish landscape gardening. '*Ut neque planis porrectus spatiis, nec multae prodigiis herbae*' (There should neither be a great extent of open space, nor an excess of vegetation), he wrote in a letter to the Prime Minister, Mr Balfour, inviting him to stay at Derreen.[14] It was sad when the house was looted and burned in his eighty-seventh year during the Troubles of 1922. It was rebuilt, however, after his death in 1923, and after a long period of dormancy the garden has now been redeveloped. In the early 1950s it was inherited by Lord Lansdowne's granddaughter, Viscountess Mersey, a keen gardener, who restored and extended the plantings, especially of subtropical plants – tender rhododendrons of the Maddenii and Edgeworthii series, and tender Mexican pines, *Pinus montezumae* and *Pinus patula*. Her plantings of large-leaved *R. macabeanum* are splendidly at home and in scale with the curling contours of the mountains behind.

Across the bay from Derreen a retired Indian Army Surgeon-Major, Samuel Thomas Heard (1835–1921), bought an island in 1873 and made a garden at the same time as Lord Lansdowne. Rossdohan, as it is called, was then a plateau of peat-covered rock off the northern shore of the estuary and buffeted by the strongest of Atlantic gales, which periodically sweep up the bay. This unfriendly and uninhabited island, with but a single twisted hawthorn on it, must have attracted him by its singularly uninterrupted views of the long bay between the mountain ranges, described by John Montague in his poem, 'Rossdohan, Co. Kerry':

> Caha to the South, McGillycuddy to the North,
> This bay lies, like a giant bowl
> Of blue water, held reverently
> Between monstrous palms

Samuel Heard had been born in West Cork, thirty miles from Rossdohan.[15] His family's seat of Ballintober, near Kinsale, is now a lost demesne, and its elaborate and distinguished formal gardens of the late seventeenth century are known to us only through a contemporary bird's-eye view.[16] He was interested in gardening in his youth, when exotic plants were already being grown successfully in many Co. Cork gardens: James Hugh Smith Barry was collecting trees at Fota; the Earl of Shannon was planting camellias at Castlemartyr; and Lady Doneraile (to whom Curtis dedicated a volume of his *Botanical Magazine*) was grafting rhododendrons at Doneraile Court.[17] Heard graduated in medicine and then spent some time in Paris, when the experiments of Barillet-Deschamps in bedding out subtropical foliage plants in the parks were causing a stir in the gardening world. The influence of these experiments was to be far-reaching, for they were not only to inspire William Robinson to write his first two books, *Gleanings from French Gardens* (1868) and *Parks, Promenades and Gardens of Paris* (1869) but were also to influence the fantastic paintings of subtropical jungles by le Douanier Rousseau (1844–1910). In fact, the woodland garden which Heard laid out at Rossdohan was to become reminiscent of the waterside jungle in Rousseau's *La Charmeuse des Serpents*. During the 1860s there was even an attempt to emulate the subtropical gardening of the Parisian parks in Merrion Square, Dublin. The principal progenitor was John Adair (see p. 148) who published a delightful period piece entitled *Hints on the Culture of Ornamental Exotic Plants in Ireland* (1870),[18] which combines a high moral tone with practical suggestions for culture. He extols the Emperor Napoleon III for his patronage and largess in connection with the subtropical gardening in Paris, exhorts his fellow Irishmen to go and see it, and invites those who cannot do so to read William Robinson's accounts of it.

After his period in Paris, Heard spent fifteen years in India before he returned to make his own subtropical garden at Rossdohan. Joining the East India Company and being stationed as a surgeon at Madras, he became familiar with the exotic plants in the Madras Horticultural Gardens.[19] Lord Mayo, then Viceroy, records that these gardens 'had a good collection of flowering shrubs and plants, the greater number of which are well known in our hothouses'.[20] Heard was later to grow tender East Indian ferns out of doors at Rossdohan; but the greatest single influence on the garden he was to create was his marriage in 1862 to Kate, daughter of William Bradley of New South Wales, as it was for his importations of Australasian trees and shrubs and for the unique size and proliferation which they attained on his Co. Kerry island that Heard was later to become so well known.

By the time he had retired from the army in 1873 and bought Rossdohan in the frost-free climate of the Kenmare peninsula, Heard had obtained a broad and sympathetic experience of the subtropical plant world in its native habitat. First of all, he built a curious house to the designs of the architect J. P. Seddon on the inland side of the island.[21] It stood on an outcrop of rock jutting into the bay, its base washed by the waters of the rhinestone inlets on either hand, and given an exotic eastern air by a glazed verandah decorated with lunettes of coloured glass. Protection from Atlantic gales was his first concern in laying out his garden, so he planned a series of dense shelter-belts round the house, cut through by narrow curving walks of coral, which opened occasionally into dappled glades. The two main walks ran out from the house, one under the landward side of the long narrow ridge which follows the spine of the island, and the other across the island to the stable courtyard on the western shore.

In the first place Heard planted native gorse and Chilean escallonia in large groups to take the initial brunt of the south-west gales, as he knew of the success of Lord Carbery (1810–89) who had planted gorse to shelter his wind-blown demesne at Castlefreke on a headland in West Co. Cork. He was then able to grow some of the first flush of the great rhododendron hybrids produced by Waterer's Nursery at Bagshot (1855).[22] He must equally well have known of the garden of the Knight of Kerry (1808–80) at Glanleam on Valentia Island not ten miles away. In this remote place the Knight, with the shelter provided by escallonia, fuchsia and other wind-hardy shrubs, had succeeded in growing a scintillating range of South American plants – myrtles, fuchsias, drimys, escallonias and embothriums.[23] These were new to Europe at the time, having been collected by William Lobb (1809–63) in Brazil and Chile and distributed through the nurseries of Messrs Veitch and Sons. The Knight's successes with them were well known in the popular gardening press of the time, but neither Castlefreke nor Glanleam was in such an unfriendly locality as Rossdohan, so Heard also planted extensive areas of Monterey cypresses and pines. The former were by then common in Ireland and had been planted at Derreen twenty years before, but the Monterey pine had been experimented with only by the Dorrien-Smith family at Tresco Abbey, a similarly wind-swept garden in the Scilly Isles.

Within the areas created by his shelter-belt Heard planted many species of Australasian, South American, Himalayan and southern European trees and shrubs, and so they became jungles of exotic vegetation, like those at Tresco, Oporto, the Azores, the Canaries, and Madeira. All of these places were on the old sea route around the Cape to the east and had similar climates. Commerce in plants along this route flourished long before the nineteenth-century plant-hunting expeditions began, so one finds there are remarkable specimens of eastern Australian pittosporums at Rossdohan which had been naturalized in the Azores since the early nineteenth century. *Acacia melanoxylon* (Black Wattle), prolific around Funchal in Madeira where they were introduced from Australia, is just as common at Rossdohan as is *Clethra arborea* (Lily-of-the-Valley Tree), wild in the woods and thickets of Madeira.

The garden at Rossdohan, therefore, belongs to a world of rarefied vegetation confined to a few small areas along the eastern shores of the Atlantic. The Cape-route exotics were intensified by a variegated cordyline, a South African virgilia, a North African lycium (Box Thorn), East Indian ferns, an enormous clump of

Arundinaria simonsii (Simon's Bamboo), and an *Aralia chinensis* from Manchuria.[24] This polygenetic exoticism was reinforced by a dense enclosure, since the need for shelter precluded any open vistas to the surrounding coastal landscape as was possible at Derreen; but there was some relief in the many native plants which were able to establish themselves, for the first time, on the island in the shelter of the Californian conifers, and so were able to give the authentic Robinsonian character to the garden.

Through the woodland walks today the Australasian plants, light of habit, bark and leaf, are set off beautifully by the dark masses of the conifers. A tall spreading eucalyptus dominates the main path: Silver and Black Wattles soar in clusters about its head, forming a complex tracery against the sky. Their seed is shed upon the ground, from which young colonies rise about them. Bristling cordylines smite the sky. In the upper reaches of the shade one sees the tall fans of the old tree ferns waving slowly in the wind. These enormous primitive plants, both *Cyathea dealbata*, the Silver Tree Fern of New Zealand, which is said to have covered the globe once, and the green *Dicksonia antartica* of Australia, shed a moving kaleidoscope of light and shade, through the complex architecture of their fronds, on the floor below and on their young, which grow in clefts of rock or in the rough bark of olearias, and make rings of tongue-like ferns round the mossy trunks of the soaring trees. The floor is also littered with young plants of native ferns – Royal, King and Hart's Tongue – crowding on to the path. Such a place as this, where nature has taken over from man, would have exceeded Robinson's wildest expectations when he wrote *The Hardy Fern Garden*, for this is a world of fancy and daydreams. One marvels at the crowding growth as one listens to the music of the leaves when the wind rises off the bay or observes the long fronds and branches oscillating in compound rhythm against the sky. As one passes through the shelter-belt of conifers, one enters the world of reality again on the shores of the light-filled bay. Here the wide seascape of the Kenmare river stretches out, with its bright skies, moving horizons, delicate patterns of water and clear humid atmosphere such as are found in the landscape paintings of Daubigny (1817–78), which were so much admired by Robinson.

ROSSDOHAN, CO. KERRY. *A grove of Silver Tree Ferns.*

ROSSDOHAN, CO. KERRY. *The Bamboo Grove.*

The path which leads to the stableyard flanks a long, winding lawn backed by deep borders of trees and shrubs among outcrops of rock, all seen against a dark-green frieze of pines. This reach of the garden is today a much newer creation, for on account of its greater exposure it has been destroyed more than once in south-westerly gales. Plants of fine architectural form give rhythm along its length. Sheaves of the sword-like *Phormium tenax* (New Zealand Flax), green, variegated and purple, contrast with the tiered platters of the Chilean gunnera, while *Beschorneria yuccoides*, arundinarias and palms contribute their own sculptural forms. In between, the less shapely of the Australasian plants, olearias, hakeas, callistemons, cassias, kunzeas, boronias and leptospermums, of which Heard once had the best collection in these islands, each contribute its flowery mass. Outcrops of Old Red Sandstone coated with lichens and moss periodically emerge from the borders and are gardened with rock plants in nature's way. Coral paths intensify the subtropical ambience, and a lily pool, surrounded by a terrace, lies quietly in a corner.

A volume of *Curtis's Botanical Magazine* was dedicated to Mr Heard after he died in 1921. He had not only grown many rarities of the temperate and warm-temperate world but had tried in cultivation in Europe a number of plants for the first time, among them the tender *Eucalyptus viminalis* (Ribbon Gum) and *E. stellulata*, both from his wife's homeland in New South Wales.[25] His house was burned down in the Troubles in 1923, and the garden was grazed by cattle and sheep until 1941, when the island was bought by Nicholas I. Fitzgerald, who built a new house in the Dutch Colonial style to the designs of Michael Scott. This was also burned down. The tall ruin of Old Red Sandstone is now maintained as a romantic focus for the garden. High on a terrace looking down the full length of this blue, mountain-clad bay, one can climb the ruined staircase to the floor of the top storey and gaze across that superbly unaltered view.

Some gardens are lucky to have been continually maintained since their inception; others die a rapid death. It takes only a short period of neglect for this to occur, but few gardens can be said to have been rescued at the last moment from extinction. This is what has happened at Rossdohan, for it was bought in 1955 by Ralph Walker, a past President of the Royal Horticultural Society of Ireland, and his brother Philip. In the last twenty years they have revived this neglected garden, often against overwhelming odds, and have brought it to a point of perfection which it might well have never achieved. They have renewed the essential shelter-belts, especially after disastrous losses from the storm in 1958, they have cleared the old woodland garden so that Heard's achievement can again be recognized, and they have added to the planting, in the Heard tradition, by trying out many new and rare plants.

Near Rossdohan is Garinish Island, acquired about 1860 by the 3rd Earl of Dunraven, the noted antiquary and scholar. It lies in a romantic position some hundreds of yards off the mainland at Parknasilla. The island was clothed with a wood of indigenous sessile oak and was divided by a high ridge of rock, in the lea of which Lord Dunraven built a lodge designed by J. F. Fuller, the architect of Derreen. This was perched on a plateau of rock, its wide overhanging eaves and sloping roofs reaching almost to the ground in the manner of an Alpine lodge, a perfect complement to the Alpine and rock-garden which was later laid out about it. The 3rd Earl used the lodge as a base for yachting, archaeological expeditions, and entertaining his learned friends.[26] In 1868 one of his daughters married Lord Barrymore of Fota, and so on inheriting Garinish in 1871 the 4th Earl (1841–1926) would have become familiar with the growing collection of trees and shrubs in his brother-in-law's arboretum near Cork. He spent much of his life abroad, however, at one time being an under-secretary for foreign affairs in London, where he would have worked with Lord Lansdowne, his neighbour across the estuary at Kenmare. It was not until his retirement at the age of sixty that Lord Dunraven began the development of the subtropical wild garden on the island, when the gardens of Rossdohan and Derreen were already thirty years old.

The island is characterized by a series of parallel glens which run across it from east to west, terminating in rocky creeks by the shore and separated by high ridges of limestone. The geological structure has been brilliantly exploited in the design of the gardens. The sheltered glens were filled with soil from the mainland to provide level or softly undulating lawns at the bottom. In each, a wide range of subtropical trees and shrubs was placed, carefully spaced to allow each to grow to its full, natural shape – a matter considered of great importance by William Robinson. Each valley was treated differently in that each was planted predominantly, but not exclusively, with one genus – a further point upon which Robinson insisted. One now is a magnolia glade, filled with pink and white blossoms in spring; another has become a woodland of palms and cordylines. A rare New Zealand palm, *Areca sapida*, was also tried; it was flourishing in 1926 but has since disappeared. Yet another glen glows with Japanese maples and has a great eucalyptus as sentinel at one end. A kitchen garden occupies another, but the most entrancing is a wooded one in which a long avenue of *Dicksonia antartica* (tree ferns) grows, many of them removed from Rossdohan after its sale in 1923[27] and now large and handsome specimens. Associated with them, as at Rossdohan, are broad underplantings of exotic and native ferns – woodwardias, king, royal and hart's tongue ferns – the combinations of which give to this glade the character of an enormous outdoor fernery. Under each of the lawns an extensive drainage system was necessary, but difficulty was turned to advantage by conducting all the drains into a single glade at a lower level, there to form a natural rock-pool, where Asiatic primulas luxuriate and seed themselves along the margins, and water-lilies flourish.

GARINISH ISLAND, CO. KERRY. *The tree fern avenue.*

Threaded through these glens are brilliant Himalayan rhododendrons and seas of colourful azaleas. Many tall trees of pittosporum and myrtle add an evergreen rhythm from glen to glen. A tall variegated *Pittosporum eugenoides*, 30 ft high, and a sweet-scented *P. tobira* were remarked upon in 1926.[28] Bamboos tower above, and a climbing hydrangea scales the summit of a tall Scots pine. These are Robinsonian wild gardens – 'the placing of perfectly hardy exotic plants in places where they will look after themselves' – *par excellence*.[29]

There is, however, another aspect of Robinsonian gardening which cannot be seen in the gardens we have mentioned so far, and that is the natural rock-garden. In 1870 Robinson published *The Wild Garden* and also *Alpine Flowers for English Gardens* which was the fruit of a visit to Switzerland the previous year. In Geneva M. Henri Corrévon had initiated a new idea in gardening – the use of natural constructions of rock and stone as a setting in which a variety of mountain plants from many parts of the world could be grown. Robinson wished to introduce this to the British Isles. Its emphasis on the simulation of a natural setting of rock appealed to him, and he castigated the artificial cement and 'refuse brick rockeries' which were the common currency of the time. The natural ridges of rock which formed the valley's sides at Garinish, over which one clambers to get from one sheltered valley to the next, provide ideal settings for a series of such rock-gardens. Narrow paths and winding flights of steps were first cut into the rock faces, and along the ridges much of the soil and overlying scrub was removed to lay bare the beautiful grey limestone which had been waterworn into the most wonderful hollows, shelves and

116

ravines. Many of these were then filled with gritty soil preparations by Mr Robertson, Lord Dunraven's gardener, so that in time they came alive with sheets of Spanish gorse. Near-by shelves carried groups of cistus;[30] rare saxifrages mixed with hanging sheets of the commonest pink oxalis; groups of blue lithospermums spread among the boulders along the plateaux, mingling with colonies of heathers; and curtains of *Vitis coignetiae* (Crimson Glory Vine) hung over a steep vertical face. Here the rare Kerry lily still finds a home. Nothing compares with the excitement in this garden of climbing up the paths to one of the ridges only to discover yet another subtropical glade laid out below. It is a garden of constant surprise, none greater than the occasional view from a high point of the clear waters of the bay and the soft blue of the Kerry mountains framed by a pine tree. The brilliant exploitation of the natural features of the island to provide an alternating series of rock-gardens and subtropical glens suggests the directing hand of an overall designer.

A planting book on the island lists all the plants which were so generously given to Lord Dunraven by other gardeners:[31] a large collection of bamboos from Lord Lansdowne and a rare *Acacia falcata* from Dr Heard. Much came from Fota and from Lord Dunraven's garden at Adare Manor, but quantities of plants were bought from nurseries in the milder climates of Cornwall, the Scilly and the Channel Islands, and a collection of hydrangea species was even imported directly from Japan in 1913. The majority of Lord Dunraven's plants came from the Daisy Hill Nursery, Newry, Co. Down, which specialized in designing many rocky stream-gardens in Ireland at the time in a style similar to those designed by Messrs Veitch and Sons of Exeter. In addition, quantities of pernettya hybrids arrived from the famous breeder, L. G. Davis of Hillsborough, Co. Down. The island remained the property of the Dunraven family until the 1950s when it was bought by Mr Reginald Browne who maintained, extended and renewed the garden, which is now owned by his sons.

The coastline round Kenmare boasted a host of smaller wild gardens at the time, including that of Captain Wyndham-Quin, Lord Dunraven's cousin, at Derrynane Cottage,[32] also that of The O'Mahony round his great Gothic castle of Dromore which still hides deep in its forest by the shore,[33] and, above all, Colonel Hartley's small garden at Reennaferraha.[34] Here a row of cabbage palms had their trunks clothed with a number of different clematis varieties, the collection of bamboos rivalled that of Rossdohan, and the gunnera had leaves much bigger than anybody else's! Over the Caha Mountains at Glengarriff, Lady Ardilaun started a garden of rhododendrons and South American plants but abandoned it. Glengarriff Castle had fine eucalypts,[35] and Mr Bryce began the making of the island garden at Ilnacullin (see Chapter 4). Further along the coast at Bantry House Gerard Leigh White was planting Waterer's rhododendrons, and at near-by Ardnagashel House the Hutchins family, guided by the then Director of Kew, was making a fine arboretum, which now boasts some immense trees, the finest *Podocarpus salignus* in these islands, a large *Cryptomeria japonica* and the most beautiful cork oak.[36] Ardnagashel is owned by Captain Ronald Kaulback, who accompanied Captain Frank Kingdon-Ward on his famous plant-hunting expedition in the Himalayas in 1924–5 and he and his wife have added many Himalayan trees and shrubs to this sheltered wooded valley by the shore of Bantry Bay.[37]

A new phase in Robinsonian gardening in Ireland was begun by Mr and Mrs Reginald Bence-Jones not far away at Lisselane, near Clonakilty, Co. Cork. Robinson, in his early works, had addressed himself to the subjects of subtropical, Alpine and wild gardening; but in *The English Flower Garden* (1883) he widened his system to include many other types of gardening design, some of his chapters being entitled 'The New Rose Garden', 'Water Gardens', 'The Bog Garden', 'The Orchard Beautiful' and the 'Hardy Flower Border'. All of these themes, which were to become the common currency of the best of modern gardens, were represented at Lisselane where Mr Bence-Jones's planting of each even corresponded closely to that recommended by Robinson in his book.[38] From the turreted house stretched a long and wide terrace lawn, margined with herbaceous borders and bounded by a stone

balustrade over which one looked down on the garden 30 ft below. 'There are bold spirits who do not mind setting their houses among rocks and heather, but we must cultivate a flower garden', said Robinson in this latest of his books. Furthermore: 'The garden near the house must be laid out with formal beds.' His earlier disciples, Lord Lansdowne and Mr Heard, must have been disappointed by this; bold spirits that they were, they had set their houses amidst the rocks and the heathers. From the terrace to the lower lawn at Lisselane sloped a rock-garden in the natural style, over which cascaded a host of dwarf plants relieved at intervals by taller subjects such as yuccas, palms and groups of kniphofia. The broad list of plants, each of which was recommended by Robinson in *The English Flower Garden*, exhibited what he acclaimed as 'the charm of endless variety'.

Below the rock-garden stretched the lower lawn which was bounded by the Arigadeen river. Opposite the house it had been widened to form a lake upon which was an island where bamboos, rhododendrons and fine-foliaged plants luxuriated, while at its edge *Astilbe chinensis* var. *davidii*, recommended by Robinson for water margins, spread itself in self-sown colonies. At the back of the river-side lawn was a pergola 70 yards long, covered with profusely flowering roses and terminated by a thatched summer-house smothered with jasmine nightshade. Robinson would have approved of this simplicity, for a classical temple of a gentleman's park as a focal point was to him, as it was to Constable, an aversion. The pergola formed a background for the rose garden, which was filled with bushes, standards and climbing varieties trained to tall poles. In 1909 a bog-garden was made by a newly formed lakelet and here again its wide variety of planting was based on that recommended for such places in *The English Flower Garden*, including *Pinquicula grandiflora*, the Irish butterwort, from the damp mountains around Bantry Bay, which both Robinson and Gertrude Jekyll adopted for garden cultivation. Beyond the garden proper lay a long walk at the foot of a steep bank, which was covered with evergreen and flowering shrubs planted in large groups. Beyond this was the orchard, decorated with roses on trelliswork, and the kitchen garden, through which a broad walk extended. This was flanked in traditional style by wide herbaceous borders filled with Robinson-approved plants, especially the Dropmore variety of anchusa, so beloved both by Robinson and Miss Jekyll. Distributed around the garden was a collection of rare and tender trees and shrubs. By 1909 Bence-Jones already possessed the new *Hydrangea arborescens* 'Grandiflora', introduced from Pennsylvania by M. Lemoine only two years before, which demonstrates how resourceful a collector he was.

There were many collectors round the shores of Cork Harbour in those days. Besides Lord Barrymore at Fota and W. E. Gumbleton at Belgrove on Great Island (see Chapter 2), Ebenezer Pike and William Crawford, on their neighbouring demesnes of Besborough and Lakelands, respectively built up significant collections of newly introduced exotics. Besborough was remarkable for its specimens of *Desfontainea spinosa*,[39] and at Lakelands *Magnolia campbellii* flowered for the first time in cultivation.[40]

On a Red Sandstone hill that overlooks Cork Harbour at Glounthane, Mr R. H. Beamish began as early as 1900 an Alpine and subtropical garden.[41] The drive was flanked by masses of exotic vegetation – cordyline palms, bamboos, drifts of Ghent azaleas and embothriums – standing out against the dark background of pines. From the house a long straight path led under a series of yew arches alternating with pairs of cordylines to the rock-garden. Its site had been an old quarry, to one side of which was a bare steep rock over 40 ft high; in the crevices of this, soil was placed and free-growing subjects like dianthus and erigeron were planted. Climbers – among them a huge *Mandevilla sauveleons* – were also used to clothe the bare masses of rock. Below the wall vistas of many artificial, rugged hills and deep vales opened out, clothed with Alpines grown, as they should be, in masses several yards across. Among them were saxifrages, lithospermums and campanulas – difficult subjects to cultivate – and *Haplocarpha scaposa*, which Mr Beamish himself introduced from the Cape. A stream dashed in torrents from the top of the quarry to run through one of the valleys, appearing and disappearing, dividing round an island, widening into a pond, and finally ending in a morass or bog-garden. On its margins were planted meconopsis, rodgersia, primulae, herbaceous senecios and other stream-side plants. In the pond an artistic arrangement of nymphaeas was bordered by masses of *Iris laevigata* and *Arundo donax*. Close by was a fine arbour covered with two forms of *Wisteria floribunda*. An upper walk, along the rim of the quarry, gave a view of the rock-garden below, and from there one walked upwards to a collection of rare Mexican pines, among which is a *Pinus ayacahuite*, the tallest in these islands.[42] Along a small upland valley were numerous tropical plants: *Musa japonica* or basjoo, aloes and various succulents, *Caesalpina japonica*, *Genista fragrans*, *Gevuina avellana* and *Dendromecon rigida*. There were also many plants introduced from China by E. H. Wilson and others brought back from New Zealand by Captain Dorrien Smith of Tresco.

When Richard Grove Annesley of Annes Grove, Co. Cork, began his garden in 1907, he was continuing in this fine Co. Cork tradition. He had many horticulturalist connections, including his lifelong friend, the Marquess of Headfort, a cousin of Earl Annesley and of Mr Armytage Moore of Rowallane, while his wife was a cousin of Lady Aberconway, 'whose husband was then laying out his garden at Bodnant in Wales. The house of Annes Grove was built in the early eighteenth century with its back to the picturesque gorge through which the river Awbeg flows. It faces a gently undulating park encircled by trees, among which at one point is a castellated gate-lodge by the Pre-Raphaelite architect Benjamin Woodward. The park was decorated with sombre conifers in the late nineteenth century, and the walled garden was made into a Victorian flower-garden, with flower borders in a box-edged scroll-work pattern, and a garden house, decorated with applied twig-work, perched on a mount. At the height of the fashion for wild woodland gardening a rich vein of peaty soil was discovered in the wood beyond this garden. It runs for a distance along the rim of the gorge and some way down it to the river valley. Richard Grove Annesley began by planting showy hybrid rhododendrons here, advised, among others, by Gerard Leigh White of Bantry House, who recommended Waterer's hybrids and introduced him to John Annan Bryce of Ilnacullin. White wrote to him of Bryce in 1920: 'He is a real walking encyclopaedia, and nearly as good at names as Sir John Ross, but with a more catholic range of interests'.[43] In 1924 Annesley subscribed to the first of a series of syndicates established by garden owners to sponsor the plant-hunting expeditions of Captain Frank Kingdon-Ward in Burma and Tibet. Financial participation in these must have been exciting for the gentleman gardener, who received interim reports from the expeditions as they trekked through remote Himalayan valleys. Some of these, still at Annes Grove, describe the trials of collecting. One gives news of the murder of Kingdon-Ward's mail-runner, another that the Tibetan government had refused to allow the white members of his expedition to enter the country as it feared they might be spies. Many letters are lyrical in their descriptions of the rhododendrons, alpine and herbaceous plants growing in these majestic mountain valleys. On the botanist-explorer's return, each subscriber received a packet of the seed collected, all numbered in reference to the field notes which accompanied each batch of seed. For example:

KW 5687: Rhododendron species. Triflorum
Lusha; 10,000 ft. 19/4/24.
This is No. 5648 at its best. Flowers pure yellow or flushed ochre, mahogany or almost salmon pink. Abundant in birch copse, on the half sheltered slope of the mountain, extending then up into the pine forest, where smaller plants flower freely.[44]

Each owner was then faced with the problem of raising the seeds. Mr Moore of Rowallane was apparently an expert in this operation and wrote frequently to Mr Annesley with advice and encouragement. There were frequent disappointments, as many seeds failed to germinate. Over-germination of others encouraged the subscribers to exchange duplicates. As well as Mr Moore of Rowallane, the Marquess of Headfort in Co. Meath, Sir John Ross of Bladensburg at Rostrevor, Co. Down, Mr McCausland of Drenagh, Co. Londonderry, and Mr Lecky-Watson of Altamont, Co. Carlow, all had young seedlings to exchange, some of them obtained from Sir Frederick Moore of Glasnevin. Often plants from other expeditions such as those of Forrest, Rock, Farrer or Purdom were offered as enticements.[45]

ANNES GROVE, CO. CORK. *Richard Grove Annesley and* Cornus kousa var. chinensis.

In spring the woodland garden at Annes Grove is alive with the colour of these Himalayan rhododendrons which are grown in large coppices of a single variety, as one might find them in the wild. To these have been added all the familiar exotics of a woodland garden of the period: South American embothriums, crinodendrons and eucryphias, Australian olearias and North American dogwoods. Annes Grove was the first woodland garden in Ireland to include among its spring-flowering shrubs a wide range of autumn-colouring trees, such as acers, dogwoods, enkianthus and disanthus. An enormous *Cornus controversa* 'Variegata' stands by the entrance. A background and canopy of fine old native trees provide a kaleidoscope of dappled light and shade to play on the blossoms and foliage of the plantings underneath. Its simple design, the fine fall of the ground, its glimpses of the gorge in the background, and the sparkle of the river through the trees make this the most exquisite of Irish woodland gardens.

One descends to the river bank by a winding path cut into the steep cliff side. Here Mr Annesley made a natural rock-garden by clearing the trees, leaving only those suitable for the rock-garden, exposing the rocks by clearing them of undergrowth and then planting in the fissures and crevices.[46] The unique feature of the garden, however, is the wild water-garden along the river, the only one of any extent in Ireland. Robinson in *The English Flower Garden* devoted a chapter to the subject of the water-garden, and a further chapter to the bog-garden which was to be an extension of the water-garden on to its wet and muddy banks. Here the native rush and sedge, the flag iris and butterwort, the hanging willows and poplars of our stream- and river-sides would be used as backgrounds for the planting of exotic introductions from the wet woods of America, the little bogs of the high Alps and the swampy meadows of the Himalayas. The beauty of marsh and river bank had become integral to the late Victorian imagination through the romantic poetry of Tennyson and the painting of the Pre-Raphaelites. Water-gardening had gained a further impetus through the creation by M. Latour-Marliac, a modest amateur from Bordeaux, of a spectacular breed of hybrid water-lily, which was popularized with enthusiasm by Robinson. Manias for certain plants have always been an important influence in garden history. The late nineteenth century saw one of these for water-lilies, which reached its climax in the paintings of *Les Nympheas* by Claude Monet, in which the artist used the life of the water-lily as a complex symbol of the life of man and his world. Of the views in Monet's own garden at Giverny in Normandy one is constantly reminded as one walks along the river at Annes Grove.

An island had been made in the river opposite the house in the eighteenth century and this was restored by Richard Grove Annesley, after many years of neglect, with

ANNES GROVE, CO. CORK. *Richard Grove Annesley on the bridge in the river garden.*

121

the help of a battalion of soldiers from near-by Fermoy barracks soon after he inherited the property. Along its watery banks he planted waving poplars, willows and dogwoods, whose ember-like glow warms the eye in winter. Colonies of fine-foliage plants at intervals along the bank make luscious backgrounds to the flowering plants. Most notable are the bands of quivering bamboos which fringe the river, their nodding plumes constantly in motion on a windy day. Bold clumps of pampas grass and New Zealand flax stand as unchanging reference points along the edge, be the river low or in spate. The waters rush over rocky weirs and swirl around the bases of cordyline palms. Spray glistens on the stiff leaves of the yucca. The great leaves of gunnera, the pert green rosettes of the water saxifrage, and the heart-shaped leaves of *Senecio clivorum* overhang the water and provide shade for fish and nesting-grounds for waterfowl. The twisted goblets in white and yellow of the American and Chinese skunk cabbages (*Lysichitum americanum*, *L. camchatense*) arise miraculously from the mud each spring, sweet colonies of Asiatic primulas (*Primula japonica*, *P. rosea*, *P. florindae*, and *P. wardii*), many of them raised from Kingdon-Ward's Himalayan seed, decorate the margins, and little fleets of water-lilies sail in the backwaters of the river. Tibetan and Chinese poppies have naturalized themselves in groups, and bridges of rustic paling, one hung with wisteria, like those in Monet's paintings, cross the river and its sidewaters to the island and back again. Above, the cliffs of the gorge are crowned with a thick line of mature beech and pine trees silhouetted against the sky.

Rising to the house level again, one enters the walled garden which is subdivided into compartments. A centre walk leads between herbaceous borders to the Victorian summer-house on its mound. It is crossed by another path, flanked by scroll-work beds which are bright with bedding plants, and then by an avenue of Irish yews, their sobriety relieved by the glaucous foliage of the iris borders round them. Between these paths the simple compartments are edged with borders devoted to a single flower species at a time – delphiniums, dahlias, arum lilies and hemerocallis for example. One compartment, however, contains a curving pool overhung by a weeping birch and fringed with rare Asiatic poppies and delicate primulae. Ornamental grasses, hostas, rodgersias and small groups of other waterside plants form a green frame for the water on which rare lilies float, and a funerary urn gives to this secluded corner a sweet melancholy.

The garden at Annes Grove represents Robinsonian gardening in three of its aspects: the flower-garden, the wild woodland garden and the water-garden. If not the largest of these gardens in Ireland, it is certainly the most exquisite. Its elegant simplicity harmonizes with the grace of its early eighteenth-century house and that of the curving Awbeg river, the poet Spenser's sweet Mullagh:

> Where Colin Clout sat piping and keeping his sheep
>   amongst the cooly shade
> Of the green alders by the Mullaes shore.[47]

Three years after his dramatic exodus from Ireland in 1861, William Robinson returned to write some articles on Irish gardens.[48] One of these, surprisingly, was on Colonel White's garden at Killakee, Rathfarnham, Co. Dublin, which had been laid out by Ninian Niven, who was the representative in Ireland of the Barry and Nesfield school but who had never been as thoroughgoing a gravel and brick gardener as his colleagues in England. After this initial visit, Robinson returned frequently to visit gardens and friends. We know that he felt his ideas might reach their truest expression in Ireland, for the country possessed two of their most essential components – superb natural scenery to provide effective counterpoint to the highly cultivated garden within, and a mild, and in some places, subtropical climate which would allow the naturalization of a wide range of exotic plants. As early as 1873 a correspondent in *The Gardeners' Chronicle* noted that Co. Wicklow, on the East coast of Ireland, enjoyed a climate as mild as that of Co. Cork and Co. Kerry.[49] The first to exploit this potential was Mr Phineas Riall of Old Conna Hill, Bray, Co. Wicklow.[50] His father had built a fine Gothic mansion, to the designs of the architects Lanyon and Lynn, high on a rugged hill overlooking the mountains and the sea, and had planted dense, encircling belts of timber to shelter the wind-blown park. In 1860, the year after the house was completed, he began to move tender plants from his conservatory out-of-doors: *Metrosideros floribunda* and other New Zealand shrubs in 1860; a young *Eucalyptus globulus* in 1873; and, most important of all, in 1878 a *Cordyline australis*, the first to be grown out-of-doors in the British Isles,[51] where, in a formal enclosure surrounded by 14-ft high yew hedges it became an object of admiration in later years. Like every other Victorian planter, Riall made a collection of coniferous trees but relieved their dark, matt masses by interplanting a collection of shining hollies. His son, Captain Patrick Riall, extended the range of subtropical planting by sending back from the Mediterranean subjects like *Acacia dealbata* (Mimosa) and *Eriobotrya japonica* (Loquat Tree), and by obtaining from India a large collection of rhododendron seed, unfortunately of unnamed species.[52]

Near by is the similar sloping site of the garden at Fern Hill, Co. Dublin, begun by the Darley family *c.* 1860, but adapted and expanded by Mr and Mrs Ralph Walker over the last thirty years. The Victorian villa with its Swiss tower is the focus for an Alpine garden of enormous boulders and a stream falling through a chain of pools, abundant in mimulus whose seeds are carried downhill on the descending stream. From here a Victorian *allée* traverses the hillside and is flanked by a 'laurel lawn' from which rise fine conifers – a *Picea smithiana* and a *Pinus sylvestris*, the latter said by Mitchell to be one of the largest recorded. The *allée* crosses a network of lanes leading from the granite quarries and the stonecutters' village on the hill. In Robinsonian fashion these once functional paths provide the basis of the present ornamental layout. Fern Hill is one of the Irish gardens which has gained much from Glasnevin's difficulty in growing calcifuge plants and has obtained many rhododendrons from this source over the years, beginning with *Rhododendron arboreum* 'Fern Hill'. The rocky slope makes an ideal site for viewing large-leaved mountain rhododendrons from the Himalayas, interplanted with Headfort and Exbury cultivars. In the more remote parts of the garden the Walkers have planted seedlings from their subtropical garden at Rossdohan (see p. 108), among which are *Hakea salignus*, vestia, brachyglottis and pseudopanax, and the black and silver acacias are flourishing. In contrast to the intensity of horticulture in the garden there are always breathtaking views over or through the trees to a panorama of Dublin Bay. Near the old-fashioned kitchen garden Mr and Mrs Walker's son, Robert, has added a herb garden and nursery. The continuity which this development at Fern Hill augurs for the future has long been a feature of Mount Usher, the most important Robinsonian garden in Co. Wicklow.

Mount Usher lies in a narrow, sheltered valley between the mountains and the sea in the north of the county. Here in the early eighteenth century the Tighe family laid out an ornamental park, which was begun by Mr William Tighe after visiting the early *ferme ornée* of Philip Southcote at Wooburn Lodge and the landscape park of Charles Hamilton at Painshill. The valley retains its early eighteenth-century design to this day.[53] In one corner of the park was an old tucking mill, which continued in operation until 1868, when it was bought as a weekend retreat by Edward Walpole Sen., a member of the famous Dublin family whose linens were then, as they are now, much admired. The mill was situated in only an acre of ground, but Walpole planted trees and laid out a simple Victorian flower-garden with gravel walks and a fountain at its centre. In 1875 he gave the property to his three sons, Edward and George who were keen gardeners, and Thomas, an engineer, who was to contribute in another way by the design of the many graceful bridges and weirs which now span the river. Edward and George were particularly interested in acquiring rare and unusual plants, and for the first few years they contented themselves with embellishing the 1-acre plot round the house with such plants as they could find. Unlike many others at the time, they worked, secateurs and trowel in hands, in the garden themselves.[54]

When Sir Frederick Moore, then Director of the National Botanic Garden at Glasnevin and a great influence in late Victorian gardening, first visited Mount Usher in 1885, he was impressed by the number of beautiful and rare plants which the Walpoles had managed to acquire and grow in their ten years there. Among the many tender plants he noted berberidpsis, *Buddleia colvilei* and *Mandevilla sauveleons*, in particular.

My first impressions were that it was an exceptionally favoured situation both as regards soil and climate, and that practically any plant which would live outdoors in the British Isles would grow there, which impressions were subsequently proved to be accurate. It occurred to me that the brothers, or rather the two, Edward and George, who concerned themselves about plants, had not fully grasped the possibilities of the place. From that day on I kept them supplied with the names of interesting plants which I thought might succeed. These they generally acquired, and to their credit be it said, that they never complained when such things as Dryandra, Acokanthera, Hovea, Eleacarpus, Michelia fuscata, Thiboudia acuminata and Tibouchinia failed to survive and discounted my recommendation.[55]

Edward ransacked nurseries in Great Britain, France, Italy and Germany for desired plants. Consignments of seed came from New Zealand and Australia, and a large importation of plants from the Yokohama Nurseries in Japan, which proved to be a successful adventure.[56]

Mount Usher might well have become a mere botanical collection of rare plants if the Walpole brothers had not become aware soon after of the writings of Robinson who himself frequently visited the garden. It may have been F. W. Burbidge, Curator of the botanical gardens at Trinity College, Dublin, a friend of Robinson and a contributor to the first edition of *The English Flower Garden*, who introduced Robinson to them. Alternatively, it may have been Sir Frederick Moore, who contributed articles to later editions and whose father, David Moore, had befriended Robinson in the aftermath of the Sir Hunt Johnson-Walsh affair. From then on Mount Usher was to become a living exemplar of the Robinsonian style, though still a small garden of only an acre or so. Robinson writes:

MOUNT USHER: a quaint creeper laden mill house at Ashford, with an acre or two of ground, partly wooded, through which the silvery Vartrey flows, gentle as it falls over its little rocky weirs in summer, but swollen and turbid after wintry storms. The place is really an island at the bottom of the valley; the hilly country round it is beautifully diversified, and is graced by the finest of native trees. The garden is quite unlike any other garden that I have seen, and to see it in the time of Lilies, Roses, Paeonies, Poppies and Delphiniums is to see much lovely colour amongst the rich greenery of the rising woodlands. In autumn the colour is less brilliant but equally satisfying as the eye wanders from the Torch Lilies and Gladioli, to the Blue Agapanthus, and thence to the Pine and Fir clad hills.

Mount Usher is a charming example of the gardens that might be made in river valleys, especially those among the mountains and the hills. In such places there is often delightful shelter from the violent winds, while the picturesque effect of the mountains and the hills offers charming prospects from the garden.[57]

The garden was then becoming crowded, and this meant expansion into the eighteenth-century park of Rosannagh. In 1888 Walter Stuart Tighe, an interested friend, gave them a lease of the wood across the river from the mill, and in 1889 and 1905 further sections of his park.

The wood was an area of mature oak and Scots pine which sloped up the hill to the high road. To get to it Thomas Walpole designed a suspension bridge, made by his firm, Ross and Walpole, which is so light and slender that occasionally it seems to disappear from view. Only five years previously Robinson first proposed woodland as a suitable place for modern gardening and suggested planting in it, in a natural fashion, many hardy shade-loving plants from all parts of the world. The Mount Usher woodland was one of the first to be planted in this new style. Today, when one crosses the bridge to the wood, birdsong fills one's ear as the sound of water recedes. Narrow paths wander in the half-shade among striking plantings: tall conifers, *Agathis australis* (New Zealand Kauri Pine) and *Cupressus cashmeriana* (Kashmir Cypress) contrast with native oaks. Tall Scots pines shelter Himalayan rhododendrons; deeply divided leaves of the Chilean *Lomatia ferruginea* appear prehistoric in silhouette; and hanging branches of *Dacrydium cupressinum* wave slowly, as if on the ocean floor. Below these, wild bluebells and wood anemones merge with sheets of American wood lilies and veratrum. Many-headed palms with their sprays of sword-like leaves compete with the trumpet bells of *Cardiocrinum giganteum* (Giant Lily) on 10-ft stems.

As mentioned previously, further extensions were made in 1889 and 1905, with two long reaches of the river bank. The Walpoles could now make a tree collection to add to the flower and woodland gardens, and set about planning the new areas as an integral part of the whole. From the broad informal lawns on the river bank in front of the house they laid out two long, grassy rides into the new areas, each one stretching as far as the end of the garden where handsome views of the park at Rosannagh opened. These lawns became flowering meadows in spring, with thousands of snowdrops, myriads of daffodils, groups of crocus cups and, occasionally, the delicate nodding bells of snake's-head fritillary waving in the wind. In the background early flowering cherries and magnolias brightened the awakening woods. Robinson recommended that there were hints to be gathered for such bulb planting from the way wild plants arrange themselves, and even from the sky: 'Often a small cloud passing in the sky will give a very good form for a group, and even be instructive in being closer and more solid towards its centre, as groups of narcissi in the grass should often be.' In *The English Flower Garden* he illustrates two such plantings, one at Belmont, Co. Carlow, and another at Straffan, Co. Kildare.

From these Robinsonian lawns the rides stretch out, that on the west side lined with azaleas and backed by striking groups of mountain rhododendrons which have today reached tree size. The azalea line is broken by eucryphias and embothriums; but the glory of this part of the garden is the great collection of eucalypts, for which Mount Usher is famous, dating from the year 1905, when the seeds were obtained from the botanical gardens at Sydney. The collection was augmented by importations from the Melbourne botanical gardens in the 1950s. The slender grey trunks of the eucalypts lean and twist among blue-grey conifers such as *Chamaecyparis lawsoniana* 'Wisselii', and a large *Cedrus atlantica glauca* contrasts with the masses of dark-green trees like a tall *Tsuga heterophylla* (Western Hemlock), and breaks forward over rhododendrons to dapple the Azalea Walk with shade. The gorgeous foliage of the

South American *Pinus montezumae* (Montezuma Pine), planted by the 7th Viscount Powerscourt in 1909, and the green tinsel of *Podocarpus salignus* add further grandeur and interest to this area.[58]

The matching ride on the east bank of the river was lined with *Trachycarpus fortunei* (Chusan Palm). Robinson devoted a chapter in *The English Flower Garden* to the beauty of the foliage of tree ferns, palms, yuccas, bamboos and the like, but regretted that palms in our climate could not achieve the same beauty as those on the banks of the Ganges or the Nile! On one side of the Palm Avenue is a collection of eucryphias, amongst which enormous clumps of the 'Mount Usher' hybrid are prominent. *Eucryphia × intermedia*, a hybrid which first occurred in Sir John Ross's garden at Rostrevor, is also grown here and throughout the garden. On the other side is a corresponding collection of southern beeches which was begun by E. H. Walpole in 1928. Although not among the earliest in these islands it is the most extensive. The collection, as Robinson proposed, is grouped together not, as in a botanical garden, to the exclusion of other families of plants, but intermixed with others which would contrast and set off their particular characteristics. The eucryphia collection is interspersed, for example, with plantings of fragrant rhododendrons, and among other trees – with two Lawson cypresses of a rare and wonderful colour – are the silver *Chamaecyparis lawsoniana* 'Silver Queen' and the lime-yellow *Chamaecyparis lawsoniana* 'Elegantissima'. The nothofagus collection is interplanted with olearias and a tall pagoda-like *Picea breweriana* (Brewer's Weeping Spruce), and the limes of the old back avenue to Rosannagh provide a background. Trees and shrubs are carefully spaced to allow each to grow into its full, mature shape and size, a matter constantly insisted upon by Robinson, rather than forming part of a pattern or shape designated by man's design, as was the purpose of Victorian planting. The trinity of vistas was completed in 1928 when the Maple Walk to the north-west of the house was laid out.[59] In this the rows of Japanese maples, underplanted with autumn-colouring deciduous azaleas and enkianthus, were placed so that their combined blaze of colour was repeated by reflection in a still reach of the river.

A new house was erected in 1928 by E. H. Walpole to the designs of J. Mansfield Mitchell on the site of the old mill. It was designed with a series of projecting bays, each of which was to look up one of the grass rides, and a central belvedere from which the surrounding garden and its mountain backdrop could be viewed. The river forms the principal axis of the garden. A long curving *allée* of water, it enters the garden in a series of calm shallow pools, linked by weirs which were designed by Thomas Walpole. As it passes the house, it changes character, becoming a noisy rapid tumbling over its rocky bed, and then flows quietly on again into the shade of the tree collections and the quiet park of Rosannagh. It is crossed by a chain of bridges of delicate and different designs, and its flow is broken by a series of shallow cascades. Its banks and shallows form a Robinsonian wild water-garden, thick with mimulus, ferns, gunnera and umbrella saxifrages, and overhung by curtains of prostrate conifers and branching cotoneasters. These conifers, in particular *Taxus baccata* 'Doyastonii Aurea' and *Tsuga canadensis* 'Pendula', are among the most outstanding plants in the garden. Above them a pair of Chinese firs break the skyline, lifting one's eyes to the hills. The river is fed by a series of old mill streams which virtually encircle the house. Dextrous use has been made of these: in one there are stepping-stones placed along the bottom, over which one can pass to a rock-garden on its banks; another, which passes under the shade of an old copse, has been made into a fernery; and a third, which winds its way from the entrance gate to the river by a large lily pond, is decorated with waving bands of brightly coloured primulae and astilbes. It is consistent with Robinson's view of the need for simplicity in garden design that these old mill streams, and even the walls of the old potato patch, in this, the oldest part of the garden have never been changed for more elaborate, decorative elements as the garden grew.

During E. H. Walpole's time the garden grew yet again. The kitchen garden was enclosed by its tall beech hedges; two further bridges were thrown across the river; and what is known as 'The Riviera', a long reach of river bank on both sides which

MOUNT USHER, CO.
WICKLOW. *The river
garden today*.

stretches towards the village of Ashford, was acquired in 1946. A bridge, dedicated to E. H. Walpole's first grandchild, Penelope, makes a circuit at one end. By it one may rest in a pavilion erected in 1946 to the memory of Charles Fox, the great head gardener, who was in charge of the gardens at Mount Usher for forty years. Then one takes a long walk back to the house by sunny banks mainly planted with Mediterranean cistus, species roses, callistemon and varieties of buddleia.[60]

Since 1956 the garden has been in the care of Robert Walpole. The Robinsonian garden needs to be continually recreated for it is a living and natural thing. The great joy of Mount Usher is that this process has now been carried on by four generations of one family, each with its own vigour and personality, but, none the less, within a broad Robinsonian frame. It is this unique continuity of gardening in the same style which makes Mount Usher one of the most interesting gardens that has ever been created.

The newcomers were skilfully associated with the native trees and the varied wild growths around the place, and by picturesque grouping, and the absence of anything like striving after purely artificial effects, or apparent botanic system or scientific collection in their choice and placing, many of these, now trees in their proportions, play their part in a scheme where Nature still dominates and artifice is her handmaid faithfully falling into her ways.[61]

Near Rathdrum, about ten miles south of Mount Usher, lies the demesne of Kilmacurragh, whose history is as tragic as that of Mount Usher is happy. Its great garden, laid out by Thomas Acton (1826–1908), fell into decay during the First World War, when it suffered the loss of two successive owners within a period of a year. Its ownership was then for more than a quarter of a century the subject of a legal dispute, from which the garden has only been recently rescued by State intervention. It is now being reclaimed by the State Forestry and Wildlife Service.

The Acton family had lived at Kilmacurragh for nearly three centuries, the house dating from 1697, when Thomas Acton and his sister Janet began what Mr Watson of Kew was to call in 1906 the most interesting garden in Ireland. Its setting

127

was that of the formal park of the early eighteenth century, with battalioned lines, its quaint Dutch ponds and its heronry.[62] Three noble avenues lead to the house, from which the ground slopes gently away to lake, stream and sea, and commands fine views, especially to the east, of the Welsh coast. By 1893 the entrance gate, by a pretty lodge smothered in great rhododendrons, opened on to an avenue of great silver firs backed by a double avenue of monkey-puzzles varied along its length by such trees as *Cupressus lusitanica* (Cedar of Goa), *Cryptomeria japonica* 'Elegans' (Japanese Cedar), *Araucaria araucana* (Monkey-Puzzle) and arresting groups of great tree rhododendrons. From this one passed through a rock-fringed avenue, heavy with masses of *Gaultheria shallon*, on by a weeping beech and past a group of giant ash trees into an Arcadian landscape of hill, park and great trees. The giant sycamores and the enormous beeches would have delighted a landscape painter.

At every turn F. W. Burbidge in 1893 was reminded of the paintings of Corot, Daubigny and Diaz, and the great ash boles would have delighted Constable or De Wint.[63] The lawn in front of the house was, and still is, carpeted in February with a glowing mass of almost-nocturnal purple crocuses. Underneath the trees was the most complete series of the Sikkim, Bhutan and Nepalese rhododendrons then known. One could wander in the lush grass, gazing up into the great trusses of blood-red bells of *Rhododendron roylii*, the red stems of *R. falconeri*, the blue-green leaves of *R. eximium*, the moonlight effect of *R. triflorum* and a host of others, all featured in Hooker's *The Rhododendrons of the Sikkim Himalayas*, which lay ready indoors for reference, should any doubt as to specific identity of plants arise in the garden. They were said to bloom at Kilmacurragh more happily and freely than they would 'if below the everlasting snows and heights of Kinchinjinga'. To these were added groups of hybrids raised by the great Victorian nurseries of Waterer and Cutbush, or by the Irish nurseries of Smith of Newry and Davis of Hillsborough.[64] The most precious were those which had been sent back to M. Vilmorin of Paris from the remote mountain valleys of China by French Jesuit missionaries. Among others Mr Acton had acquired *Rhododendron delavayi* and *R. wightii fictolactea* from M. Vilmorin in 1884,[65] and the *R. delavayi* was the first to flower in these islands twenty years later.

There is a splendid avenue of rhododendrons here, great bushes 10' to 12' in height, all of which were rooted from cuttings by the owner's sister, and which now form one of the characteristic features of the garden. They are still in luxurious health and vigour, covered with flowers and the margins of the walk below are stained red and blush, or white by the myriads of fallen flowers, amongst which the bumble bees are constantly busy in the sunshine.[66]

Many tender plants were first tried at Kilmacurragh in the open air: the Chilean *Laurelia aromatica*, *Ceratonia siliqua* (Algerian Karouba) and an enormous embothrium were planted in 1876. The southern beech, *Nothofagus moorei*, was first tried here in the open in 1887. Among the rhododendrons were many rare species of Indian berberis, and what is still a most magnificent specimen of *Magnolia campbellii* which opens its pink goblets against the March sky.

In the glen below the wood the 'quaint Dutch ponds' were converted into a wild water-garden, connected to one of the early eighteenth-century beech avenues by a pair of walks lined with English yews. In the enclosed garden behind the house Mr Acton's sister planted old roses about a sundial, anticipating Miss Jekyll's revival of this genre. In the garden she planted *Rosa spinosissima* (the fragrant Sweetbriar), *R. indica*, the single China rose, *R. bracteata* (Macartney Rose) and *R. microphylla plena*, a rose then extinct in most gardens but which had been well known since Elizabethan times. Such old, and indeed, wild roses had been an integral part of the Pre-Raphaelite imagination, and had been restored by them to the public consciousness through their paintings, particularly in Sir Edward Burne-Jones's Briar Rose series. It was appropriate, therefore, that this rose garden should remind Burbidge of the Paradise garden described in Parkinson's Herbal (1629).[67]

Thomas Acton, like the Walpoles at Mount Usher, was his own gardener, but there was never much 'keep' about the place, as he preferred a wild setting of long grass and wild flowers – foxgloves, forget-me-nots, veronica, woodruff, and ferns for his exotics. After he died in 1908, and after the tragic events of the First World War, the care of the garden was left to one old man who had worked in it since 1889. In 1929 Lady Moore, whose husband, Sir Frederick, had given many plants from the gardens at Glasnevin, wrote:

The plants are looked after by the same old man who has looked after them for the past forty years. When one blooms he sends a postcard: "Let yez come soon, rosydandry falconyera or lowther (Loderi) is an admiration". The summons is obeyed and his verdict is proved true.[68]

Kilmacurragh, today, with its house rotting and its park divided still reveals the poignant magic which it exercised on F. W. Burbidge over eighty years ago, when in the dusk a swan fussed his wings on the lake below, deer wandered away to rest, wood-pigeons started from a blue pine, while high above, in the tallest beeches, the great grey herons fed their young ones for the night:

After seeing a broad and beautiful old garden and domain of this kind, one feels an exaltation of the mind, and a consciousness of its being a something more pleasant and satisfying than a jam-tart like garden of carpet beds, or a crowded flower show, or than an exhibition of painted pictures, because here the pictures are alive and real, and ever changing in the sunshine and air from hour to hour. To thus see the cool lush grass and flowers, and the noble trees against the sky, and to see the great herons wheeling slowly overhead laiden with fish dinners for their nestlings, and to catch just one last glance at the dappled fawns and their young ones in the bracken, is to feel that Pan is not yet dead, and to be assured in one's heart that there is something Arcadian left to us in the world after all.[69]

Thereafter, Robinsonian gardens continued to be made, at least until the start of the First World War. Some were inland where the climate was not so kind. Those at Belmont, Co. Carlow,[70] and at Straffan, Co. Kildare, were particularly well known. The garden at Straffan was laid out by Major and the Hon. Mrs Barton, and was famous as early as 1880[71] for its wild plantings of daffodils and snowdrops under the red-twigged limes in the park. Mrs Barton's brother, Lord Clarina, had brought back the Straffan Snowdrop (*Galanthus nivalis grandis*) from the battlefield of Tchernaya, where the allied troops were victorious on 16 August 1856, towards the end of the Crimea War.[72] In 1893 the Bartons made a wild garden on an island in the river Liffey opposite the house, which was reached from either bank by suspension bridges like those at Mount Usher. A mossy-stoned rockery surrounded a thatched summer-house and was planted with rare hardy and native ferns, bulbs and alpines, many of which had been collected in the wild by Mrs Barton herself. She was the first to collect *Narcissus bernardii* from the slopes near Gavarnia, *Asplenium fontanum* from the Pyrenees, the giant *Orchis latifolia* from Kilmarnock, the dark-red form of *Anemone pulsatilla montanum* from Royat, and many others. The bog-garden on the banks of the river sported a host of exotics, which included the *Polygonum sachalienense* (the Giant Knotweed of Japan), and was aglow with rich colouring in winter – golden and cardinal willows, crimson dogwoods, silver birch and yellow reeds – and augmented in summer by such trees as the purple plum and golden elder.

The torch of Robinsonian gardening passed to the north of Ireland to Co. Down, where Sir John Ross of Bladensburg, Captain Roger Hall of Narrow Water Castle whose rocky valley was laid out by Smith of Newry, and Mr Armytage Moore added Robinsonian sections to their garden. Mr Hugh Armytage Moore by 1936 was obviously a fine gardener who had added to and embellished the estate which his uncle had bought in the nineteenth century, though he himself did not start until 1903 and did not live at Rowallane until 1917. During the Second World War much of the garden was looked after by only two of the six gardeners and was therefore

NARROW WATER
CASTLE, CO. DOWN.
*Captain Roger Hall's
children and a gunnera,
c. 1910.*
NARROW WATER
CASTLE, CO. DOWN.
*The wild garden designed by
Thomas Smith of Newry,
c. 1918.*

ROWALLANE, CO.
DOWN. *The Walled
Garden, c. 1940.*

neglected. In December 1954 Mr Moore died, and the next year the Committee of
the National Trust for Northern Ireland, with a grant from the Government, took
over the garden and brought it back to its previous excellent state under the very
skilled direction of Lady O'Neill of the Maine.

Six miles from Strangford Lough, too far to avoid late frosts, 300 ft above sea-
level, with 36 in average rainfall, Rowallane is set in undulating, gorse-covered
country – Co. Down at its best, with light, rather poor, lime-free soil and frequent
outcrops of hard whinstone (basalt) rock. By the 1930s about 40 of the present 50
acres were under cultivation – a walled garden near the house, a reclaimed hillside
of gorse and rocks, and mixed plantations in what were stone-walled fields outside.

ROWALLANE, CO.
DOWN. *A group of
cordylines, c. 1930.*
ROWALLANE, CO.
DOWN. Picea brewerana.

The Walled Garden with climbers smothering the walls, choice shrubs, perennials and herbaceous plants spilling on to a network of narrow, straight paths, with large specimen trees underplanted, is divided into rectangular compartments with small lawns, sometimes box-edged. Once used for fruit and vegetables, the garden is now all a plantsman could wish for: magnolias, abutilons, camellias, *Buddleia colvilei*, fremontias, davidias, olearias, *Solanum crispum*, *Azara mycrophylla* (cut back by the severe winter 1962–3), *Deutzia veitchii*, and a glorious *Magnolia dawsoniana*, planted on the other side of the wall but draping rose-pink flowers over it – these are but a few.

Many plants and shrubs here and elsewhere in the gardens bear the famous Rowallane name: *Viburnum plicatum* var. Rowallane, *Primula* 'Rowallane Rose' the tender *Hypericum* var. Rowallane Hybrid, the original Royal Horticultural Society's medal-winning *Chaenomeles superba* 'Rowallane Seedling', etc. In this Walled Garden there is a tiny stream – hardly conspicuous – which flows between beds of meconopsis, hostas, rodgersias and other moisture-loving plants. On top of the gate-pillars at the entrance to this garden two baroque stone urns have been placed which seem too large for the brick wall and narrow path leading into the garden. Part of the stable-block appears above another wall – a small brick tower with Gothic glass slits, like a Church of Ireland church. These are the only structural ornaments in the grounds other than some charmingly original, conical piles of large, smooth stones from the beach at Newcastle. These enhance the drive, which ends in a fine *Abies magnifica* (Red Fir), 70 ft by 7 ft 11 in (1968), on the lawn in front of the un-distinguished house.

To step from the Walled Garden through the farmyard and iron gate into the wildness of the Spring Garden is to enter another world. Wide grass walks, like the fairways of some celestial golf-course, are bound by entering and receding banks of hybrid rhododendrons, azaleas, cherries, magnolias and davidias which, according to a correspondent of *Country Life*, 'merge into the natural background of conifers, thorn and gorse'.[73] With this we would disagree, for in May the strong polychroma-ticism of these masses of rhododendrons, including hundreds of *R. triflorum* cultivars

131

in blue, pink and purple, overpowers any background. It is surprising that tonalities known to an artist, whereby adjacent colours and blocks of colour are placed after deliberation in a picture, are ignored by many collector-plantsmen. How much more necessary when dealing with Nature and polychromatic flowering shrubs, whose colours are so much stronger than a painter's pigments, that a horticultural and pictorial unity be consciously achieved by skilful planting.

To the south of this garden an acre of natural rock-garden, created by much blasting and carting of rock outcrop, has become so successful that dwarf rhododendrons, Alpines and primulas with many other plants now appear naturally placed. The configuration of these huge smooth rocks, which are quite unlike the usual jagged limestone rocks, repeats the smooth markings on the trunks of beech and nothofagus. The rocks have been placed superbly well, and this garden, after its neglect in the Second World War, looks ageless. Further on the route round, after the rhododendrons and pines in the Old Wood, the Hospital, so-named from the days when sick calves were treated in this sheltered valley, today houses many healthy and tender plants, among which we noticed a splendid *Desfontainea spinosa*, 100 ft in circumference, with its fascinating tubular scarlet and yellow flowers for many months. Among other rare shrubs a large *Embothrium coccineum* 'Longifolia', by the exit gap in the stone wall, apparently came from Sir John Ross's original at Rostrevor and therefore may be the oldest of these plants in Ireland.[74] In a further paddock there are more fine nothofagus,[75] said to be the finest collection in Ireland. Beeches and pines in the Home Wood are underplanted with tender rhododendrons, eucryphia, lomatia and magnolias. Throughout the gardens the straight sheep walls of the original fields are strangely anachronistic, yet Robinsonian, in their unpretentiousness in the midst of all this exoticism, and it is a pity there are now fewer views into the surrounding countryside than there were twenty years ago.

Further west the garden of the Manor of Tempo forms a rare unity with the house, for the exoticism of the architecture gives the keynote for the exotic planting of its Robinsonian garden, and its sequential composition of gables and bell-tower anticipate the sequential composition of the garden as it curves around the spring-fed

lake with its mirror-like reflections. Laid out by Sir Charles Langham in 1913, it was continued and improved by his son Sir John Langham, the botanical artist, and is now in turn maintained by his wife, after whom the daffodil 'Christabel Langham' is named.

In the 1850s and 60s Mr and Mrs Henry Hart, well-known gardeners of that time, lived at Carrablagh, Portsalon, Co. Donegal. Their eighteenth-century house overlooked Lough Swilly toward the seaward end, where the surf could be heard as it dashed on the beach and rocks far below. So it does today, with one of the finest unspoiled views from any garden in Ireland over the deep lough to the mountains to the east, with 25 acres of planting on cliff-top intertwined with paths opening and closing the views over the water. Near the house a walled garden, on an inner slope protected by a taller bank between it and the lough, houses some tender plants but does not prevent the fierce east wind from parching the tops of ginkgos and preventing their full growth. Yet in this walled garden a magnificent *Drimys winteri*, planted by the Harts, now thrives, as do huge old bushes of fatsia, eupatoria and cotoneaster, and tender *Grevillea rosmarinifolia* and *Prostanthera rotundifolia* (Mint Bush) which have only recently been planted. Outside this, garden paths on or near the cliff edge lead through a glorious jungle where one sees huge old specimens of *Rhododendron sinogrande*, *R. grande*, *R. falconeri*, tall *Clethra arborea*; and a large *Olearia macrodonta* 'Rossii', which came from Sir John Ross at Rostrevor, was lost and has recently been found again. The present owners, Captain and Mrs Harmon Watt, have a flourishing market garden and are keenly planting on the estate, having dug out all *R. Ponticum* plants, as well as clearing up after losing 3,000 trees in hurricane 'Debbie' – and that in itself is no mean achievement.

A few miles from Carrablagh as the crow flies, but about twenty-three miles round Milford Bay by road, lies the estate of Mulroy, bordering the bay. A Victorian house with drives and causeway was built and added to by successive Earls of Leitrim, but not until 1936 did any extensive planting start. Ideal climatic conditions and complete shelter produced speedy growth of *Eucryphia* var. *nymansensis*, *E. moorei*, *E. cordifolia*, *E. lucida* as well as many magnolias, especially *M. campbellii*, *M. hypoleuca*,

133

M. tripetala. Lady Leitrim, after Lord Leitrim's death in 1952, has carried on much planting, but her work was almost totally wiped out in a few hours by hurricane 'Debbie'. Our constant repetition of this disaster as it occurred in Irish gardens must become tedious, yet in a garden like this at Mulroy it virtually destroyed the garden in a few hours. Much of the area at Mulroy, especially in the Peat Garden, was not cleared after the hurricane, and until recently no one with horticultural knowledge, with the exception of Lady O'Neill of the Maine, has entered the area. She writes to us of her exciting finds there:

For years I have been longing to plunge into the complete thicket which the old garden at Mulroy has now become. . . . To get to the middle of the thicket is virtually, if not literally impossible. One has to fight one's way through apparently impenetrable Rh. ponticums, brambles etc. Every few yards there is a deep ditch (to drain the bog these were necessary criss-crossing the area). So what with bushes above and ditches below I was in great danger of breaking my legs! Here and there I found small clear areas. The undergrowth which has grown up is now, of course, more than adequate protection for the plants which have survived. These are so large that they now dominate the scene. The most spectacular were

Rh. falconeri in full vigour 20/30 ft
Rh. thomsonii in full vigour 18/25 ft
Rh. triflorum species growing as thickets
Rh. ciliatum growing as part of the undergrowth.
Drimys aromatica in thickets up to 20/30 ft across.
Styrax japonica 30/40 ft
Tricuspideria hookerii nearly 30/40 ft across
Eucryphia cordifolia 50/60 ft
Eucryphia nymansensis 50/60 ft.
Fine species of many other Rhododendron species, Parrotia, Stuartia. Magnolias and *Drimys winterii* demolished by the hurricane growing from the base.

All Rhododendrons were very well budded.
The above list is a sample of many plants which if cleared would be found to be in first-class condition.

After Lady Leitrim's remarkable efforts in replanting it is to be hoped that one day all the garden will be cleared.

In a book largely concerned with gardening matters it might seem far-fetched to mention the Bauhaus, the most famous school of architecture, craftsmanship and design of our times. But such has been the influence of the training of this art school, founded in Weimar in 1919 by Walter Gropius, the architect, that the planning of gardens, with all other arts, has been influenced. Notable among such gardens is St Columb's, Churchill, Letterkenny, Co. Donegal, started twenty-five years ago by Derek Hill, the well-known painter. During his Bauhaus-inspired training at Munich Mr Hill says he had to make 'abstract designs with different materials to show contrast between rough and smooth, hot and cold (in colour), light and dark, round and angular, tall and short, and any other contrasts we could imagine. All the students had to go through this course, whether they specialized in architecture, fashion, stage design or pottery. It was one of the most important lessons I was ever taught and when I came to plan my garden in Donegal, this early training was what influenced me most.' On the practical side, however, he did not try to grow plants which could not stand up to frost, bitter salt-laden wind and thin, acid soil.

No better example of variations in microclimate in Ireland can be seen than at Glenveagh Castle and St Columb's which are only four miles from each other as the crow flies. In the winter St Columb's, which stands on high ground, looks over frozen lakes across which icy winds blow. Glenveagh has none of these climatic disadvantages, yet at St Columb's in summertime, with the wind stirring the trembling leaves of a white poplar which reflects the sunshine from the lake, there is an animation which one rarely sees in a sheltered valley like Glenveagh. Unfortunately, the low ground by the bank of the lough is a frost-pocket and cannot be protected by a

ST COLUMB'S, CO. DONEGAL. *The bust of Bacchus. Photograph by the late Charles Gimpel.*
ST COLUMB'S, CO. DONEGAL. *The cast-iron loggia.*

134

shelter-belt; Mr Hill has therefore wisely planted waterside plants which completely die down in winter: gunnera, rodgersia, rheum and *Osmunda regalis*.

As in all good gardens, the view is two-way: the house, washed a rich Venetian red, stands on a steep bank 'as if in the dress-circle', and not only has a different view from each window but is itself frequently a focal point. From one window a lovely feature is a mature beech tree whose white trunk is reflected in the lough water, and elsewhere *Pinus radiata*, *Tsuga heterophylla* (Western Hemlock) and *Cupressocyparis leylandii* are carefully placed – tonally to relate to their companion trees and bushes, and spatially to form masses of contrasting foliage. Each detail is perfectly worked out: the pretty bust of Bacchus is placed with fine judgement to form a key point from the house amid the greenery; Dawyck beeches up the avenue give an essential formal touch; and dogwood breaks the excessive green of Donegal.

The artist's eye of the owner shows throughout: a cage of Victorian ironwork applied to the side of the house and covered with polythene in winter forms a miniature conservatory. 'Wrong to add such a structure to a Georgian house', say the purists; 'right aesthetically to adorn the dull side of the house', replies Mr Hill. In many gardens today colour in planting is regarded as a purely decorative and non-structural exercise. Colour is the process of light reflection, and the form of plants can be released only by the quantity and quality of light reflected from them. Only when the eye is trained to appreciate form with colour can a garden be satisfying, and Mr Hill as an artist has achieved this through his imagination at St Columb's.

Dargle Glen, Co. Wicklow, made by Sir Basil Goulding in the last thirty years, is similar in spirit to St Columb's but very different in its site. This steep and dramatic picturesque glen, with the river dashing through the bottom, has a mild climate and is richly planted. A diagonal vista, the main feature of Sir Basil's design, sweeps up to some extraordinary tent-like structures in metal, called the Aislands. They are used for entertainment purposes related to the near-by summerhouse, a glass-fronted and -sided building cantilevered over the side of the glen. Beyond and above this the

DARGLE GLEN, CO. WICKLOW. *The Summer-house designed by Michael Scott and Partners.*

ground rises through an orchestrated tapestry of changing colour to a field and sky-line coppice. Below the Aislands the glass summer-house cantilevers precipitously over the boulder-tossed torrent, and on the cliff-like slopes of the glen are poised large modern abstract sculptures, including a group of standing columns in studied disarray, by the Irish sculptor Ian Stuart. These are in a setting of trees and shrubs chosen not for their horticultural rarity nor for their bruited provenance, but for their visual contribution to the whole effect. On the north-facing glenside Sir Basil has planted a collection of over 250 rhododendron species and cultivars. On the drier, south-facing glenside he has planted the same number of rose species and cultivars. Large numbers of autumn-colouring trees and shrubs – nyssas, parrotias and maples – have been planted to succeed the summer-flowering roses, and finally groups of conifers etch a pattern against the winter sky.

Sir Basil writes to us of his unusual approach to the garden:

My observations, starting as a non-gardener, were that most gardeners seem to know nought of method, little of layout and scenic design; are suckers for rarity, curiosity and elphin delicacy; buy on visual accident; plant in curious gaps; ignore eventual form, and above all are slaves to speedy effect.

Thus, in a variety of forms the influence of William Robinson lives on, and usually in areas outside the compartmental garden which today surrounds the house.

6 'Gardens where a Soul's at Ease'

John Butler Yeats (1839–1922), the poet's father, when an undergraduate at Trinity College, Dublin, used to spend many happy hours at Sandymount Castle, the home of Robert Corbet, an uncle on his mother's side of the family. This castle, now in a suburb of Dublin overlooking the sea, was an eighteenth-century house which had been Gothicized in the 1830s with tower, battlements and cloister. J. B. Yeats describes the owner and his gardening:

Before I was born, he bought or leased, I never knew which it was, Sandymount Castle, and then began creating all around him beautiful gardens . . . Every morning he rose early, and would wander all over the grounds, sometimes with a small saw and hatchet, making among the trees what he called 'vistas'. He employed four or five gardeners; and as long as I knew Sandymount Castle, none of these men ever left him and no one ever interfered with them. So treated, they were gentle, pleasant and diligent, and gardens were lovely.[1]

The poet himself was born in 1865 in a small house near by in Sandymount Avenue, and as children, his sister and he were often wheeled in their prams through the grounds of the castle. There was a small deer park, a lake with an island, lawns and vistas through the trees to the Dublin mountains. It was Robert Corbet's chief interest, but unfortunately he spent too much time and money on this and not enough on his business so that as an old man he was obliged to sell the estate.[2]

After a visit in 1900, the poet declared he could scarcely recognize the Sandymount grounds, which had largely been built over, with the castle converted into a boys' school. Yet his pride in his Protestant ancestors, particularly the Butlers and the Corbets, and his admiration for the way of life of these Protestant gentry never left him. Their elegant houses and well-cultivated gardens symbolized for him the best of the eighteenth century in Ireland. But one of the tragedies in the lives of many of the richer members of the Anglo-Irish ascendancy during the late nineteenth century

SANDYMOUNT CASTLE, DUBLIN. *The Corbet family in the garden. 'I vividly recall those photographs . . . of a great door suggesting not Abbotsford but Strawberry Hill— the door that my dream recalled.'* (*W. B. Yeats*)

was their belief that they should divide their time between London and their Irish estates. It was calamitous for their tenants to suffer an absentee landlord's agent, and painful for the family to attend a London season when the plants in their Irish gardens were at their best.

> Some that had gone on Government work
> To London or to India came home to die,
> Or came from London every spring
> To look at the may-blossom in the park.[3]

Typical of these families were the Gore-Booths of Lissadell, ten miles from Sligo. Their elegant neo-classical house built in Ballsadare limestone, with its great bay windows to the south, looked over Drumcliff Bay, past Rosses Point over to Knocknarea and a fifty-mile sweep of the Ox Mountains. Though very open to the winds, the house and its lawns were superbly sited near the shore and backed by trees. In the nineteenth century the demesne was often enlarged, and even by 1850 the roads within its bounds were thirty miles in length. 'The surface is beautifully broken, and the woods, lawns and rocky banks clothed with wild plants, seem endless.'[4] The 4th baronet, Sir Robert Gore-Booth, is remembered in the long Irish memory as the landlord who added the Seven Cartrons to his estate. These were 800 acres in the neighbouring townland of Ballygilgan, on which lived some poor fishermen and landholders, many of whom chose to take a passage to America rather than accept inadequate compensation and a less desirable place in which to live. Tragically, the emigrant ship sank with all hands in Donegal Bay. Nevertheless, in the aftermath of the Famine Sir Robert spent nearly £40,000 to relieve the sufferings of his tenants. He kept the estate as a bird sanctuary; but his son, Sir Henry, more often at home than his father, periodically used to hunt bears and whales in the Arctic when he grew tired of wild life at Lissadell.

By the end of the century plantations of hard wood for shelter from Atlantic gales had grown well, although along the shore, to which the drive runs parallel, the trees can be seen to be suffering from the salt spray. Yet they provided a sufficient shelter for the Gore-Booths to have elaborate flower-gardens. In 1905 two acres of garden inside walls were added, which with their herbaceous planting showed the contemporary influence of Gertrude Jekyll. It was sheltered from the north-east and designed as a summer garden, where one visitor saw *Meconopsis cambrica* bordering the beds, in which were planted, among other flowers, the crimson *Astilbe davidii*. He also noted

Romneyi coulteri along the base of a wall, and the deep purple *Buddleia davidii veitchiana* and *Magnolia lennei*, the beautiful and richly coloured variety of *M. × soulangiana*. In between the beds, somewhat formally planted, were standard roses, chiefly Wichuraiana ramblers. The most sheltered part of the demesne, at the back of the house in the woods, was called the Glen, in which a stream forced its way from Ben Bulben to the sea.

In old times the stream was in bad odour and received the name of Brenoigne, or stinking runlet, but by cleansing it and altering somewhat its channel; by turning into it an additional supply of water, by making several small cascades where the levels admitted them; and by planting its banks with fragrant shrubs and flowers, the Gore Booths have so altered its character, that it is now the gem of the demesne, and deserves the name of the Sparkling Sweet-scented Streamlet. Owing to the shelter and warmth of the deep glen, and to the running water, delicate exotics that would hardly live a day in most parts of the neighbourhood, thrive here the whole year round, as in their native habitat.[5]

When Yeats was a child and staying with his grandmother at Merville on the outskirts of Sligo, he once decided to walk the ten miles to Lissadell, where the Gore-Booths welcomed him and gave him cast-off shoes and stockings to replace his own which appeared to be worn out.[6] After living at Merville, set in about 60 acres, with a marvellous view of Ben Bulben, Yeats 'learned to love an elaborate house, a garden and trees'.[7] He must, therefore, as a young man in 1894 have been pleased to receive an invitation to stay at Lissadell. There he met Sir Henry Gore-Booth's two daughters – Constance, a superb horsewoman whom he had sometimes seen as she rode to meets of the Sligo Harriers, and the delicate Eva who wrote poetry in a manner not unlike that of AE (George Russell). All of them were in their twenties, and the girls listened while Yeats told them of the excitements of the Irish Literary Revival and of his writing *The Countess Cathleen*. On a second occasion he stayed for two weeks

CONSTANCE AND EVA GORE-BOOTH, *in the garden at Lissadell. Oil painting by Sarah Purser.* CONSTANCE GORE-BOOTH (*later Countess Markiewicz*).

during which they discussed their hopes for Ireland in the fight against the English. He never went there again, yet he never forgot his visits, and twenty-two years later he wrote to Eva: 'your sister and yourself, two beautiful figures among the great trees of Lissadell, are among the dear memories of my youth'.[8] In 1927, after they were both dead, he wrote his great elegy, 'In Memory of Eva Gore-Booth and Con Markievicz'.

> The light of evening, Lissadell,
> Great windows open to the south,
> Two girls in silk kimonos, both
> Beautiful, one a gazelle.
> But a raving autumn shears
> Blossom from the summer's wreath;
> The older is condemned to death,
> Pardoned, drags out lonely years
> Conspiring among the ignorant.
> I know not what the younger dreams –
> Some vague Utopia – and she seems,
> When withered old and skeleton-gaunt,
> An image of such politics.[9]

Both sisters rebelled against the landed class in which they had been brought up, and supported the underdog, the Irish against the English or the poor against the rich, with such passionate intensity that in Yeats's opinion it consumed them. Symbolically, he thought, they had forgotten the simplicity and purity of the waterfall on Ben Bulben's side down which the stream pours into the Glen at Lissadell.

> There is a waterfall
> Upon Ben Bulben's side
> That all my childhood counted dear;
> Were I to travel far and wide
> I could not find a thing so dear.[10]

Until the First World War the Alpine gardens at Lissadell were excellently kept up. In 1911 Henri Corrévon, a famous Swiss gardener from Floraire near Geneva, reported in *The Gardeners' Chronicle* that the high Alpine species – *Eritrichium namum* (the king of the Alps, always difficult to establish) and many androsaces – were growing well despite the very moist air of the Sligo climate. He also noticed walls covered by *Abutilon vitifolium*, crinodendron and *Solanum crispum*; and some 'new' Asiatic primulas (meconopsis), especially a recently raised hybrid, *Primula bulleyana*, which had been exhibited by Sir Jocelyn Gore-Booth, 'the happy owner of this paradise'.

One of the commonest phrases about landowners in Burke's *Landed Gentry of Ireland* is 'formerly of . . . '. We should be thankful, therefore, that the Gore-Booths still struggle on at Lissadell and personally guide the public visitors around. It has not become a hotel, religious house or mental home, nor has it been burned down. Though the garden is neglected, the bluebells in spring still bloom abundantly under the silver birches; but the woods have been decimated.

> *Nous n'irons plus aux bois*
> *Les lauriers sont coupés. . . .*

Three large houses in Co. Sligo fascinated Yeats as a young man. One was Markree Castle, Collooney, deep in its woods with picturesque lodges, walls and Gothic entrance gates, which:

had always called to my mind a life set amid natural beauty and the activities of servants and labourers who seemed themselves natural, as bird and tree are natural. No house in a town, no solitary house even not linked to vegetable or beast by seasonal activities has ever seemed to me but as 'the tent of the shepherd'.[11]

Although there is no record of his having been invited to Markree in his youth, he must have seen the planting there by Colonel Cooper, of an arboretum and rhododendrons, and maybe heard of the extensive rock-garden with Alpines. Many entries in the account books of the National Botanic Garden, Glasnevin, refer to seeds and plants sent to Markree in the 1890s.[12] The second house in Co. Sligo was the great grey Palladian building of Hazelwood, the home of the Wynnes, set with its gardens on a peninsula into Lough Gill, three and a half miles from Sligo. Fine trees grew there, silver firs of great size, arbutus from Killarney, with shrubberies left wild rather than cropped; two grottoes, the one 'prettily laid out, and another with seats of Irish bog-wood, and a pavement of small stones, intersected by horses' teeth'.[13] But Yeats mentions this estate but once. Lissadell meant more to him than these others.

John Butler Yeats brought his family back to Ireland from London, where Willie had been at school, when Willie was fifteen. They had little money, and as the war between tenants and landlords was at its height, J. B. Yeats gradually lost all the rents he had been getting from their small property in Co. Kildare, which had been theirs for many generations. They settled in Balscadden Cottage, 'a long thatched house' on the cliff edge at Howth looking out over Ireland's Eye and Lambay Island; each day W.B. journeyed to the Erasmus Smith High School in Harcourt Street, Dublin. Not being in the least academically inclined, he found the whole experience depressing, especially reading 'Shakespeare for his grammar exclusively'. Enjoyable moments in his life were expeditions such as sailing over to Lambay island from Howth, after which he thought: 'I would like to live here always, and perhaps someday I will.' Fortunately his wish never came true. At that time he had what he called 'a literary passion' for the open air. As well as removing the glass out of his bedroom window so that in stormy weather the salt spray would soak his bed, he used sometimes to sleep out at night among the rocks and rhododendrons of the wilder part of the grounds of Howth Castle, until his father thought he was not getting enough sleep, and one of his schoolmasters, noting his tiredness, placed a different interpretation on his nocturnal excursions.

No estate in Yeats's life was as important to him as Coole Park, Co. Galway, where he stayed during the summer months for twenty-five years. John Masefield, who stayed at Coole in 1905, wrote in his *Memories of W. B. Yeats*:

At Coole, one felt that nothing had ever died there; all was near by, the ancient gods, the fairies, the heroes, the hawthorn of all the Springs, the swans of all the waters, and the Rose of Ballylee, the beautiful. At night, the moonlight and the woods seemed full of an intensely living past.

The best time to walk from Gort to Coole Park is when the angelus bell is ringing and the sun is setting behind the Burren. From the entrance to the Coole estate the track leads to a dark, arched avenue of ilexes and limes before it twists through woods to the spot on which the house once stood. The impact of this lost demesne is most melancholy in its memories of past glory. For what is now a narrow track bounded by falling walls was once a wide drive through undulating parkland; and where 'saplings root among the broken stone', up to the very site of the house, was likewise a splendid sweep of park with noble elms and limes.[14]

In its setting of wood and open parkland without ha-ha the sturdy plainness of the house did not signify it had been built for defence like many Irish houses, but rather as an accessible dwelling where all were welcome. From the west side, where half-octagon windows had been added in Victorian times, one could look down to the lake, and even after the trees had grown, the shining waters could be seen from the house. The stable buildings near by were two-storeyed, and above them towered a magnificent dovecot in a gable which still soars to the sky. All these are now a sad, ivied ruin, for many of the largest stones have been removed for building the new Galway cathedral. Having survived Whiteboys, Land Agitation, Troubles and Civil War, the house deserved a better fate than to be pulled down in 1941 by a building contractor in need of stone. The foundations of the walls have recently been

MARKREE CASTLE, CO. SLIGO. *The Italian well-head.*

141

uncovered in an act of dilatory but useless contrition. The house now befits only an archaeological study, though the garden justifies horticultural restoration.

From the days of Richard Gregory, a younger son of the nabob in the East India Company who brought objects of *virtu* from Italy, until 1932 when Augusta Gregory, the widow of Sir William Gregory, died, Coole was always a place of peace – the home of a Protestant family living in amity with tenants and at peace with Catholic neighbours. In 1892, at the age of forty, she devoted the second half of her life to making Coole a place where the greatest writers in Ireland could meet or have peaceful surroundings in which to work. There she was able to plan the Irish National Theatre and to write her many plays, stories and articles.

Sean O'Casey, one of her most unlikely admirers, noted her two loves: books 'nearest her mind' and trees 'nearest her heart'. One of the six favourite books in her library was John Evelyn's *Silva* in a calf binding and with exquisite coloured plates of larch and 'Silver Firr', trees which both she and previous Gregorys had planted so freely. Among other 'beloved' books was Hooker's *Pomona Londonensis* (1818), with forty-nine plates printed in colour, which was finished by hand and bound in contemporary polished calf.

Her finest horticultural creation was the walled garden of about 3 acres, planted with trees, ornamental shrubs and flowers. In the lower part of the garden was a well of about 12 ft in diameter, never dry, and shrouded in dark evergreens; near by, the long grey walls supported glasshouses for the grape vines and nectarines; and a bastion of *Taxus baccata* (English Yew) guarded these vineries from northern storms. In fact, the whole garden was enclosed in a high stone wall with only two gates, thus protecting it from ocean salt carried by the force of the Atlantic gales from Galway Bay. At the end of a flower-bordered gravel walk, on the lower side of the garden beyond the vineries, stood a large marble bust of Maecenas on a simple stone plinth. It was framed in ivy and had an iron seat in front which retained the summer's heat after the sun had set. If on entering the garden by the gate from the house side a visitor walks down to the right, the woods, if invoked, will throw back an uncanny echo, which is awe-inspiring in its solemnity, its length and single repetition. Despite a limy soil, certain large trees such as *Quercus ilex* (Holm-Oak) and *Catalpa bignonioides* flourished. Lady Gregory describes her favourite of these which grew over the long path:

...coming as I believe from the gentle Pacific zone has no fault to keep it outside the garden walls. The clean limbs, spreading over garden bench and border give no noxious shade, for the leaves larger than the palm of a man's hand – I have but now brought one in and tried it with a measuring tape – nine inches across, ten from pointed tip to stem, – are but a few beside these of our native trees. The trusses of white bloom add beauty to their pale green. They cast a pleasant shadow on the long bench and a part of the flower border, yet not such darkness as to check the blossoming of tulip or larkspur, or anemone, or the growth of that delicately leaved laurel painters lay on a poet's brow; or of rosemary and the sweet tufted herbs.[15]

At once visible today is the Autograph Tree, a *Fagus sylvatica cuprea*, on which Lady Gregory used to invite famous visitors to inscribe their initials, and discourage others from inserting them. The method used is amusingly described in Edith Somerville's *Diary* written when she was staying at Coole in August 1901:

Today Augusta made me add my initials to a tree already decorated by Douglas Hyde, AE and more of the literary crowd. It was most touching. WBY did the carving for me, I smoked, and high literary conversation raged and the cigarette went out. I couldn't make the matches light and he held the little dingy lapels of his coat out and I lighted the match in his bosom.[16]

The tree had been mutilated before the present owners fenced it in. But it is just possible to discern the initials of W. B. Yeats, his brother Jack and his father J. B. Yeats; Augusta Gregory and her son Robert; the lyre-cypher of John Synge; AE's colophon; and the large initials 'G.B.S.'. It is said that Augustus John climbed high up the tree to carve his initials. Future generations may puzzle over the name of Bernadette Devlin. In spring all the garden was 'so radiant, so decorated, the great white horse-chestnut in bloom, the smaller red ones, the leaves so fresh, the paths carpeted with the brown blossoms of beech.'[17] It was not a neat or tidy garden, although there was a maze in box; in parts it was sufficiently wild for pheasants to nest in cortaderia (Pampas Grass) and wild duck in a clump of bamboo.

Edith Somerville, who so charmingly described the ceremony of the cutting of initials on the Autograph Tree, had herself a sensitive eye for landscaping, as is shown by her description in *The Real Charlotte* (London 1972, Chapter XLVIII) of a typical country-house garden in the west of Ireland at the end of the last century.

At the back of Rosemount kitchen-garden the ground rose steeply into a knoll of respectable height, where grew a tangle of lilac bushes, rhododendrons, seringas and yellow broom. A gravel path wound ingratiatingly up through these, in curves artfully devised by Mr Lambert to make the most of the extent and the least of the hill, and near the top a garden-seat was sunk in the bank, with laurels shutting it in on each side, and a laburnum 'showering golden tears' above it. Through the perfumed screen of the lilac bushes in front unromantic glimpses of the roof of the house were obtainable – eyesores to Mr Lambert, who had concentrated all his energies on hiding everything nearer than the semi-circle of lake, and the distant mountain held in an open cut through the rhododendrons at the corner of the little plateau on which the seat stood. Without the disturbance of middle distance the eye lay at ease on the far-off struggle of the Connemara mountains, and on a serene vista of Lough Moyle . . .

Throughout the years Sir William, and Lady Gregory after him, constantly planted at Coole in a pinetum beyond the walled garden and in an orchard by the stables. She describes the pinetum and her work there:

Going out from the garden to that path by which one sees the rare foreign conifers planted by my husband and that are now great towering pyramids I come to, and look upon with pride, some acres of my own planting that with less of strangeness have in their planter's eyes an equal beauty in the white stems of the silver fir, the rosy blossoms, the delicate green branches of the larch. Many an hour I have spent among them, – for in a nursery of trees, as of children, one may run the whole gamut of joy and anxiety, of pride and of fear; my companion and helper an old man now passed away. Many a time in winter snow we have gone out together with tar and brush to make the bark distasteful to hungry rabbits, or in summer time he with slasher, I with spud, to free our nurselings from the choking of brambles or of grass.[18]

This is corroborated by Anne Gregory's account as seen through her eyes as a grandchild:

Grandma adored the woods and taught us such a lot about them. Every year she planted a lot of young saplings and endlessly walked round looking at her young plantations, tearing away from the older ones, and seeing that the wire netting was safely around the smaller ones to keep the rabbits away. The weather had to be very bad indeed to keep her from visiting at least the nearest seedlings. She always wore galoshes over her shoes, cotton gardening gloves over her mittens, and armed with her spud went forth daily to wage war against thistle, ivy, nettles, convolvulus and rabbits. I think one of the few times I saw her really furiously angry was when she found that several of her beautiful young larches had been cut down and taken away.[19]

She was a great plantswoman, and in 1898 at the centenary celebrations for the rebellion of the United Irishmen she recommended that 'every Nationalist should plant at least one tree in this year of '98 and every Unionist in 1900, and every waverer or indifferent person in the year that separates them, and the face of the country would be as different in the new century from what it is now as a head covered with soft waving hair from a head that is bald or close shaven'.[20]

Yeats came to know the woods and garden 'better than any spot on earth', and to record many of the chief happenings there. The hurricane of 1903 struck Coole especially severely. Acres of tall conifers in Pairc-na-Carraig suffered as the wind cut a swath through. Lady Gregory was in London with Yeats at the time, and she received a letter telling her that 'nine great limes [were] felled between house and stable yard; our demesne wall broken by falling trees' and the large ilex on the lawn was split in half. In 1906 Yeats dedicated to Lady Gregory his long dramatic poem 'The Shadowy Waters', that describes the Seven Woods of Coole in detail as he saw them:

> I walked among the seven woods of Coole:
> Shan-walla, where a willow-bordered pond
> Gathers the wild duck from the winter dawn;
> Shady Kyle-dortha; sunnier Kyle-na-no,
> Where many hundred squirrels are as happy
> As though they had been hidden by green boughs
> Where old age cannot find them: Pairc-na-lee,
> Where hazel and ash and privet blind the paths;
> Dim Pairc-na-carraig, where the wild bees fling
> Their sudden fragrances on the green air;
> Dim Pairc-na-tarav, where enchanted eyes
> Have seen immortal, mild, proud shadows walk;
> Dim Inchy wood, that hides badger and fox
> And marten-cat, and borders that old wood
> Wise Biddy Early called the wicked wood:
> Seven odours, seven murmurs, seven woods.[21]

COOLE PARK, CO. GALWAY. *W. B. Yeats on the shore of the lake. Photograph by George Bernard Shaw.*

The derivations of these names are not entirely clear: Shanwalla, according to the son of Lady Gregory's Irish tutor, derives from 'sean balach', as that signifies the old road which ran through the wood before the Gregorys made two new avenues. Kyle-dortha (Coill-Doorada) was the dark wood about which local inhabitants told tales of its having been burned early in the nineteenth century, but which had been replanted by Lady Gregory's time. Pairc-na-Laoigh was the calves' field and Pairc-na-Carraig, the Rock Field – but known to estate workers as the Fox Rock. Thousands of trees were destroyed in this wood in the 1903 hurricane. Subsequently, it became a wild unplanted area by which the river Cloon flows under high poplars on a steep bank. Pairc-na-tarav was the bull field or park, and Inchy Wood (Incha Wood) was haunted.[22]

For many years Lady Gregory planted trees. In February 1909 Yeats wrote in his *Journal* that 'for a year they have taken up much of her time. Her grandson will be fifty before they can be cut . Then he compares an artist's or a writer's life with that of a landowner: ' . . . do not we also plant trees and it is only after some fifty years they are of much value.' His admiration for Lady Gregory constantly shines through in his poems. In one of his finest tributes to her it is the sound of his feet on the gravel path in the garden and the most prominent trees alongside it that he chooses for his imagery.

> If you, that have grown old were the first dead,
> Neither catalpa tree nor scented lime
> Should hear my living feet, nor would I tread
> Where we wrought that shall break the teeth of Time.
> Let the new faces play what tricks they will
> In the old rooms; night can outbalance day,
> Our shadows rove the garden gravel still,
> The living seem more shadowy than they.[23]

When Yeats was staying at Coole in the 1890s, he had walked over to a sturdy but ruined medieval tower, guarding a bridge over a stream, which had once been in Coole demesne. The history of this tower fascinated him:

I have lately been to a little group of houses, not many enough to be called a village, in the barony of Kiltartan in County Galway, whose name, Ballylee, is known through all the west of Ireland. There is an old square castle, Ballylee, inhabited by a farmer and his wife, and a cottage where their daughter and their son-in-law live, and a little mill with an old miller, and old ash trees throwing green shadows upon a little river and great stepping-stones.[24]

Twenty years later Yeats bought Thoor Ballylee, and while repairs were being effected, he took up residence there with his wife and small daughter in the summer

COOLE PARK, CO. GALWAY. *Lady Gregory under a catalpa.*
THOOR BALLYLEE, CO. GALWAY. *Drawing by Alan Fenn, 1970.*

145

of 1919. It had a walled garden sheltered between two cottages, where roses and apple trees grew, and across the road was a grove of lime trees. To his friend Clement Shorter he wrote, while he waited for repairs to be finished: 'We shall live on the road like a country man, our white walled cottage with its border of flowers like any country cottage and then the gaunt castle.'[25] On 11 July 1919, in a letter to John Quinn, his patron and friend for many years and a rich New York lawyer, he described his tower which 'needs another year's work under our own eyes before it is a fitting monument and symbol, and my garden, which will need several years if it is to be green and shady during my lifetime.'[26]

Until 1929 the Yeats family used to visit Thoor Ballylee each summer, and it became of immense importance to Yeats's poetic development. There he wrote many of the great poems in his book entitled *The Tower*, which became a recurrent and paramount symbol for him of solitude and introspection. Dr T. R. Henn wrote of Thoor Ballylee as:

It satisfied his desire for a rooted place in a known countryside, not far from Coole and his life-long friend Lady Gregory. . . . Many aspects of the wild life about it, and the stony pastures beside, were pressed to serve as emblems: otter, moorhen, heron, trout; the trees that stood against the gales coming in from the Atlantic; the thorn of the crags . . .[27]

Lady Gregory's strength to work for Ireland was also 'constantly renewed' in solitude in the Coole garden which she created. As friend to Yeats, Synge, Douglas Hyde, O'Casey and other Irish writers, she admirably fulfilled the role of patron. Each reacted differently. O'Casey, the Dubliner, described the trees as 'ripe in age and kingly in their branchiness';[28] unlike Yeats he disliked the gloom of the woods, preferring to wander through the wild heath where the air was filled with clouds of blue butterflies. Lady Gregory was convinced that one of Synge's finest pieces of writing, at a climactic moment in *Deirdre of the Sorrows*, must have been inspired by his autumnal visit to Coole:

Who'll pity Deirdre has lost the twilight in the woods with Naisi, when beech trees were silver and copper and ash trees were fine gold.[29]

The last years of Lady Gregory's life were tragic, but she bore it stoically. In January 1918 her only son Robert was shot down while he was on active service with the Royal Flying Corps. She wrote to a friend:

The machinery of my life has not changed. Last month I was planting for Robert now I am planting for Richard [her grandson aged eight], but my heart is very sore. . . .[30]

By 1921 the excessive Irish land rates had forced the Gregorys to sell more land, leaving only about 300 acres, which was insufficient to support an estate that in 1878 had been more than 4,800 acres.[31] In October 1924 she drove over to Roxborough House, her childhood home near by. Already the garden was becoming totally overgrown.

Yet the road by the deer-park and the avenue most beautiful, river and hills, and the trees in their autumn foliage. All silent that had been so full of life and stir in my childhood, and never deserted until now. The garden is grass and weeds, but some phloxes that Kathie had planted not yet choked, and I am bringing them here, a great enrichment to my borders.[32]

Five years later she paid another visit, her last, and was saddened to see that the fine beeches had been felled along the river, which was choked with reeds, and in the garden she could scarcely find her way. She felt 'like Oisin on his return to Almhuin, for he was the last of the Fianna, so am I of my generation, the brothers, the sisters; and now the homestead that had sheltered us all a deserted disconsolate ruin'.[33]

An examination of her *Journals* reveals her indomitable spirit. In March 1927 she put her signature to a deed of sale to the Ministry of Lands and Agriculture. The

146

estate still belonged to the Gregory family, and she was allowed henceforward to live there on payment of a nominal rent. Her diary records it:

April 1st. I have just put my name as witness to the sale of Coole – all – house, woods, gardens.[34]

But she evidently still hoped the estate would be safe in the future in the hands of a Government department, for she wrote in her *Journals* on 6 May 1929:

'The beauty, the romance of the Seven Woods, the mysteries of the ebbing and flowing of the lake are dear to me, have been well loved, and are now in hands that will care and tend them it is likely for ever.'

But Yeats knew it would not be thus: it would become, he wrote, 'an office and residence for foresters, a little cheap furniture in the great rooms . . .'. Lady Gregory died in 1932 after a long and courageous fight against cancer. Yeats, in lines of prophetic insight in his great poem 'Coole Park 1929', bids us remember her.

> Here, traveller, scholar, poet, take your stand
> When all those rooms and passages are gone,
> When nettles wave upon a shapeless mound
> And saplings root among the broken stone,
> And dedicate – eyes bent upon the ground,
> Back turned upon the brightness of the sun
> And all the sensuality of the shade –
> A moment's memory to that laurelled head.[35]

In November 1922 Yeats was elected to the Seanad to advise Government on matters concerning education, literature and the arts. In the previous winter Mrs Yeats had bought 82 Merrion Square, and for the following six years they lived there. The square, the second largest in Dublin, was splendidly planted with trees and shrubs. It had all been well planned because an act of the Irish Parliament in 1757 had set up Commissioners for Making Wide and Convenient Streets, so that when John Ensor, the architect, started a few years later to lay out the square for the landlord, the 6th Earl Fitzwilliam, it was done on a generously elegant and extensive scale, larger than contemporary squares in London. When Yeats lived there, the gardens, as is often the custom, were for the use of the residents of the square only on payment of an annual subscription to the Pembroke estate which then owned the property. Yeats spoke with passion in the Seanad in March and April 1927, advocating that the gardens should be open to the public, and that if, as was proposed, the National War Memorial Fund were to erect there a war memorial to the Irish dead in the Great War he could see no harm in that – in fact there would be a positive advantage if the square were then opened. He had been into the square gardens, he said, only once in the past year, though he walked almost every day round the pond of St Stephen's Green: 'I know the great delight that that Square and these waters give the children. It must enter into their life and memory for ever.' Nor did Yeats regard the siting of the war memorial in Merrion Square of any great import: 'in a hundred years the Square will be there if this scheme is carried out for the health of the Dublin children and the delight of all the citizens.'

However, the scheme did not go through because the Pembroke estate, which was the landlord, asked £110,000 for the garden (a large sum in 1927), and the Government then offered the Islandbridge site for a war memorial, agreeing also to landscape it.[36] Yeats's far-sighted suggestion for opening up the Square garden has at long last come about. In 1939 the Catholic Archdiocese of Dublin bought the garden as a site for a cathedral, but public opposition to this scheme and to others involving building on the garden was so determined that the idea was abandoned. The Archbishop then presented the square to the Dublin Corporation. Not until then was the general public allowed in the garden.

Merrion Square had been laid out in the late eighteenth century as a *jardin anglais* with informal clumps of trees and shrubs standing on an undulating green sward, all enclosed within a perimeter belt of trees. The sward was traversed by curving paths, sunken so as not to interrupt the vision of green. It made a perfect complement in style to the famous terraces of Georgian houses behind. During the 1860s John Adair, a barrister resident in the Square, planted masses of subtropical plants among the existing trees and shrubs in attempted emulation of the great subtropical planting which was then being carried out in the parks of Paris (see p. 111). Most of these in Merrion Square through time and neglect have died. He also planted groups of evergreen trees, chiefly hollies, to demonstrate that, contrary to popular opinion of the time, evergreens would survive and grow in the middle of a heavily polluted Victorian city.

This planting in Merrion Square was done within the earlier framework of trees and shrubs, so that the park survived as a typical example of its period until recently, when it was taken over as a public park by Dublin Corporation. Although the Corporation has, by clearing and replanting, miraculously restored it after many years of neglect, it has recently departed from the original style by planting Victorian formal bedding schemes on the lawn, introducing crudely designed play and service areas, as well as unsympathetic statuary and furniture. It is sad that so much well-intentioned effort should contribute to the destruction of the park's original style. Would a similar destruction of the original Georgian terraces which surround it be tolerated by the same Corporation?

St Stephen's Green gardens, where Yeats said he walked 'almost every day' while he lived in Merrion Square, were designed by J. F. Fuller and William Sheppard, who were employed through the benefactions of Sir Arthur Guinness (later Lord Ardilaun). The gardens differ little from comparable parks in a metropolis – excellent planting of standard Victorian evergreens and trees, a pond for wildfowl, curving tarmac paths, bedding-out and artificially raised areas to break up the original flat terrain, including natural outcrop rock-work by Pulham & Sons.[37] But the park in Yeats's time was redeemed from ordinariness by a splendid equestrian statue of George II (1758)[38] by John van Nost the younger, who had lived in Ireland for some years and was the greatest seminal influence on Irish sculptors in the second half of the century. Yeats would also have seen Henry Foley's fine statue of Lord Ardilaun, but not the bust of the Countess Markievicz (died 1927) which was erected

in 1954. (In helping to dig trenches in the park at the start of Easter Week, 1916, the Countess must have spoilt its beauty temporarily.) How much Yeats used to see was questioned by George Moore in *Ave* (1911) in which he remarks how Yeats as a young man seemed too preoccupied in his walks through the gardens to notice children playing or ducks in the pond. Since Yeats's time the gardens have been further enhanced by a bronze bust by Henry Moore in Yeats's memory, and by a dramatic statue of Wolfe Tone by Edward Delaney (1969) at the north-east corner.

Coole had meant more to Yeats than any other house and garden, and significantly he includes both his Coole Park poems in the *Oxford Book of Modern Verse* which he edited in 1936. The subsequent history of Coole is appalling. Nothing remains now but a few floor tiles, the old garden walls and the ruins of the stable-block. The great catalpas have gone, and the garden has been planted with rows of *Picea abies* (Christmas trees). Successful efforts by voluntary workers have recently been made to tidy it up by trimming box hedges and restoring its form.

The story of Thoor Ballylee is heartening in comparison. By 1952 it had fallen into decay – cattle rested in the ground-floor rooms, water poured in through the roof, and vandals had torn planks from the oak door. Then in 1961 the Kiltartan Society, founded by Mrs Mary Hanley, aided by Bord Failte Eireann, started to restore it, and Mrs Yeats and her son and daughter placed it in a trust's hands. Today all is weather-proofed, cottages re-thatched, garden cleaned up. Thousands of visitors come annually to see it.

> An ancient bridge, and a more ancient tower,
> A farmhouse that is sheltered by a wall,
> An acre of stony ground,
> Where the symbolic rose can break in flower,
> Old ragged elms, old thorns innumerable.
> The sound of the rain or sound
> Of every wind that blows.[39]

ST STEPHEN'S GREEN, DUBLIN. *The Yeats Memorial by Henry Moore.*

After Lady Gregory's death Yeats bought 'Riversdale', Willbrook, Rathfarnham, four miles south-west of Dublin. It was ideal – a small early-nineteenth-century house set in an estate of 4 acres with a pleasant garden well stocked by a previous tenant – conservatory, croquet lawn, roses, herbaceous borders, walled kitchen garden, orchard and gardener's cottage. As at Sandymount Castle, there were views to the Dublin Mountains to the south-west. One would have thought that Yeats would have been happy and settled at 'Riversdale' for the closing years of his life, yet the voice of Plato's ghost, the daimon who takes part in the conversation of the soul with itself when death is approaching, disturbs his peace:

> All his happier dreams come true
> A small old house, wife, daughter, son,
> Grounds where plum and cabbage grew,
> Poets and Wits about him drew;
> 'What then?' sang Plato's ghost. 'What then?'[40]

Nevertheless, it was at 'Riversdale' that he wrote many of his *Last Poems*, which establish with granitic certainty his place as the greatest poet in the English language of the twentieth century.

> Gardens where a soul's at ease;
> Where everything that meets the eye,
> Flowers and grass and cloudless sky,
> Resemble forms that are or seem
> When sleepers wake and yet still dream.[41]

149

7 Modern gardens: Japanese, Robinsonian and Compartmental

In the first decade of this century it was thought fashionable to have things Japanese, including gardens. But the making of these – only a handful on a large scale – must not be dismissed as being merely the result of 'a search for picturesqueness rather than any real interest in Japanese philosophy and symbolism'.[1] At that time many people in all walks of life were intrigued by Japonaiserie: Joseph Conder, an English architect living in Japan, had written his great work *Landscape Gardening in Japan* (1893); W. B. Yeats was avidly reading translations by Ernest Fenollosa of Japanese Nöh plays; merchants were exploiting the opening up of Japan for trading during the previous thirty years; politicians extolled the Anglo-Japanese Alliance (1905) which suited an internationally isolated Britain; artists were delighted in the appearance of prints by Hokusai and others; and horticulturalists were excited by John Gould Veitch's bringing back collections of seeds of conifers from Japan.

The commercial side culminated in the Japan-British exhibition in London (1910), after which a replica of Chokushi-Mon, the Gateway of the Imperial Messenger, which had been in the exhibition, was erected in Kew Gardens where it still stands. Japanese gardens in varying sorts and shapes became the fashion, and among these was one made in 1909 by the 3rd Lord Egerton at Tatton Park, Cheshire. Compared with the Japanese garden made by Lord Redesdale in the 1880s at Batsford,[2] in which there was a huge collection of Japanese plants, Lord Egerton's was concentrated on a Shinto temple, imported from Japan, which he placed on an island approached by an Oriental bridge, with an arboretum as a background. A charming scene which was observed by his friend and neighbour in the county, Colonel Hall-Walker of Tarporley, Cheshire, who had already been inspired to make a Japanese garden of his own. His chief interest in life was bloodstock breeding of racehorses, and this he carried out successfully at Tully, near Kildare. What better idea, as he already owned a nursery chiefly of Alpines at Tully, than to make a Japanese garden too? A gardening correspondent was interested to find at Tully a feature of which he had never seen before: 'a Japanese garden partaking also of the nature of an Alpine one. . . . Alpines are grown at Tully in immense quantities in pots'.[3] There were, in fact, 30 acres of nursery with millions of seedlings handled annually. But the Japanese garden was always kept private by Colonel Hall-Walker. As the millionaire Managing Director of Peter Walker & Co., brewers of Warrington, the Colonel was in a position to make the garden with no expense spared. He therefore employed Tassa Eida, a Japanese gardener whose work he had apparently seen in England, and established him with his wife and two children, Minoru[4] and Khaji, in Curragh House near by. The construction of the garden, which is only about an acre and a half, an average size for an authentic private Japanese garden, was started in 1906 and took four years to complete, with forty labourers carting limestone rock from some miles off, transplanting semi-mature pine trees, sinking a well, draining the bog, constructing waterfalls and pools, and erecting a tea-house (prefabricated in Japan). In addition, a boat was chartered to bring stone lanterns, bonsai, trees, shrubs and a tiny model village, carved in Fujiyama lava, from Japan to Ireland.

In general terms Japanese gardens, with over a thousand years of tradition, are landscapes made by artists in which little hills, bridges, islands, small trees and shrubs, streams and cascades represent larger landscapes of rocks, mountains and woods. A central hill and stone with resting-place may command the whole garden, as does one master tree, usually a pine. In a quiet corner to give shade there may be an oak by a stone seat; on one of the smaller hills on the perimeter a wild cherry with brilliant foliage; and intermixed with rocks round the lake numerous dwarf conifers.

150

This garden at Tully is often criticized for not being entirely Japanese in planting and layout; yet when it was created in 1906 the tradition of gardens in Japan was being strongly eroded by western influences and horticultural introductions. The traffic was two-way, and so a garden made by a Japanese expert at that date was more representative of the period if it contained occasional western plants and even grass lawns and horticultural colour, rather than just green-ness. Therefore Eida planted Scots pines and beeches which were designed to have the same symbolic effect as his own trees but which were not Japanese in origin.

As well as these aesthetic and horticultural mixtures between east and west in gardening, the Tully gardens carry a further symbolic addition, which must have been the idea of Colonel Hall-Walker or his gardener Eida: a Yugen, a hidden meaning, of a journey through life of Everyman or the Pilgrim Soul. He enters at the Gateway of Oblivion among the trees and passes into the open where there is a small cavern, the womb. Thereon all the details of Everyman's life are plotted in the guide to the gardens – the Path of Childhood, with stepping-stones above water (a very common feature in Japanese gardens for practical reasons), the Hill of Learning, the Bridge of Matrimony (two separate planks interlocked side by side, again a common feature in Japanese gardens), until he passes the Gateway to Eternity. All this sounds delightfully Japanese, but nowhere in Joseph Conder's *Landscape Gardening in Japan* nor in Teiji Itoh's more recent *Space and Illusion in the Japanese Garden* is such symbolism so much as hinted at, and these are two definitive works. There are azaleas everywhere at Tully, also a beautiful wisteria-clad pergola and many plants one associates with Japan – kerrias, mahonias, fatsias and chaenomeles, as well as some Alpines from the original Tully nurseries and saxifrages sent from Glasnevin in 1910 in 'ninety-seven packets of unspecified seed'.[5] Further seeds from Japan have recently been acquired by the National Botanic Gardens, Glasnevin, and many have germinated at Tully.

The Tea House,[6] standing on a hill, has frosted glass windows, traditionally to prevent tea-drinkers from looking out into the beauty of the garden and being distracted from the tea ceremony. But this usually took place at night and, paradoxically, to a westerner the custom of tea-drinking was founded on a Zen-Buddhist belief in the beauty of nature, so why was one not allowed to see the surrounding garden? There are some splendid moments along this garden-path at Tully: the

JAPANESE GARDENS,
TULLY, CO. KILDARE.
The Tea House.
JAPANESE GARDENS,
TULLY, CO. KILDARE.
The view from the cavern.

lantern by the clipped yews on the Hill of Learning, the maples by the stream, *Cryptomeria japonica*, with dark-green leaves and peeling reddish bark, and the bubbling of the miniature cascade seen from above.

In 1915 Colonel Hall-Walker gave his Tully Stud Farm to the nation to form the National Stud, and in 1919 he received a peerage, taking the title Lord Wavertree (the first and last as he had no heirs). Until 1943 the gardens were not particularly well cared for by the British National Stud; after that they were handed over to the Irish Government which two years later formed the Irish National Stud, and restored the gardens to some of their former glory. The problems of the Director today are taxing: a small path-type garden, made for tranquillity and meditation, where the leaves of a willow brushing the waters of the stream might have been the only sound, is now visited annually by thousands. But the future of this garden is assured by State patronage, and in the hands of its director, John Colleran, it is now more Japanese in planting and design than it has ever been.

The O'Donovan, the present owner of Hollybrook House, Skibbereen, Co. Cork, tells us that the large Japanese Water-Garden was laid out there in 1903 by two Japanese gardeners for his great-aunt Mrs Morgan, who had sailed in her yacht to Japan and brought back the lanterns. In her house, designed and built by R. S. Balfour at the same time, she also had a Japanese room. Unfortunately, this garden today is an overgrown jungle, but not apparently irreparable. From its 3½ acres in a woodland setting it is still possible to stroll along a tributary of the Ilen river which is the main axis: a peaceful stream with side-waters, islands, remains of bridges above a ruined sluice, all of which must have been in the best Japanese 1,000-year-old tradition. Stepping-stones and paths can still be traced to two pavilions, one of which was a tea-house with its verandah over the water and stone water-basin near by. Both houses were sited with views over the water and near two flat-topped stone lanterns. Though snow must be rare in Co. Cork, one of these, a *yukimi* or snow-viewing lantern, on a base set on three legs with a light box crowned by a wide flat top to catch falling snow, still looks very beautiful, with or without snow, as it hangs gracefully over the water. Two gates (*torii*) with free-standing uprights and a cross-beam in the best Shinto shrine tradition are totally ruined, as is the roofing of a well of spring water made of three slabs of stone.

Bamboos, especially the smaller Sasa varieties, have taken over, rhododendrons are uncontrolled, and irises and water-lilies, once graceful in old pools, appear in summer; much overgrown, but still just recognizable, are a *Thujopsis dolabrata*, a once-fine evergreen that has been a forestry tree in Japan for 2,000 years, a *Cryptomeria japonica*, not so large as either of the pair at Derreen, and a *Chamaecyparis*

HOLLYBROOK, CO. CORK. *The snow viewing lantern, c. 1935.*

pisifera squarrosa. The common *Acuba japonica*, the hardy evergreen with scarlet berries, survives admirably in the shade.

The garden was maintained until 1943 but six years later, when the present owner's parents inherited the estate, it had in their opinion declined too far for restoration. Schemes have recently been mooted locally to revive the garden as a tourist attraction, but so far through lack of funds these have come to nothing. Handsome bronze cranes, those Japanese symbols of life and happiness, therefore remain in store; and the way is not lighted to the tea ceremony.

After the making of the three examples at Tully, Powerscourt and Skibbereen, the fashion for Japanese gardens seems to have committed *hara-kiri*, although there are scattered examples of the Bypass Japanese Style[7] with the odd bridge, stone lanterns and tea-house in public parks. No eastern influence is traceable in the compartmental gardens we shall now consider, except that sometimes a mild flavour of things Japanese is sprinkled over water-gardens influenced by Gertrude Jekyll.

The first book in modern times to advocate and outline a new English formal movement in gardening was John D. Sedding's *Garden-Craft, Old and New* (1895). This appeared in the middle of the period of William Robinson's strongly worded exhortations towards woodland gardens, and with its exquisite illustrations of English formal gardens, both ancient like Levens's and modern like Sedding's own designs, was a passionate plea for a reassessment of the whole relationship in gardening of Art and Nature. In the middle of the Victorian era Sir Gardner Wilkinson had seemed a lone voice when he wrote that 'common flowers, the weeds of the country are apt to be despised because they are common; they also have the advantage of being hardy, and rare flowers are not always those suited for beds'.[8] It was the early Renaissance gardens with their simple country flowers in formal patterns to which Sedding tried to reintroduce gardeners, especially in areas round the house. A forecourt with yew hedges, after early Renaissance models, is a place to walk on bleak days, where the earliest spring flowers can bloom comfortably and where later in the year hollyhocks, paeonies, poppies, tritomas and tulips can be seen at their best against a dark-green hedge. Such enclosures, often perfect squares in Tudor quadrangles, bounded by espaliers, clipped box hedges and ornamented with vases, fountains, and statuary, were the formal garden designs which Sedding thought should be revived.

This book was followed by the more influential *The Formal Garden in England* by Reginald Blomfield and F. Inigo Thomas, who also traced traditional garden crafts back to medieval and early Renaissance gardens; and though there were no medieval

WESTPORT HOUSE, CO. MAYO. *The Italian Garden, c. 1930.*

KILLARNEY HOUSE, CO. KERRY. *The house and terraces, c. 1900.*

KILLARNEY HOUSE, CO. KERRY. *The parterre, c. 1900.*

KILLARNEY HOUSE, CO. KERRY. *The fan parterre, c. 1900.*

154

gardens left, there were many detailed accounts and pictures which could serve as guides. These, they wrote, showed a series of walled or trellised enclosures with simple formal plans, distributed round a house and related to each other informally rather than axially in the French manner as at Westport House. Each compartment was often simply planted with fruit trees trained on espaliers against walls, and with old-fashioned or even wild flowers in formal beds. The culmination of this style was reached in England in the gardens of Sissinghurst and Hidcote.

Blomfield did not work in Ireland, but Sedding laid out gardens for his friend George Devey, the architect who had designed Killarney House for the 4th Earl of Kenmare. Its façade was architecturally broken down into gables and bays, and the garden was similarly fragmented into separate compartments, informally linked in the Early English style, and planted with old-fashioned flowers rather than the usual Victorian bedding-plants. Some of these areas were enclosed by high hedges; others opened up magnificent views across the Lower Lake of Killarney. In the Western Garden arcaded yew hedges were a backdrop for a box garden of beds planted with old-fashioned pinks and marguerites; the Lower Fan Garden had lavender hedges and sweet-smelling herbs; the Middle Terrace designs were made in *Viburnum tinus* (laurustinus) and the Upper Fan Garden had bedding-plants. Although the Sunken Garden with the Kenmare Arms and the Prince of Wales feathers worked in box might seem Italianate, a closer inspection showed the beds to be planted with cottage flowers.[9] Arthur Bourne Vincent in 1906 laid out a similar parterre at Muckross House, also on the Lower Lake, designed by R. Wallace, who was later to assist Sir Edwin Lutyens in making the formal cellular gardens with great yew hedges at Castle Drogo, Chagford, Devonshire. These gardens, derived from early Renaissance gardens and often planted with cottage flowers, were well suited to changing social conditions even in Edwardian times, for an owner, man or woman, could cope with the small areas into which the garden was divided, and found it much less expensive than employing labour for bedding-out or mosaic culture.

One of the most interesting of compartmental gardens is at Lambay Island, four miles off Rush, Co. Dublin, which was constructed by Sir Edwin Lutyens. In 1904 the Hon. Cecil Baring[10] bought this square mile of black rock and turf with a ridge rising to 400 ft in the north-east.[11] The only material for building was a sort of blue-green porphyry with feldspar crystals. A blockhouse had been built on the island in the fifteenth century to keep pirates away, and this was the basic structure to which Sir Edwin Lutyens was commissioned in 1907 to add extensive farm buildings, cottages, a garden and eventually a double house for the Hon. Cecil Baring's daughters. No one was more famous at that time than Lutyens for the successful use of traditional local materials for building, and no architect showed such refreshing vitality in his treatment of surface textures, such a rare touch in his relation of solids to voids, and such a sense of fitness in the design of walls, staircases, pavements, pergolas and terraces in a garden. The overall result at Lambay was austere in tone when new, because the sun and salt had bleached the old blockhouse and farm buildings. Fortunately, Gertrude Jekyll collaborated once again with Lutyens to clothe walls and gardens with hanging creepers and bright herbaceous plants.[12] The soil is a dark loam, and trenching was difficult owing to rock. To keep the new additions to the house low and out of the wind Lutyens altered levels and made a terrace to the North Court. Much Silurian shale was removed and taken to construct a large mound to the north-west, on which was planted a copse. Old stone pillars found in the farm buildings were effectively used for a sturdy pergola, a feature he constantly repeated in his garden designs.

After stepping off the boat at the quay on the south-west of the island, one sees a row of cottages huddling near the jetty, and beyond these the Chapel, a rough Doric temple. A short walk across an open field by a grass path, and a Lutyens bastioned gateway to the main entrance of the house confronts one. Across the top of this rampart gate – a superb design in oak, like all the others – a rampart on the inner side has been constructed so that one can walk uninterruptedly in medieval fashion along the walls, with a breast-high parapet, covered with *Cotoneaster horizontalis*, escallonia and buckthorn on the outward side. In one of the bastions of the inner side

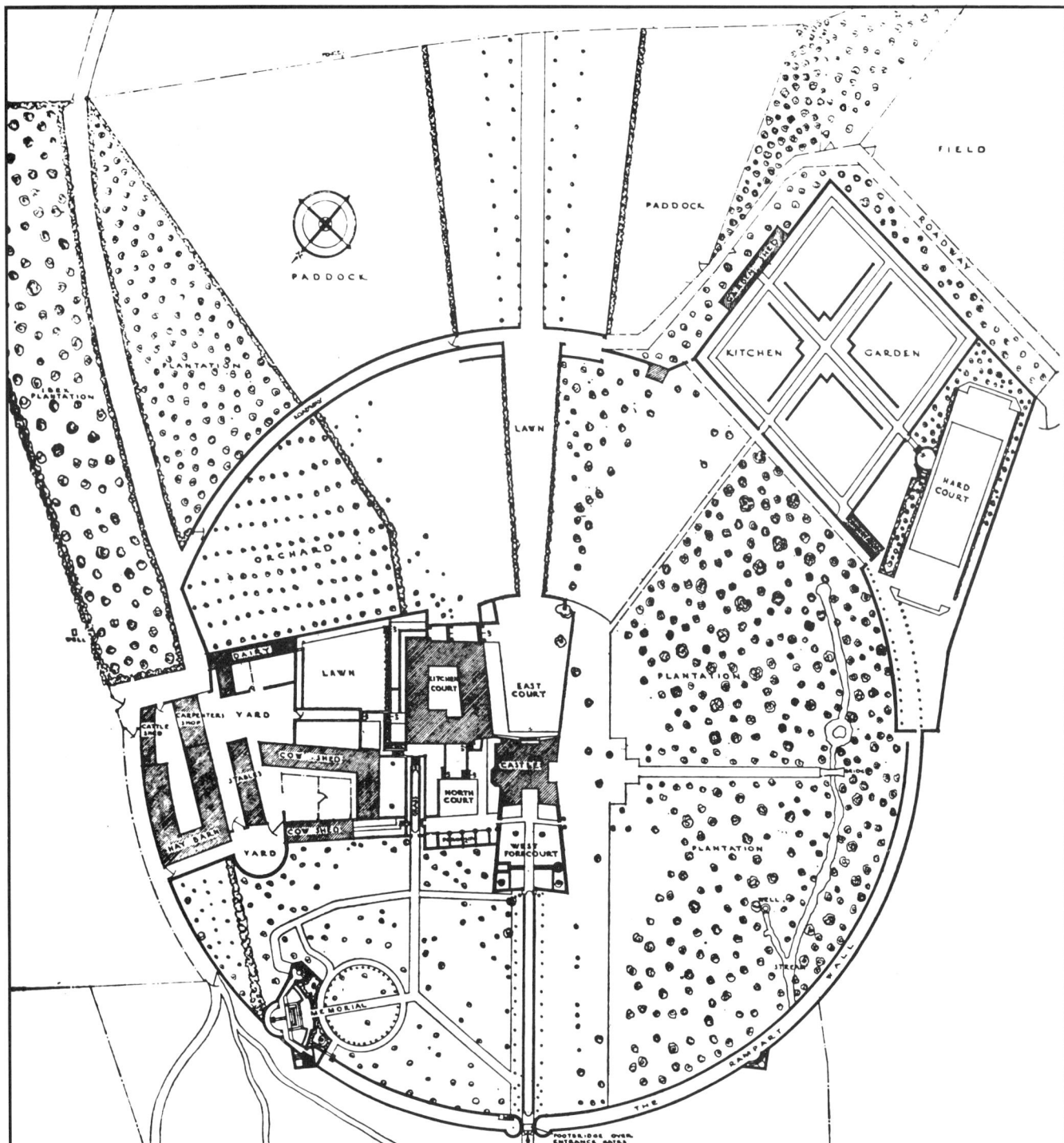

The plan contains various labels: PADDOCK, FIELD, PADDOCK, KITCHEN GARDEN, ROADWAY, PLANTATION, UPPER PLANTATION, LAWN, HARD COURT, ORCHARD, DAIRY, LAWN, KITCHEN COURT, EAST COURT, CARPENTERS YARD, CATTLE SHED, COW SHED, STABLES, NORTH COURT, CATTLE, HAY BARN, COW SHED, YARD, WEST FORECOURT, PLANTATION, MEMORIAL, STREAM, WALL, THE RAMPART, FOOTBRIDGE OVER ENTRANCE GATES, WELL

of this wall a large, austere altar-tomb with steps in dove-grey stone has been erected to the memory of Lord and Lady Revelstoke, the creators of the garden. Nearer to the house, after passing through a grove of widely spaced ash and sycamore trees, stands another wall, though less tall than the perimeter one. The whole area is an *enceinte* divided into compartments: wild garden outside with grove, brook, bamboos and iris patch; farm buildings, kitchen garden with pantiled walls; and other smaller walled divisions herbaceously planted. Each garden bears out Lutyens' contention made at that time that 'a garden scheme should have a backbone, a central idea beautifully phrased. Every wall, path, stone and flower should have its relationship to the central idea'.[13] Or as A. S. G. Butler, in his definitive work on Lutyens, so beautifully describes its secret: 'replay of little walled spaces within that great bounding circle that gives Lambay much of its architectural character. They are almost like large roofless rooms'.[14]

LAMBAY ISLAND, CO. DUBLIN. *Sir Edwin Lutyens's compartmental plan.*

On one occasion when Lutyens was on Lambay he was unable to reach the mainland for two days on account of rough seas and high winds. Since the science of aerodynamics was almost non-existent in 1908, he would not have known of the effects of wind. Indeed, he must have been misinformed, for he thought that if he built high perimeter walls in addition to inner compartmental walls all would be well, although any countryman knew and still knows that this is impractical. As has since been proved, gales on confronting a solid wall leap over the top and drive down the inner side with renewed force. The only possible defence against them horticulturally is a thick and wide belt of trees which can withstand salt and spindrift, filtering the wind as if through a lattice. Since 1908 the grove of ash and sycamore, those sturdy trees, has grown little and slowly above the height of the wall, and an avenue of mulberry trees planted to the front door was torn out of the ground after thirty years' growth.

During the mild winter of 1910–11 *Coronilla glauca* at the foot of a southern wall had flowered from October to April, but gales later in April turned the green grass brown, destroyed foliage of red currants, killed tarragon roots planted in November and decimated bamboos.[15] Some years after this the outer wall was heightened but with little apparent benefit. As in the west of Ireland, fuchsias thrive, escallonia and cotoneaster prosper, stonecrop and samphire grow naturally. But the salt burns all, and the house is constructed with small doors and few casements so that the inhabitants seem, on rough days, to be sheltering like monks. Their excursions into the garden are often to trim, prune, tie and strap plants to the walls and to stakes, or to cut them down to ground level. But on the inner side of the rampart it is a pity that shrub-killer has been used so ruthlessly on a wall which fifty years ago was gloriously clothed with escallonia and cotoneaster. However, fallow deer and grey seals still flourish.

Howth Castle stands on a peninsula at the north-east end of Dublin Bay within sight of Lambay. In 1910 Sir Edwin Lutyens worked here on the house and garden by adding a huge square tower with typical stepped Irish battlements to match the castle – the oldest inhabited house in Ireland. Joining old and new, Lutyens designed a loggia with massive, plain piers. On the south front where his tower, containing a new library on the ground floor, is the terminal at the western end, he laid out a formal parterre in the Early English style with stone-flagged paths, box edging and formal beds raised 6 in above the walk so that flowers could be better seen.[16] There

HOWTH CASTLE, CO. DUBLIN. *The Sidney parterre designed by Sir Edwin Lutyens, c. 1935.*

sun-loving shrubs thrive: *Solanum jasminoides*, a climbing *Lonicera tellmanniana*, myrtles, and a large, fragrant *Pittosporum tobira* with dark leaves and white flowers against a grey wall. A smaller formal area beneath the west tower, the Sidney garden, intersected with paths, is also planted freely, with nepeta, lavender, paeonies, rosemary, agapanthus and a large *Buddleia colvilei*. The only other formal area is on the northeast side where the famous seventeenth-century beech hedges, not so trim as they used to be, lead the eye along vistas to Lambay and Ireland's Eye.

Outside the formal enclosures from the south front one looks over a wide lawn to a landscape of meadows rising to the rhododendron-covered hill of 'Muck Rock'. To reach the summit of this one climbs by paths through dark tunnels of rhododendrons, past a cromlech hidden among the trees to the bare rock at the top. The castle below nestles in trees, and a panorama from the Wicklow Mountains to the Mourne Mountains unfolds above the many rhododendrons. It is all an excellent example of the planting of a wild garden in conditions which are suitable – on a very steep northern slope, sheltered from the sea, so that the light comes over the hill on to the flowers, filtering through a veil of atmospheric humidity which gives it a unique Irish quality. The hill, which is of micaceous granite, is covered by a deep peaty soil; natural drainage, a misty air, few frosts, and shelter from the sea complete the perfect picture; in addition, the rhododendrons have laid a rich and deep mulch from their leaves. For twenty-five years before his death in 1909 the chief planter was the Earl of Howth, although *Rhododendron ponticum* had been introduced as early as the 1790s. He left these where they made a sturdy wind-break, but when whole areas began to be smothered in rosy mauve he took them out and replanted. In the 1920s there were about 1,000 rhododendron and azalea plants, half being species and half cultivars. H. G. Wells, not usually famed for describing the natural scene, was impressed:

green and quiet, restful and fragrant, without any glaring colour, the Rhododendrons being up the hill-side half-a-mile away, and there the gorgeous blaze of sun-lit colour is toned and softened by greens and browns and greys innumerable, and overhead the everchanging sky.[17]

Another compartmental garden by Lutyens in Ireland was at Heywood, Ballinakill, Queens County (1906) for Lieutenant-Colonel William Hutcheson Poë (created a baronet in 1912). Once again Lutyens designed a garden related to the eighteenth-century house – terraces, pergola with Ionic colums, pleached alley, yew garden and an elliptical pool with a loggia, all on different levels round the house. But unlike Lambay, the site was very steep, with the house overlooking its

HEYWOOD, CO. LEIX. *Sir Edwin Lutyens's compartmental plan.* IRISH NATIONAL WAR MEMORIAL, ISLANDBRIDGE, DUBLIN *One of the Book-Rooms designed by Sir Edwin Lutyens.*

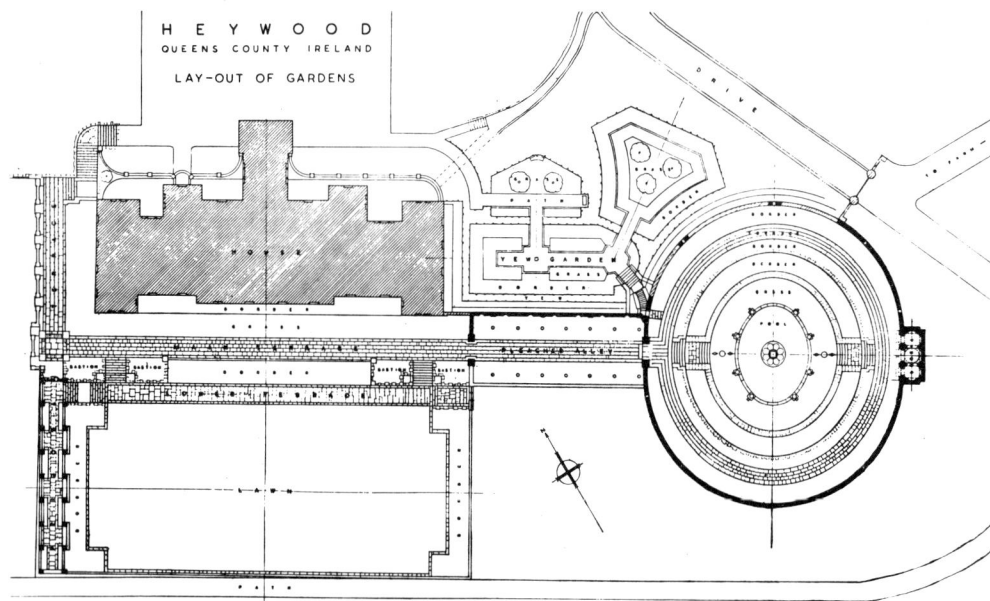

HEYWOOD
QUEENS COUNTY IRELAND
LAY-OUT OF GARDENS

eighteenth-century landscape, and this meant that Lutyens had to devise some way of dealing with the sharply falling ground. A terrace in front of the house was constructed with a pair of stone bastions to another lower paved terrace, and on the west side the garden fell away to a pergola terrace which ended in an apse and statue. The main terrace in front of the house had to be shored up with a high retaining wall with massive buttresses. In the Jekyll manner all the walls were constructed in roughly finished stone to allow wall plants to colonize and seed. As in many of Lutyens's works, the final accounts presented to the owner were far in excess of the estimates; in this case the increase was obviously related to the huge retaining wall without which the terrace would have sunk.[18]

Lutyens's finest work in Ireland is the Irish National War Memorial at Island-bridge, Dublin. The commission was given to him as early as 1918 when it was proposed that the site should be in Merrion Square, but the question was not settled until 1933 when agreement was reached and 10 acres were given over at Island-bridge. Trees were planted by the Board of Works, and the Memorial Gardens opened on Armistice Day, 1940. The main axis of Lutyens's plan was to lead to a bridge across the river aligned to the Wellington Testimonial in the Phoenix Park, but this was never built. The gardens therefore face east across the river, and the main enclosure, after much levelling, is parallel to the bank of the Liffey. Circular sunken gardens, 200 ft in diameter and in separate compartments are reached by a majestic flight of wide-stretching steps. Within this enclosure, flanked by two obelisks, basins and fountains, is the plain, uninscribed Stone of Remembrance, and behind, up another large flight of curved steps, stands the Memorial Cross. On the perimeter of the enclosure four Book-rooms – pavilions housing the names of the dead – are joined by unadorned pergolas. All is very properly monumental in granite; but its present state is pitiful. The 49,000 Irish dead lie neglected, graffiti desecrate the walls, large urns have fallen from walls, and a bypass road has cut along the edge of the gardens.

> Know that we fools, now with the foolish dead,
> Died not for flag, nor king, nor emperor,
> But for a dream, born in a herdsman's shed,
> And for the secret scripture of the poor.[19]

CASTLETOWN COX, CO. KILKENNY. *The parterre.*

At Castletown Cox, Co. Kilkenny, a compartmental garden was made in 1909 in the style of Norah Lindsay, the Irish-born garden designer, who was a cousin of Mrs Wyndham-Quin (later Lady Dunraven). Around a collection of old English garden statuary from Clearwell Court, Gloucestershire, a series of separate gardens was laid out, the most successful being the box garden, which has the scale and complexity of Serlio's designs. In 1906 the competition for the design of Herbert Park, Dublin, was won by J. Cheal and Sons, who had previously designed the Anne Boleyn garden at Hever Castle, and a new formal garden was made at Westport House, which owed more to the style of the gardens of Lake Como and Maggiore. This was perhaps due to the fact that a member of the Browne family, while on a Grand Tour in the mid-nineteenth century, bought the Villa San Remigio on Lake Maggiore and made a remarkable garden there. A cellular garden was later created at Knockmaroon, Co. Dublin, the seat of Lord Moyne, and near by at Farmleigh, the seat of the Earl of Iveagh, the Countess, a friend of Gertrude Jekyll, laid out a sunken garden in the same Early English style with topiary peacocks.

Many demesnes which have been gardened by a succession of family owners have had each generation's gardening activity adapted or swept away by the succeeding generation. Not so at Farmleigh, whose garden represents an anthology of old and new gardening styles and where the solemn avenues of conifers, clock-tower, *jet d'eau*, lake and exquisite fernery, recently restored, bespeak the Victorian period; the Winter Garden, the Robinsonian garden and the bog-garden representing the Edwardian age; the Early English-style garden already mentioned, the 1920s; and, not least, the planting of ornamental flowering trees and the division of the walled kitchen garden by yew hedges, into a series of formal compartments with borders of harmonizing colour compositions by the present earl and countess, in turn show clearly the garden history of the last hundred years.

Many smaller modern gardens have been built in Ireland in a cellular style round a house, with Jekyll herbaceous planting and low hedges or walls as boundaries to each part. From these immediate gardens one can often walk into Robinsonian areas of mixed woodland, which is sometimes used as a shelter-belt. One such modern garden which reveals astonishing growth in a short time is Mrs Reginald Farquhar's at Ardsallagh, Fethard, Co. Tipperary. When she started to garden here in 1951, her elegant Regency house and present garden were a farm with chickens in the backyard and rough pasturage round. As Ardsallagh is on a slight rise in the middle of the horse-breeding plains, she immediately planted shelter-belts to the west from which direction most prevailing strong winds blow. To walk today through these shelter-belts on grass paths does not mean passing banks of *Cupressus macrocarpa* or Scots pines, but meandering by griselinia, berberis, *Ilex serrata* (deciduous Japanese Holly), magnolias, beschornerias, *Myrtus lecheriana*, *Hypericum* 'Rowallane', with notable *Acer griseum*, that most beautiful of small trees, and koelreuteria, all growing splendidly and underplanted with primulas and meconopsis. At the back of the house in a paved courtyard on the south side, where the hens

GUINCHO, CO. DOWN
The Villa from one of the garden compartments.

used to be, enclosed on two sides by a stable wall and another wall and therefore doubly protected, Mrs Farquhar has planted *Jasminum polyanthum*, a *Magnolia soulangeana* (small and therefore in scale), *Embothrium coccineum*, crinodendron, *Wistaria sinensis*, *Mutisia oligodon*, *Fremontia mexicana*, abutilons, and eucalypts in holes in the centre of the *pavé*. Leading from this a lily-pool garden, with a small, stone-lined, rectangular pool in the centre, is paved round and margined by 2-ft walls and a wide border of trees, shrubs and flowers together: *Acacia alpina*, eucalypts, *Leycesteria crocothyros*, a carpet of *Leptospermum prostratum* and, near steps to the pool, *Myosotium nobile* (Chatham Island Forget-me-not). From this lily-pool garden at Ardsallagh an iron gate leads to 2 acres of high walled garden – one half shrubs and trees, the other half kitchen garden with two greenhouses. Sophora, eucryphria, hoheria, *Nyssa sylvatica* and other tender shrubs all grow strongly. It is a compartmental garden and, except for a central axis, has all the essential elements of the best gardens present: variety, each piece leading easily to another, and the connection between garden and house through the courtyard most welcoming. On a neutral soil, with strong winds and by no means frostless climate, Mrs Farquhar has made after about twenty-five years an enchanting garden.

Another compartmental garden, begun in 1947, lies around Guincho, a villa in the Portuguese style, near Helen's Bay in Co. Down. Informally arranged round the house are a sunken circular lawn, a pool garden and a formal paved garden with raised beds and a remarkable Victorian seat of cast iron in an acorn and oak-leaf design. From here a vista opens down a flight of steps to a great sloping lawn backed by trees and ringed with shrub borders. At the bottom of the slope lies a woodland garden in a dell watered by a winding stream. The compartments provide a series of linked surprises in the manner of Frances Hodgson Burnett's *The Secret Garden*. Although a horticulturalist's garden, the form of the compartments at Guincho is retained even in winter through Mrs Frazer Mackie's interest in and particular skill with foliage plants. The exposed site is ideally suited to the light and loosely slung foliage of the Australasian plants, and their muted colour tones are admired by Mrs Mackie more than the riot of colour often obtained by growing numerous cultivars.

A windy site and a dislike of colour riots were also shared by Lord Talbot de Malahide at Malahide Castle, and therefore an exchange of plants often occurred between the two gardens. Large leptospermums, callistemons, melaleucas, drimys and idichiums provide enclosure and backgrounds in the compartments, and give shelter to a great range of interesting plants, including a collection of hostas from Japan, a *Paeonia ludlowii* from Major Sherriff's seed, a guevina, and tree ferns in the woodland dell, and perhaps the rarest plant in the garden, *Todocarpa thymifolia*. A great *Sophora tetraptera* covers a corner of the house, and there are many charming plants – the hedgehog holly, the dwarf evergreen oak, the double blackberry, the holly-leaved rhododendron and a group of Chilean *Puya alpestris*, whose peacock-blue flowers carried on striking spikes are reminiscent of the designs and colours used in their artefacts by the South American Indians. Guincho is characterized by the quiet restraint derived from growing only species and excluding 'man-made' cultivars, and by a sense of unusual balance – the formal enclosures contrasting with the outlying wilder areas, the woodland balancing the open lawn, and the evergreen foliage defining the summer flowers.

Kilmokea, a simple neo-classical house built in the 1790s as a rectory, stands high amid mature trees five miles from the deep inlet of Waterford Harbour. In the last twenty-eight years Colonel and Mrs David Price have laid out a series of gardens, compartmented round the house and leading to woodland. Most people think of the gardens of Co. Cork and Co. Kerry when subtropical conditions are mentioned, but here at Kilmokea there is little frost, and many tender plants associated with the west thrive with exceptionally fast growth. Great Island, on which Kilmokea is situated, is a large peninsula jutting into the harbour, five miles from the sea and surrounded on three sides by tidal waters. This accounts for the mild climate and also perhaps for the choice of the site as a trading-post by the Vikings. One of the principal features of the garden today is a Viking mill-pond, recently excavated, in which the remains of a horizontal mill were discovered and are now preserved near by.

Peacocks and fan-tailed pigeons strut and frolic round the house amidst spring borders and the curving lawn which lines the short drive up from the road – a rare sight in season, with massed plantings of daffodils, sky-blue *Ompalodes cappadocica* and flowering cherries. Under tall old beech trees ferns, bergenias and hostas flourish as well as a fine *Drimys winteri*, *Hoheria stylosa* and some eucalypts. Tender shrubs and flowers also thrive in the sheltered Dovecot Garden to the north of the house; *Jasminum polyanthum* and Schizophragma scramble up walls which shelter camellias. After a formal paved garden with Italianate loggia and pool, one arrives at the west façade at the back of the house. Once the kitchen garden of the rectory, it is now a lawn surrounded by stone walls. Fully planted herbaceous borders, climbing roses and ceanothus sweep in front of the wall at the farthest end, through which one steps down into a wild garden with old horse-pond under the shade of mature oaks and chestnuts. In front of these the golden foliage of a swamp cypress, a tall embothrium and *Acacia dealbata* stand out. Below this, across a small highroad, a 4-acre woodland garden is a surprise. The upper part is occupied by the Viking mill-pond from which water spills over a small dam to flow down through the woodland, forming picturesque ponds and falls on the way. The wood, of mixed hemlock, Douglas fir, spruce and pine, planted only fifteen years ago, provides shelter from the wind which whistles off the estuary. As can be seen, this is a garden which is horticulturally interesting in small compartments near the house, leading to the Robinsonian woodland area. If one had to exemplify any trend as typical in modern gardening, this would be the format, and Kilmokea is an exemplar, set in a mild climate.

Perched on a cliff-top at Drumleck, Co. Dublin, on the peninsula of Howth overlooking the bay and mountains to the south, laid out recently by John Hunt, the medievalist, this garden is the last of the compartmental gardens of any size to be laid out in Ireland. It is distinguished by a series of compartments on an axis which is some distance from the house, and although the garden is axial, each compartment is entirely separate and hidden from the next by being linked by flights of steps on a steep slope. From the lawn in front of the house one looks down over a balustrade into a quarry which has been made into a formal rose garden around a circular fountain which has as its centre a figure by Bernini or one of his followers. From here flights of steps flanking a water-staircase rise to a plateau, on which a formal lawn with a tank at its centre forms the centre of the garden. Then a further flight rises to a landing, from which one can look back on the path by which one has progressed so far. Here one turns once again up the hill and climbs, by a series of staircases flanked by free-standing columns set into the shrub-borders on either hand, to reach a panelled door with pedimented doorcase set into a wall and rescued from ruins of the eighteenth-century Home for the Incurables, Dublin. Through it one passes into yet another compartment.

One further garden which cannot be categorized as fitting a compartmental design nor as one made by an artist-owner, is Marble Hill, Port na Blagh, Co. Donegal. We mention it in order to illustrate how much can be achieved in a garden in a short time by using modern methods. When Mrs Jobling Purser bought the property in 1970, the neat neo-classical house stood between mountains and Sheephaven Bay with nothing but a jungle round it. Fortunately, there were some old sycamore, beech, sorbus and fruit trees but little else, except for a deserted vegetable garden near the beach and a converted barn. After clearing saplings, brambles and weeds, she enlarged a forecourt in front of the house by constructing two small terraces, to the design of Mr Lanning Roper, below which she asked him to plant shrub roses and to advise on further planting of hostas, bergenias, rodgersias, kniphofias, agapanthus, lilies and Californian poppies, with francoas giving winter colour in the mild climate. The prettiest feature, alongside the house, is a walled garden with tall, conical dovecot strung over an angle in the wall. Flowering shrubs covering the walls or against them include *Abutilon vitifolium, Itea illicifolia*, ceanothus and many clematis. It is a superb site, and had been enjoyed for summer holidays in the past by such friends of the Law family, who owned it, as Augustine Henry and AE.

It would appear that the compartmental style, deriving as it does from the simplicity of the Early English style, answers many of the questions one might ask of a gardening style for today. It is adaptable to a garden of any size, larger ones having simply more compartments; it is flexible in that it can respond to an owner's changing circumstances by allowing subtraction or addition of compartments without seriously affecting the overall design; it gives a method of organizing a large range of plant material into distinct areas, while allowing for a maximum use of architectural and sculptural features as focal points; and, lastly, being an enclosed system, it is an admirable style for a period when few people have control over development beyond the immediate vicinity of their house.

As a climax to these modern gardens, we have chosen to discuss four gardens made for the greater part since the Second World War by owners with outstanding artistic and horticultural ability. These demesnes are on a magnificent structural scale as well as being unique horticulturally. In plan they do not fit into either a loose Robinsonian jacket nor into a Lutyens-Jekyll compartmental garment, though gardens near the houses in each case lead to extensive woodland areas so beloved by Robinson. The Earl and Countess of Rosse at Birr Castle, Lord Talbot de Malahide at Malahide Castle, Mr Henry McIlhenny at Glenveagh Castle and Mr Ambrose Congreve at Mount Congreve have created these majestic paradises of concentrated immensity, which will never again be made by private individuals if taxation continues at the present penal level. The National Trust (Committee for Northern Ireland) has taken over Mount Stewart gardens, and similarly in England looks after the gardens at Sissinghurst Castle and Hidcote Manor which are comparable to the four in Ireland, yet neither so large nor so interesting horticulturally. It must be evident to State, city or local authorities in Ireland that these four Irish gardens are of international importance and worthy of careful preservation, as the Dublin Corporation has recently taken charge of Malahide Castle garden, and it appears that plans have been made for the future of Glenveagh and Mount Congreve after the deaths of their owners. It would be tragic if any one of this quartet should ever become a lost demesne.

To enter the twin-towered stone gateway in the high walls of Birr Castle, Co. Offaly, is to set foot in an enchanted world of horticulture created by successive Earls of Rosse and much added to by the late Earl and the Dowager Lady Rosse in the last forty years. In climatic conditions which are not altogether kindly – average rainfall of about 33 in., frosts sometimes as low as 0° Fahrenheit, and an alkaline soil restricting the range of plants which can be grown – the achievement of Lord and

Lady Rosse is unequalled. However, they have been helped by much sunshine (for Ireland), a rich alluvial soil near the lake and river, and, above all, by a splendidly varied site: about 150 acres of gardens, lake and parkland, with the river Camcor as an axis curving past the castle and through a wooded valley.

The demesne can be divided into five sections: the courtyard in the precincts of the castle walls to the south-east; the terraces with the river garden on both sides of the Camcor; the arboreta to the west and north of the lake; the formal garden and kitchen garden across the park to the north; and the parkland itself with the Giant Telescope. In the first of these, a *giardino segreto* in the personal care of Lady Rosse, the walls provide shelter on three sides making it ideal for tender plants, but it is somewhat lacking in sunshine on account of the heavy shade from mature trees along the banks of the Camcor. The garden is designed to be looked at and approached from the rooms of the castle. Formal rose beds in the centre, with clipped edges of *Teucrium chamaedrys* (Germander), a glossy-leaved evergreen with small pale-purple flowers (a welcome change after box borders), are flanked by rising ground on which grow bushes of *Senecio laxifolius* with its bright-yellow daisy-like flowers and thick silver leaves, a handsome Spanish broom, cistus in variety, choisya, with a *Clematis spooneri* entwining the balustrade of the staircase to the Keep. The walls of the castle itself are luxuriantly clothed with roses and wistarias, *Buddleia auriculata*, providing fragrant flowers in the lean months from September to January, and *Ceratostigma willmottianum*, with pretty purple flowers in July. Below the wall facing the castle, peat was brought in for a spring border of azaleas accented by *Eucryphia nymansensis* at each end. From this private garden a path, high above the river bank in the cover of huge, mature yews and beeches planted on both sides of a romantic cascade, leads to the terraces of the river garden.

These terraces are on two levels: the upper one, a flower-garden with lawns, was constructed in 1912 in front of the walled fortifications above the castle moat, but planted and completed in its present shape by Lady Rosse in the 1930s. The formal geometrical solids, the architectural forms governed by the angular wall, all carefully interjoined, must have been influenced by the prevailing aesthetic of Cubism. As one looks down from the castle windows, this terrace, with no serpentine lines or conventional curves, has the pattern of a Cubist painting, a wholly new handling of spatial values in gardening layout. The lawns with their angular shapes and un-broken lines provide the solidness, and the tonality of the flowers in the rectangular beds is full and warm, with vigorous definition of the planes. This formation was evidently governed initially by the sharp angles of the Vaubanesque fortification limestone wall, which originally bounded the moat.

To make this garden at Birr was a brilliant conception, since the nearest flower-garden previously was a quarter of a mile away to the north-east, as was common practice in the policies of great houses in Scotland and Ireland (see Mount Stewart, p. 100). Amid bright herbaceous planting, grow large plants of ceanothus with contrasting deep-blue flowers in spring, and towards the end of the border, a *Magnolia delavayi*, flat-topped and more than 20 ft high with creamy-white flowers. Bordering the paths, accenting the straight lines and angles, stand tubs of agapanthus. The sense of formality in the design of this terrace garden, with its outlines of walls, paths and edges, may stem from the fact that William Robinson helped to design the large herbaceous borders at Nymans, Lady Rosse's childhood home; and despite Robinson having a reputation for wild informality, the borders at Nymans are punctuated strongly at the end by large, sculptural topiary work and a statuary basin, which give form to its apparent herbaceous casualness. The out-lines of the walls, paths and edges of the terrace garden at Birr also combine this herbaceous planting with a formal setting.

The river walk below the terrace is reached by steps directly leading to the pretty metal suspension bridge, built *c.* 1820 and thought to be the first of its kind in Ireland. The lower walk along the river bank is lined with red-hot pokers, gorses and brooms, including a lovely *Cytisus praecox* from Mount Usher with velvety red flowers, gorses and *Iris sibirica*. On the other side is an obvious William Robinson garden – all trees, shrubs and perennials. A path leads through shady glades to St Brendan's

Garden with his well beside the waterfall. This is not St Brendan the Navigator, but a less famous, though contemporary, saint who founded a monastery at Birr *c*. 560. In the lower parts of this garden a canal runs parallel to the river, and there seems to be water everywhere alongside of which huge clumps of bamboo and other water-loving plants flourish. On the walk on the other side one begins to notice fine trees on both sides of the river: a notable *Juniperus recurva* (Himalayan Juniper), and on the other side a huge *Populus canescens* (105 ft by 15¾ ft in 1966), possibly the largest specimen in the British Isles and certainly the largest tree in the gardens, as well as many flowering trees such as laburnums, cherries and many rare magnolias. Among these are every type of magnolia which it is possible to grow in this climate and especially plants introduced by E. H. Wilson after his expeditions to China between 1907 and 1911, subscribed to by private collectors including the 5th Earl of Rosse. This would account at Birr also for *M. delavayi*, already mentioned, and *Davidia involucrata* (Handkerchief Tree). On the gentle slopes bordering the river walk, eucryphias, including *E.* × *nymansensis*, remind one once again of Lady Rosse's home in Sussex where Harold Comber's father was Head Gardener, and whence so many plants have come to Birr, despite differences in soil. It is impossible and would be tedious to list the galaxy of flowering shrubs in this river walk at Birr, but the health of viburnums, deutzias, kolkwitzias and even *Drimys winteri*, a tender tree, is evident, as is the careful planting of white-flowered hoherias and eucryphias against a background of dark foliage.

It is quite a long walk round the far side of the lake, and as one enters the arboretum from this path one marvels at the continuity of the planting and garden construction at Birr by Lord Rosse, especially in conifers and species of acer introduced by E. H. Wilson.[20] Where else has there been such continuous planting since 1845, that unhappy year when to alleviate the sufferings of the poor, the fortifications of Birr were constructed, the lake extended and trees such as Douglas firs planted? In the tradition of all fine arboreta those at Birr lead naturally by a walk out of the gardens, and are planted with an eye to the visual excitement of the juxtaposition of certain different trees and shrubs as well as for horticultural interest in the growth of rare specimens. The acer collection is very fine, and one should see an *A. macrophyllum* (Oregon Maple) in October bright with huge golden leaves, as well as a *Berberis montana*, a very beautiful barberry, drooping yellow flowers in May, sent by Comber from seeds collected in the Andes in 1927 to his father at Nymans. Near the head of the lake the path crosses the Camcor and the Little Brosna river; from then on the arboretum is chiefly of conifers. One may notice the absence of eucalypts, as Birr is too far from the sea; but in the rich alluvial soil by the lakeside poplars do well, and one sees old beeches, oaks, horse-chestnuts, hollies, laurels and box trees. As the path crosses the bridge at the top, there is a spectacular view of the castle through 200-year-old beeches. Here the trees are more widely spaced as the path leads to the formal gardens. Many are rare, such as a *Cornus capitata*, which is tender except in the south-west of Ireland, and some fine *Quercus coccinea* (Scarlet Oaks) which produce a rich effect in autumn. By the gate in the stone wall of the formal gardens once stood a large *Paulownia tomentosa*, 44 ft by 4 ft in 1966 according to Bean, with long blue-purple flowers in May. It died shortly after this, but four other younger ones flourish.

The most successful feature in the walled garden are the pleached hornbeam *allées*, with the plants widely spaced and therefore not forming a tunnel as is usual, but rather a ribbed structure from which one can peep out. Terminating two of these *allées* are baroque statues, said to be two of the Graces. The charming baroque curves of the ribs occurred, so Lord Rosse told us, during the Second World War when pruning had to be neglected, and so, instead of growing flat-topped, the trees produced this *treillage*. Nevertheless, it took an artists' eye to see the possibilities of this growth. There are also some Bavarian stone urns, placed in Box parterres made in 1935, which are planted with shrub roses and ornamental cherries. Between the formal gardens and the kitchen garden a dark avenue of much older box trees, some 35 ft high and said to be 300 years old, is remarkable for its age, like some archaeological artefact, but not very beautiful except in its vivid green colour.

BIRR CASTLE, CO. OFFALY. *The pleached hornbeam* allées.

BIRR CASTLE, CO. OFFALY. *The parterre and baroque urns from one of the windows in the pleached* allées.

BIRR CASTLE, CO. OFFALY. *Lord Rosse directing the conveyance of the Great Speculum to its position at the base of the tube. From a drawing by Henrietta Crompton.*

There are many other smaller gardens in this area, each with its treasures, and one wonders at the extent of it all. The walk back to the castle passes under many mature limes, oaks and beeches, and in spring one sees a solid carpet of daffodils.

The Giant Telescope with its sheer walls, dressed up with crenellations resembles contemporary architecture of Brunel, and its walls are now clothed in *Buddleia colvilei*, the delicate *Abutilon vitifolium*, shrub roses and cistus. Patrick Moore's recorded voice, seemingly coming out of the bowels of the huge telescope tube, relates the exciting history of the invention.

The late Earl and Countess of Rosse without doubt were the finest owner-gardeners in Ireland today, having an encyclopedic knowledge combined with a rare artistry in the design and planting of gardens and arboreta. But what will happen to this demesne in future years if it is not possible to employ the eight gardeners who work there so successfully today?

A hundred years ago Mount Congreve was still the simple eighteenth-century house of the Congreve family, with a garden of three terraces between the house and the river Suir, five miles above, and south-west of Waterford. Between the terraces and the river lay a steep wooded bank with picturesque winding walks under large holm-oaks and sweet chestnuts. Since 1965 the house has been expanded into a palace, the Congreves are commemorated by amber memorial plaques on the white-washed walls of the Protestant church, and the 100-acre garden, with extensive parkland, is one of the fullest planted in the world, having a full-time gardening staff of thirty-five. All this is the work of Mr Ambrose Congreve in recent years. The large walled kitchen garden now has a central lawn with two wide herbaceous borders against each wall and slopes down gently to an eighteenth-century ornamental greenhouse. A riot of colour in all seasons, it is treeless except for a large old *Ginkgo biloba* (Maidenhair Tree).

In the late 1920s and 30s Mr Congreve was a regular visitor to Mr Lionel de Rothschild at Exbury, near Southampton. Here, by these wonderful oak-woods sloping down to the Beaulieu river, Lionel de Rothschild had hundreds of gardeners raising new cultivars and planting newly discovered species of rhododendron. These woodland gardens are patently the model for Mount Congreve, and what Mr Congreve learned there he explains in a letter to us:

. . . plants should not be scattered about the garden, and repetitions of the same mixtures should be avoided. Therefore, if you plant three *Rhododendron thomsonii* or twenty, plant them together in a group to make a bold colour effect, and if you can introduce an element of surprise so much the better. Woodland gardens should not have all their secrets exposed from one or two vantage points, and even formal layouts are more effective when there is an element of concealment of one part from another. Grass should be used in both informal and formal gardens. Formal lawns as well as informal ones with grass paths winding out of sight can do much to highlight shrub and tree plentings cooling down the mass colours. In any planting the question of scale ought to be considered and little groups of colour dotted about in an extensive shrub or herbaceous border do not, in my opinion, look well.

As a result, all shrubs and trees at Mount Congreve are planted in groups of sixes, and some in greater numbers. Almost every shrub that can grow in the fairly mild climate of south-east Ireland has been tried – certainly more than Lionel de Rothschild grew before he died in 1942 – as hundreds of new rhododendron cultivars, including Japanese azaleas, have been introduced, as well as about 500 different camellia cultivars. Likewise, hundreds of magnolias, especially species from Asia, such as *M. campbellii*, have been planted along the banks of the river and are seemingly protected from frosts in March which so quickly turn the flowers brown; in addition, there are specimens of *M. mollicomata*, an almost indistinguishable variety of *M. campbellii* which takes about twelve years to flower from seed, and *M. sprengeri*, discovered by Augustine Henry in Szechwan in 1885, as well as all their hybrids. No department of horticulture seems to be absent from Mount

MOUNT CONGREVE, CO. WATERFORD. *The water garden.*

167

MOUNT CONGREVE,
CO. WATERFORD.
Foliage contrasts.

Congreve: hydrangea species and cultivars by the hundred and bulbs massed by the hundred thousand. In a damp spot there are a hundred different *Iris kaempferi* forms in all tones of rosy-purple, royal purple, white to pale mauve, purple on grey ground and many other combinations – a large collection, which is the gift of Sir Peter Smithers of Lugano and here at Mount Congreve is flourishing. Tree ferns, another gift, from Mr Walker at Rossdohan, are being tried in a sheltered place as underplanting, but Mount Congreve has more severe winters than Rossdohan; they may, however, become established before hard frosts attack them. Conifers seem to grow well – even *Abies amabilis* which, in Mr Congreve's words, 'struggles on', and this is not surprising as this beautiful silver fir 'seems to be short-lived in cultivation, trees from the original introduction in 1830 being mostly dead by the turn of the century'. Alan Mitchell says it can be 'miffy, scraggy and gaunt; or make luscious vigorous, rich symmetrical trees of superb shape as at Castlewellan'. The ones we saw at Mount Congreve were clothed to the ground with delicate drooping branches, and were certainly not 'miffy'. Extensive planting of clematis has taken place on tripods and up trees in the woodland, especially up oak trees for spring flowering. Large propagating houses are being built, and the eighteenth-century greenhouse has been converted to its proper purpose – the growing of pot plants, such as fuchsias, lilies, amaryllis and nerines.

Structural alterations in the woodland include the moving of huge rocks to form a pool into which water pours and the making of a Chinese pagoda on which one looks down with the river beyond. Although well concealed, a railway runs along the river bank for the length of the woodland. Lionel de Rothschild employed twelve gardeners in the Orchid House alone. Mount Congreve cannot equal that, and one wonders how it will be kept up by the State after Mr Congreve's death, even though the latter has made provision for its upkeep.

The barely covered sharp grey rocks of the wild Donegal mountains, from their sublime skyline in the wind-blown clouds, drop steeply to a deep glen in which lies Lough Veagh. Perched on a promontory on the south-eastern shore, warmly clad in trees and tinted with *ponticums*, rise the granite towers and turreted walls of Glenveagh Castle, Church Hill. It is as though its typical Irish baronial battlements[21] and deer forest were placed there to form a landscape composition awaiting George Barret and his easel. No setting in Ireland so magnificently illustrates man's ability to transform a piece of savage mountainscape into a setting harnessed to the arts of horticulture. Fortunately, the climate in winter is frostless, as in Kerry or Cornwall,

GLENVEAGH CASTLE,
CO. DONEGAL. *The
barren setting, c. 1890.*

though an 80-in rainfall washes some of the nourishment out of the acid soil and wild winds sweep down the funnel-shaped lough. Mr John Adair, who had married an American heiress, bought the estate from the ill-fated Earl of Leitrim in the 1860s and commissioned his cousin I. T. Trench to design the castle. From that date until Mr Henry McIlhenny of Philadelphia (whose grandfather had emigrated from Co. Donegal to USA), bought it in 1937 the estate has been and still is in American ownership.

The pleasure-ground, the only flat ground, is near the castle on the north-east side, and there a large mown lawn of green Irish turf, with irregular outline, lies bordered on all sides by herbaceous plants with shrubs and trees behind them and encircled by a path. Edward Hyams describes this lawn as a 'lake substitute',[22] but the comparison, though superficially attractive, is false, for in general one looks *towards* a lake in a landscape, rather than from it to see planting, as one does at Glenveagh. The grass is in fact a *tapis vert*, a green base from which to enjoy a plethora of horticultural colour, and is essential, as green, 'the middle colour of the Seven Primary ones and consequently the most agreeable to the Organ of Sight is also the general Colour of the Vegetable Kingdom'.[23] Some of the older rhododendrons planted by Mrs Adair, a great gardener, have survived, but the sumptuous mixed planting one now sees is largely Mr McIlhenny's, advised by the garden consultant Mr Lanning Roper. Scots pines and the hillside provide shelter, and growth has been swift. Crinodendron pours its crimson bell-shaped flowers from 25 ft up, *Acacia dealbata* (Mimosa) survives all winters and flowers freely, and one round-headed specimen tree here is the finest we have ever seen: bushes of purple-flowering *Olearia semidentata* and evergreen *Hoheria sexstylosa*, flaming camellias, *Mutisia decurrens* and in the open, though sheltered, rhododendrons flourish, apart from innumerable lilies, watsonias, rodgersias, hostas and gunneras in rich profusion in the foreground. Above the lawn the Belgian Walk winds through the woodland garden leading to the Wild Garden on a steep slope with lichen-covered granite boulders like some rock-garden of the gods. Conifers have grown taller, large-leaved 'Grande' Rhododendrons drape over the path and azaleas sparkle, while one catches glimpses of palms, tree ferns and other exotics. This is an ideal woodland garden, as one can look down on flowering trees and shrubs – always an exciting experience. Further on in a rocky, fern-clad glen, rich in self-seeding *Rhododendron ciliatum*, a flight of large granite steps, Aztec-like in their steepness, rises straight up the hillside, defying one to climb. At the top one is rewarded by a long grass terrace carved out of the hillside from which the view takes one's breath

169

GLENVEAGH CASTLE, CO. DONEGAL. *The flight of steps.*

GLENVEAGH CASTLE, CO. DONEGAL. *The castle and lake.*

GLENVEAGH CASTLE, CO. DONEGAL. *The conservatory designed by Philippe Jullian.*

away, if one has any left. The castle and its rhododendrons lie below; 22,000 acres of State deer forest sweep over the distant Derryveagh Mountains on both sides of Lough Veagh which lies below like a strip of black glass.

Nearer home in the precincts of the castle walls a charming rectangular, walled *jardin-potager*, with flowers, fruit, herbs and vegetables in gridded beds edged with box, gently drops to an elegant battlemented Gothic conservatory designed by M. Philippe Jullian, which juts out from the stable wall like the prow of a great wooden ship, inside which a pink *Passiflora permeata* (bought as Antiquoiensis), datura and streletzia embalm the air amidst pretty furnishing.

Although large Italian lemon pots at the head of steps, eighteenth-century baroque urns on gate pillars, dolphins in wall fountains, tubs of clipped bay nearer the castle, and a stone-paved garden with herms and *Meconopsis grandis* provide occasional formal elements, the wild, though carefully planted, woodland throughout is the dominant characteristic. Perhaps to gain a true balance between formal and informal Mr McIlhenny has made a formal Tuscan Renaissance garden adjoining the castle, though the access is not direct. It is of a rectangular plan, with grisellinia hedges, fine Italian statues, busts of Roman emperors, stone seats, all in perfect scale, with plants of many eucryphias overhanging, but no flowers. All these are Tuscan elements, but the essentials – strong sunlight and deep shade – are beyond the control of even this garden's maker. Sometimes it seems like a room with gorgeous wallpaper waiting for a shaft of Mediterranean sunlight, but when even the Irish sun strikes, the garden is radiant and inviting – a magical creation.

A path across the *potager* and up some steps leads to the View Garden at the foot of which the Fairy Ring, round and grassed, looks up the extensive lough, exposed therefore to the wind, yet sheltered by bamboos and alder, with *Cotoneaster horizontalis* for ground cover, and interplanted with shrubs and climbing roses. The path then winds back through sheltered woodland, planted with clethra, *Eucalyptus globulus*, from seeds brought back from Lake Titicaca by Mr McIlhenny, and other choice shrubs, before arriving at the castle terrace. Glenveagh is all a tremendous achievement, for Mr Henry McIlhenny, assisted by Mr Jim Russell and Mr Lanning Roper, has wooed ill-clad Nature and wrapped her in rich and subtropical finery.

Lord Talbot de Malahide, who died in 1976, was undoubtedly the most knowledge-able Irish gardener of his time. He inherited in 1948, after which he started to garden at Malahide Castle, nine miles to the north-east of Dublin, keeping an exact and detailed series of Garden Books of all his collection of seeds and plants. From 1957 these books reveal he was able to benefit from Irish nurseries at Slieve Donard and Daisy Hill which were then flourishing. Nevertheless, his primary interest centred on Southern Hemisphere plants, not only Australasian ones connected with his estate in Tasmania (also called Malahide) but with South America also. During the 1950s he exchanged seeds with two other gardeners who specialized in growing Australasian plants – Lieutenant-Commander Dorrien-Smith at Tresco Abbey, Isles of Scilly, and Captain Neil McEacharn at Villa Taranto, Lake Maggiore. It was his ambition to emulate Captain McEacharn's botanical collection at Villa Taranto, which in 1960 had more than 4,000 plant names in its catalogue and which had been started thirty years earlier with help from Lord Headfort. Other gardeners with whom Lord Talbot exchanged seeds and plants were those who lived in the Mediterranean-type climates on the old trade route between Australia and Europe: in Portugal, Miss Tait at Oporto and Senhor Monenã da Silva at the botanical gardens of Coimbra; in Madeira, members of the great gardening family of Blandy; and in South Africa, gardens such as Kirstenbosch and the major nurseries of the Cape. He also collected seeds and cuttings from flourishing Irish gardens like Birr Castle, as well as from forgotten gardens like Kilmacurragh and Old Conna Hill.

After his return from Laos in 1958, Lord Talbot ended his career as a diplomat and concentrated on building up his plant collections at Malahide Castle. To do this

MALAHIDE CASTLE, CO. DUBLIN. *The castle, the medieval ruin and the shrub borders.*

he made extensive journeys himself; into the wilds of Australia for eucalypts, to Ethiopia (1961); Chile (1963); Kashmir and Mexico (1965); Afghanistan (1967); and Nepal (1968). During the 1960s he must have been operating one of the largest private botanical networks in the world, connecting such places as Yalta, USSR, Zagreb, Yugoslavia and Nanking in China. In the 1973 garden book one reads, for example, of two plants of *Epilobium latifolium* from seeds which Khrushchev had originally given to the King of Sweden and which had been planted in the botanical garden at Göteborg. When a bush-fire burned out all apparent traces of *Ozothamnus antenneria*, he was able to give back to Tasmania plants raised from seed which was collected in 1964 on the slopes of Mount Barrow. In 1971 Lord Talbot obtained seed from Mallorca of *Sophora japonica* 'Pendula', which is a somewhat uncommon tree except in southern England, and he himself sent quantities of fritillary seed to botanical gardens in Budapest, Yalta and the Sukhumi garden in Japan.

In the last years of Lord Talbot's life plants and seeds were collected not so much from gardens or from his own expeditions as from other expeditions in the wild, such as the Wye College expedition to Afghanistan in 1971 and those of Dr E. Martyn Rix to the Middle East. Nevertheless, Lord Talbot's planting book for 1971 records that his keen eye did not miss a *Phalaris arundinacea* from as near home as the Malahide Railway Station, and other plants from local sales for charity. Besides his collections of trees and shrubs he also bought and planted thousands of bulbs, chiefly from de Jager, though also from expeditions. In addition he collected Alpine plants and primulas in the 1960s with help from Irish collections such as those of Mr David Shackleton at Clonsilla and Professor Jocelyn Otway-Ruthven.

Lord Talbot's greatest contribution to botany was perhaps the financing of Dr Curtis's *The endemic flora of Tasmania*, illustrated by Margaret Stones. Four volumes were completed before his death, and the publication of the remaining two volumes was continued by his sister, the Hon. Rose Talbot, as a memorial to him. In the 'Genesis' which he wrote to the first volume, Lord Talbot admitted he was a born collector, and because he could not, on account of the climate, complete a collection of Tasmanian plants at Malahide in Ireland he was determined to see them fully illustrated in these books. In other volumes he wrote notes on the cultivation of some of these plants.

The gardens at Malahide Castle are not interesting visually unless one is a collector who is excited by the rarity of many of the 4,000 species and cultivars. It is excellent, therefore, that Dublin County Council will maintain the gardens as a botanical garden to be visited not by the general public but only by those concerned with botanical matters.

Today such European bodies as ICOMOS (International Council of Monuments and Sites) are listing gardens of botanical and historical value in Ireland, and the interest of the public is spreading to the preservation of gardens as well as houses. Kilmacurragh, for example, is currently receiving the kiss of life after forty years of neglect. Many of its fine and rare trees still survive, and although its eighteenth-century house has been allowed to decay, the estate could have immense amenity potential. These gardens form part of our greatest heritages yet they are more fragile than streets or buildings. In these infinitely varied horticultural elysiums 'peace comes dropping slow' and perhaps after a visit we are better fitted to tend our own modest gardens and refreshed to tackle the stresses of urban life. We should be grateful to all the owners and gardeners who currently allow us to see them, and it is hoped that this book may have done a little to open the eyes of our administrators and local authorities so that many of these gardens may be preserved for our children.

Notes

Chapter 1

1. H. Noel Humphries, *The Garden*, 1873, p. 48.
2. J. C. Loudon, *An Encyclopaedia of Gardening*, 1822, p. 1,061.
3. ibid., p. 1,097. We have attributed the garden to Loudon, as his description of it takes the form of an encomium by an artist for his patron and is the only description of an Irish garden in the encyclopedia for which he does not rely on *A Tour of Ireland*, 1811.
4. The Marquess of Hastings's ancestor and predecessor at Moira, Lord Rawdon (1662–1695), was a friend of Sir Hans Sloane, and made notable introductions of American plants into Europe through his botanist-collector James Barlow in the late seventeenth century.
5. Loudon, *An Encyclopaedia*, 1835, p. 1,094.
6. James Fraser, 'On the present state of Gardening in Ireland', *The Gardener's Magazine*, 1826, p. 14.
7. Loudon, *An Encyclopaedia*, 1824, p. 1,095.
8. Fraser, 'On the present state of Gardening in Ireland', *The Gardener's Magazine*, 1826, p. 14.
9. Loudon, *An Encyclopaedia*, 1824, p. 1,095.
10. ibid.
11. ibid.
12. Fraser, 'On the present state of Gardening in Ireland', *The Gardener's Magazine*, 1828, vol. 4, p. 216.
13. Loudon, *An Encyclopaedia*, 1824, p. 1,096. 'A house by Cockerel [sic] of London, in the Grecian style, and much natural and artificial wood, and every promise of magnificence. The proprietor is one of the best landlords in Ireland.'
14. These pamphlets, for example, *The disadvantages to the labourers and landlords resulting from denominational and sectarian legislation*, Dublin 1862, contain views which are progressive even in the context of Ireland today.
15. David Watkin, *The Life and Works of C. R. Cockerell*, London 1974, p. 12.
16. ibid., p. 167. The parterre pattern is similar to that designed by C. R. Cockerell for the Greek Revival Grange Park in Hampshire. See *The Gardener's Magazine*, 1826, p. 107.
17. J. C. Loudon, *The Gardener's Magazine*, 1829, p. 84.
18. James Fraser, 'On the state of Gardening in Ireland', 1826, p. 261.
19. Loudon, *An Encyclopaedia*, 1824, p. 1,095.
20. William Sawrey Gilpin, *Practical Hints upon Landscape Gardening*, London 1832, p. 45.
21. *The Dictionary of National Biography*, London 1908, vol. VII, p. 1,264. We quote: 'His principal works were in Ireland at Crum Castle, Enniskillen Castle, and the seats of Lord Cawdor and Lord Blayney.' We have not been able to trace with certainty the whereabouts of Enniskillen Castle or the seat of Lord Cawdor. It is possible that the former is Florence Court, the seat of the Earl of Enniskillen, or Castle Coole, the seat of the Earl of Belmore, near Enniskillen, and the latter is Farney Castle, Co. Monaghan, the estate of the Marquess of Bath, whose daughter was married to the Lord Cawdor of the time. Farney is situated close to Castle Blayney. On the death of the 11th Baron, the ancient title of Blayney died out, and the estate was bought by a son of Thomas Hope of Deepdene, from whom it descended to the Dukes of Newcastle. In latter years the house became a convent. The park and the temple remain.
22. It was destroyed by fire in 1764.
23. Gilpin, *Practical Hints*, London 1832, p. 6.
24. ibid., pp. 6 and 11.
25. Howard Colvin, *A Biographical Dictionary of English Architects, 1660–1840*, London 1954, p. 506.
26. Clive Aslet, 'Buildings of the Clarendon Press', *Country Life*, September 1978, p. 622.

27. Thomas Lacy, *Home Sketches*, London 1852, p. 258.
28. Mr and Mrs S. C. Hall, *Ireland, its scenery, character etc*, London 1842, vol. II, p. 167.
29. Thomas Lacy, *Sights and Scenes in the Fatherland*, London 1863, p. 439. The conservatory was designed by James Pierce who also designed conservatories at Lonsdale and Castlebridge, Co. Wexford.
30. ibid., p. 276.
31. Austin M. O'Sullivan, *Guide to Johnstown Castle*, An Foras Taluntais, 1969.
32. Lacy, *Home Sketches*, London 1852, p. 247, and *Sights and Scenes*, London 1863, p. 482.
33. In order to give the grounds a mature appearance Colonel Alcock soon invented a shrub-lifter, which was described in *The Gardener's Magazine* in 1837, p. 495.
34. Lacy, *Home Sketches*, London 1852, p. 241, and *Sights and Scenes*, London 1863, p. 479.
35. *The Irish Farmer's Gazette and Journal of Practical Horticulture*, 1863, p. 250.
36. ibid., p. 250. Other accounts of the garden at Castlemartyr occur in *The Gardener's Magazine*, 1830, p. 348, and *The Gardeners' Chronicle*, 1853, p. 759.
37. National Library of Ireland MSS. The park is now a race-course.
38. Wright MSS.
39. *The Irish Farmer's Gazette*, 1863, p. 250.
40. ibid., p. 92.
41. ibid., 1865, p. 405.
42. ibid., 1860, p. 239.
43. ibid., 1863, p. 250.
44. *The Gardener's Record*, 1870, p. 510.
45. Major J. G. Shirley, the present owner of Lough Fea, informs us that the gardens are shown virtually complete on a map in his possession dated 1837.
46. Harold Nicholson, 'Helen's Tower', *In Search of the Past*, London 1937, p. 96.

Chapter 2

1. Desmond Guinness and William Ryan, *Irish Houses and Castles*, London 1971, p. 24.
2. ibid., p. 18.
3. The most famous is extant at Emo Park, Co. Leix.
4. Dumbarton Oaks Colloquium on the History of Landscape Architecture, vol. III. *The French Formal Garden*, ed. Elizabeth B. McDougall and F. Hamilton Haslehurst, 1974, p. 69 *et seq.*
5. James Fraser, 'On the present state of Gardening in Ireland', *The Gardener's Magazine*, 1827, vol. 2, p. 216.
6. Ulster Architectural Heritage Society, *Antrim and Ballymena*, 1969, p. 8.
7. ibid.
8. Mr Toby Bernard of Hertford College, Oxford, informs us that Sir William Petty's gardener, called Bonet or Bonnet, who had been in his service between 1672 and 1684, went to live with the Earl of Meath in 1684. He may therefore have been responsible for the layout of the garden at Killruddery. During the restoration Sir George Hodson designed a dairy for one side of the parterre, and the cast-iron statuary was supplied by Barbezet and Co. and Kahl of Potsdam.
9. W. D. Hemphill, M.D., *Stereoscopic Illustrations of Clonmel*, Dublin 1860, p. 97.
10. Lady Waterford was also an accomplished artist and friend of Ruskin and the Pre-Raphaelites. See John Ruskin's *Sublime and Instructive, The Letters of John Ruskin to Louisa, Marchioness of Waterford, Anna Blunden and Ella Heaton*, ed. Virginia Surtees, London 1974.
11. *The Irish Farmer's Gazette*, 1862, p. 389.
12. We are indebted to the present Marchioness of Waterford for providing us with this information about the fountain.
13. Lord Cloncurry, *Personal recollections of the life and times with extracts from the correspondence of Valentine, Lord Cloncurry*, Dublin 1849, p. 189. For an illustration of this parterre see *Lost Demesnes*, p. 66.
14. *The Irish Farmer's Gazette*, 1853, p. 440.
15. *The Cottage Gardener and Journal of Practical Horticulture*, 1861, p. 90, p. 215: 1870, p. 475.
16. ibid., 1861, p. 213.
17. ibid., 1856, p. 157.

18. *The Gardener's Magazine*, 1835, p. 117.
19. Ninian Niven (Superintendent of the Royal Dublin Society's Botanic Garden), *The Visitor's Companion to the Botanic Garden in Glasnevin*, Dublin 1838.
20. David Moore, a Scot who changed his name from Muir to Moore on his arrival in Ireland, together with his son Sir Frederick Moore, who was later director of Glasnevin, was to have a profound influence on Irish horticulture.
21. *The Gardener's Magazine*, 1838, p. 533.
22. Ninian Niven, *A Prospectus of the proposed public gardens at Monkstown Castle, Dublin*, Dublin 1839.
23. This method of planting herbaceous and annual plants anticipates, at a time when most plants were grown in geometric rows, the free planting of the later herbaceous and mixed border.
24. *The Irish Farmer's Gazette*, 1862, p. 243.
25. The drawing for the proposal, in the Ormonde MSS, displays a naïve style characteristic of all Niven's drawings.
26. William Robinson, *The Gardeners' Chronicle*, 1864, p. 1,179.
27. Charles MacIntosh, *The Book of the Garden*, Edinburgh and London 1853, vol. I, p. 375.
28. Thomas Lacy, *Sights and Scenes in the Fatherland*, London 1863, p. 472.
29. *The Gardeners' Chronicle*, 1891, p. 405.
30. 'An Ornamental Plan for the arrangement of the Dublin Crystal Palace Garden', *The Irish Farmer's Gazette*, 1863, p. 405.
31. National Library of Ireland MSS. Sir Compton's extravagance was later to force him to sell the entire contents of Santry to pay his debts.
32. National Library of Ireland MSS.
33. *The Irish Farmer's Gazette*, 1866, p. 117.
34. Reeves MSS. We are indebted to Dr and Mrs Brian Morley for drawing this to our attention.
35. Ninian Niven, *Redemption Thoughts*, Dublin 1869, a poem in nine cantos, together with a few poems written in early life.
36. George F. Chadwick, *Sir Joseph Paxton (1803–1865)*, London 1961. Paxton also designed Mothel Rectory, Co. Waterford.
37. *The Gardener's Record*, 16 July 1870.
38. *The Gardeners' Chronicle*, 1884, p. 459.
39. Mr J. W. Chapman also acted as assistant to Edward Kemp, the landscape gardener, for many years, illustrating Mr Kemp's *How to lay out a garden*, London 1858.
40. *The Cottage Gardener*, 1863, p. 167.
41. Cosby MSS.
42. Tupper MSS.
43. *The Irish Farmer's Gazette*, 1863, p. 344.
44. Dunraven MSS.
45. Ormonde MSS and Anne Pollen, *John Hungerford Pollen (1820–1902)*, London 1920, p. 284.
46. Lacy, *Sights and Scenes*, London 1863, p. 491.
47. *The Garden*, 1884, p. 513.
48. *The Irish Farmer's Gazette*, 1864, p. 389. We can find no reference to this work in any of the definitive works on G. L. Bernini.
49. *The Gardeners' Chronicle*, 1873, pp. 46 and 77.
50. *The Gardener's Record*, 1869, p. 618.
51. *The Gardeners' Chronicle*, 1898, p. 202: 1902, p. 231 : 1903, p. 269.
52. *The Irish Farmer's Gazette*, 1864, p. 389.
53. James Adam and son, *St. Anne's, Clontarf*, sale catalogue, 1939.
54. *The Garden*, 1884, p. 271.
55. Katherine Everett, *Bricks and Flowers*, London 1949, p. 258.
56. *The Gardeners' Chronicle*, 1905, p. 51, and *The Irish Farmer's Gazette*, 1870, p. 266.
57. *The Cottage Gardener*, 1870, p. 278.
58. These were replicas of the Warwick Vase, recently removed from Warwick Castle by the present Lord Brooke.
59. *The Irish Farmer's Gazette*, 1862, p. 205.
60. *The Garden*, 1872, p. 505.
61. *The Garden*, 1885, p. 223.
62. *The Gardeners' Chronicle*, 1865, p. 967.
63. We are indebted to Seymour Leslie Esq. for this information.

64. A chronological list of accounts of Belgrove in gardening magazines of the late nineteenth and early twentieth centuries would include: *The Garden*, 1875, p. 187; *The Irish Farmer's Gazette*, 21 August 1875; and *The Gardeners' Chronicle*, 1890, p. 491: 1896, pp. 228, 301: 1899 (issue devoted to Gumbleton): 1901, p. 61: and 1908, p. 424.

65. *The Gardener's Record*, 1870, p. 34, and *The Irish Farmer's Gazette*, 1869, p. 188.

66. *The Gardeners' Chronicle*, 1883, p. 366.

67. *The Irish Farmer's Gazette*, 1865, p. 63.

68. *The Gardener's Record*, 1871, p. 393.

69. W. D. Hemphill, *Stereoscopic Illustrations of Clonmel*, Dublin 1860, p. 101.

70. *The Irish Farmer's Gazette*, 1863, p. 374.

71. E. Knowdlin, *Irish Life*, 25 April 1913, p. 93.

72. Hemphill, *Stereoscopic Illustrations*, Dublin 1860, p. 60.

73. *The Irish Farmer's Gazette*, 1865, p. 63.

74. *The Gardener's Record*, 1871, pp. 87 and 369.

75. *The Garden*, 1880, p. 423, and *The Gardeners' Chronicle*, 1876, p. 107.

76. William Robinson, *The Gardeners' Chronicle*, 1864, p. 1,179.

77. *The Gardener's Record*, 1870, p. 179.

78. A chronological list of descriptions of Rockville in Victorian gardening journals would include: *The Cottage Gardener*, 1862, pp. 499, 517; and William Robinson, *The Gardeners' Chronicle*, 1864, pp. 580, 603, 675, 698, 817.

79. J. C. Lyons, *A practical treatise on the management of Orchidaceous Plants*, London and Dublin 1843.

80. La Mortola, Sir Cecil Hanbury's great garden on the Italian Riviera, is now a National Botanic Garden of Italy. Unfortunately, there is at present a plan to drive a motorway through the middle of it.

81. *The Gardeners' Chronicle*, 1912, p. 349.

82. *The Garden*, 1880, p. 151. *The Gardeners' Chronicle*, 1894, pp. 99 and 569.

83. *The Gardeners' Chronicle*, 1884, p. 510.

Chapter 3

1. *The Gardeners' Chronicle*, 4 August 1962, p. 80.

2. Oscar Stephen, *Sir Victor Brooke, Sportsman and Naturalist*, London 1894, p. 247.

3. A. F. Mitchell, *Conifers in the British Isles* (Forestry Commission booklet), 1975, p. 159.

4. The tallest tree in Ireland is in the valley of the Shelton demesne: a magnificent Sitka spruce (161 ft). Unfortunately, the Government has allowed a chemical factory to be built near by, and this has caused disastrous pollution.

5. A. C. Forbes, 'The Avondale Forestry', *Irish Gardening*, July 1940, p. 100.

6. A contraction in Irish speech of Castle William. Evidently adopted.

7. *c.* 1820.

8. *Royal Horticultural Society Journal*, 1961, p. 201.

9. William Neale, Victoria & Paradise Nurseries, Upper Holloway, *The Gardeners' Chronicle*, 31 August 1872, p. 1,170.

10. *Ulster Architectural Heritage*, 'Mourne', 1975, p. 37.

11. *The Garden*, 5 October 1895, p. 258.

12. ibid.

13. *Country Life*, vol. VII, 1913, p. 272.

14. *The Gardeners' Chronicle*, 18 January 1902, p. 46.

15. Constance Annesley, *After Ten Years*, 1931, p. 187.

16. Mabel N. Annesley, *As the sight is bent*, London 1964, p. 125.

17. The builder was John Hargrave of Cork. It is castellated, two-storeyed, of rough stone, with staircase turret on a corner.

18. See *The Garden*, 25 July 1874 and W. J. Bean, *Trees and Shrubs Hardy in the British Isles*, 1970, vol. I, p. 700.

19. ibid., vol. 2, p. 71. Bean thought that the seeds came from B. J. Elwes who was in the southern Andes in 1902.

20. *The Irish Farmer's Gazette*, 1867, p. 407 and *The Garden*, 1 December 1900.

21. *The Gardeners' Chronicle*, 14 November 1903, pp. 245–6.

22. ibid., 1 November 1890, pp. 492–3.

23. Wages book for gardeners, 1877–9, MS 19, pp. 289–90, National Library, Dublin.

24. *RHS Journal*, vol. 68, p. 310 and vol. 69, p. 375.
25. Bean, *Trees and Shrubs*, p. 163.
26. A contrast with some of the private arboreta throughout the country which are 'not available for private viewing'.

Chapter 4

1. *The Letters of Percy Bysshe Shelley*, ed. Frederick Jones, London 1964, vol. 2, p. 275.
2. *Alberti*, IX ii, ed. Orlandi, p. 793.
3. These three folio volumes (1893) were rescued at the last minute from the disastrous fire in 1974, through the foresight of Mrs Ralph Slazenger, who realized their value if the house should be rebuilt. Without them this account could not have been written.
4. See Edward Malins and the Knight of Glin, *Lost Demesnes*, London 1976, p. 27.
5. Though less known than John Nash or Sir Charles Barry, Daniel Robertson was also one of those remarkable *virtuosi* who designed with equal fluency in either Gothic or Classical styles. His first commissions in Ireland, at Wilton and Johnstown Castles, both in Co. Wexford, were extended essays in the Early English style; his third, for Lord Carew at Castleboro, looks forward in designs for house and garden to those for Lord Powerscourt.
6. 'Powerscourt Plans', MSS, vol. I, National Library, Dublin, p. 39.
7. ibid.
8. ibid.
9. See Rev. Francis Orpen Morris, *A Series of Picturesque Views of Seats of the Noblemen and Gentlemen of Great Britain and Ireland*, 1866–80, London 1881, vol. 3, p. 31.
10. Viscount Powerscourt, *A Description and History of Powerscourt*, 1903, p. 80.
11. 'Powerscourt Plans', vol. I, Notes.
12. At that time Francis Penrose was architect to the Chapter of St Paul's Cathedral, London, and in 1895 became President of the RIBA.
13. Powerscourt, *A Description and History of Powerscourt*, 1903, p. 84.
14. 'I do not count the hours unless they are peaceful.'
15. Powerscourt, *A Description and History of Powerscourt*, 1903, p. 84.
16. The editor of *The Irish Farmer's Gazette*, 11 August 1859, states that Lord Powerscourt was considering a fountain like the Emperor Fountain at Chatsworth. In fact, Lord Powerscourt used the design of the Triton figure of the Sea Horses fountain (1690s) at Chatsworth, also modelled on Bernini; but instead of four sea horses he substituted two *pegasi*, and for six small jets he tried to emulate the single tall jet of Paxton's Emperor Fountain.
17. Lord Powerscourt admits, in his notes to 'Powerscourt Plans', vol. I (though not in the later *Description and History*), that a friend of his, Captain Johnson, Commissioner of Irrigation in Mysore at that time, told the brahmin that the idols were destined for the Queen. That has now happened to them.
18. F. H. Purchas, 'The Powerscourt Estate', *The Estate Magazine*, February 1911, p. 65.
19. H. E. Milner, *The Art and Practice of Landscape Gardening*, London 1890, writes: 'My father, the late Edward Milner, as the colleague for many years of Sir Joseph Paxton was concerned in all the later achievements of landscape gardening carried out by that distinguished man; and from 1850 until 1884 himself designed and completed many of the finest works of the kind that have ever been produced, not only in this country, but in various notable places on the continent of Europe.'
20. See *The Gardener's Record*, March 1870, I, p. 328 and II, p. 155.
21. ibid.
22. Reported in *The Times*, 15 January 1904.
23. F. H. Purchas, 'The Powerscourt Estate', *The Estate Magazine*, February 1911, p. 65.
24. Sheila Wingfield, *Real People*, London 1952, p. 84–5.
25. ibid.
26. The Tourism Manager of Powerscourt writes to us that it is not possible to visit the gardens '. . . after the busloads have gone. The Gardens are closed to the public at 5.30 p.m. each evening.' This is unfortunate, but the meaning of our sentence should be clear, and it is from our experience.
27. 'Ars Hortularum: sixteenth century garden iconography', *The Italian Garden*, Dumbarton Oaks, 1972.
28. Georgina Masson, *Italian Gardens*, London 1961, pp. 11–45.

29. *Trees and Shrubs Hardy in the British Isles*, vol. 2, 1973, p. 3 and vol. 1, 1970, p. 175.
30. To whom we are indebted for showing us Peto's plans for house and garden. Mr Maskell's own garden at Kilbogget has a fine collection of shrubs, beautifully landscaped.
31. Designed by Sir Charles Lanyon, it is a tall, square tower of Scottish baronial origin, in red sandstone from Scrabo Hill, capped in black basalt, with conical roofs to the main tower, and turrets at the corners. Scrabo means 'sod of the cow'.
32. *The Gardener's Record*, 1871, vol. III, p. 51.
33. ibid.
34. The Marchioness of Londonderry, *Guide to Mount Stewart*, January 1956, p. 5.
35. University of California Library. Mount Stewart, Newtonards, Co. Down MS, 1920, File No. 7, Folder 146. Items 2 to 5 are in Miss Jekyll's handwriting. Items 1 and 6 are evidently plans sent by Lady Londonderry to Miss Jekyll.
    Item No. 1 Ground floor plan of garden
    Item No. 2 Formal beds, steps etc with tank gardens
    Item No. 3 Cloister Garden
    Item No. 4 Walls of garden to north-west of house
    Item No. 5 Junction of two terraces and planting of N. W. terrace, including a raised bed of yuccas.
    Item No. 6 Further plan for garden, traced. Sent 20 May 1920
    Item No. 7 Ordnance Survey Map. Sheet XI. 7 Public Ordnance Survey Office, Phoenix Park, Dublin. 1903
36. The Marchioness of Londonderry, *Guide to Mount Stewart*, January 1956, p. 5.
37. *Notes for Blau's Atlas*, 1654.
38. See photographs *Country Life*, 1935, 78, p. 380 *et seq.*
39. Guide to Mount Stewart, pp. 9–10. As Lady Londonderry did not visit Italy, she may have seen the arches in E. March Phillips's *The Gardens of Italy*, London 1919. A similar eclectic garden said to be modelled on Gamberaia is in the Longwood Gardens, Pennsylvania. The spirit of Gamberaia is absent in both Mount Stewart and Longwood.
40. ibid.
41. Apparently these animals each represent a member of what Lady Londonderry called the Ark Club, the Ark being Londonderry House, Park Lane, during the First World War; though the concept of Lord and Lady Londonderry saving civilisation there seems somewhat far-fetched. The statuary at Mount Stewart depicts the people in caricature—authors, King's Messengers, politicians, servicemen, etc., who were called by the names of animals, birds and fishes. Without knowing the originals, it is difficult to appreciate the hilarity induced by these statues in cement at Mount Stewart.
42. They have recently been replaced by local earthenware tiles made at Portadown.
43. We can find no ceiling in the Mansion House, London, which remotely resembles the baroque design of the surround to the oval pool in this garden. In fact, Robert Adam never worked at the Mansion House, and once remarked on George Dance's restoration there with detestation.
44. Lady Gregory, *A Book of Saints and Wonders*, Gerrards Cross 1971, p. 22, describes the attributes of St Brigit: 'It is she keeps everyone that is in straits and in dangers; it is she puts down sicknesses; it is she quiets the voice of the waves and the anger of the great sea. She is the queen of the south, she is the mother of the flocks; she is the Mary of the Gael.'
45. *Explorations*, London 1962, p. 8.
46. *My Garden—an Intimate Magazine for Garden Lovers*, April 1944, pp. 313–16.

Chapter 5

1. *The Letters of John Constable*, ed. R. B. Beckett, vols 6–8, 1822, The Suffolk Records Society.
2. Derek and Timothy Clifford, *John Crome*, London 1968, pp. 37 and 47.
3. William Robinson, *The English Flower Garden*, London 1833, part 1, p. 4.
4. ibid.
5. Ruth E. Duthie, 'Garden History', *The Journal of the Garden History Society*, 1974, vol. II, No. 3, p. 12. This story, sometimes thought to be apocryphal, has been confirmed to us by Sir Hunt Johnson-Walsh's granddaughter, Mrs W. F. Walsh-

Kemmis. It originated in print in *Some Nineteenth Century Gardeners* by Geoffrey Taylor, London 1951, p. 68. The misspelling by him of the demesne's name as 'Ballykilcannan' has been followed since by many writers.

6. Robinson, *The English Flower Garden*, London 1883, p. 18.
7. See the *Weekly Irish Times*, 16 April 1938.
8. Edward Malins and the Knight of Glin, *Lost Demesnes*, London 1976, Appendix C.
9. James Franklin Fuller, *Omniana : the autobiography of an Irish octogenarian*, London 1916, p. 184.
10. Dudley Barker, *Prominent Edwardians*, London 1969, p. 150. In 1878, however, there were 94,983 acres at Derreen, whereas now there are far fewer.
11. J. A. Froude, *Short Studies on Great Subjects*: 'A Fortnight in Kerry', London 1871, p. 185.
12. The Royal Horticultural Society, *The Report of the Conifer Conference*, held by the RHS, ed. F. J. Chittenden, London 1932. A comprehensive list of the trees at Derreen is given in the appendix.
13. J. C. Weston, 'Some Irish Gardens', a lecture given at the Royal Horticultural Society, 27 May 1919, in which a comprehensive list was given of the shrubs growing at Derreen, communicated to Weston by Mr Arrowsmith, the gardener. Selected lists of plants were given by William Watson in *The Gardeners' Chronicle*, 1 December 1906, p. 368, and by J. W. Besant, *The Gardeners' Chronicle*, 26 June 1926, p. 461. *Donations from the Garden*, MS, National Botanical Gardens, Glasnevin, lists the plants received by Lord Lansdowne from Sir Frederick Moore, Director of the Botanic Garden.
14. Thomas Wodehouse, Baron Newton, *Lord Lansdowne : A biography*, London 1929, p.127.
15. *Curtis's Botanical Magazine*, 1915, vol. 141, Dedication Page.
16. Rosemary ffolliott, *The Pooles of Mayfield*, Dublin 1958, plate IX, p. 151.
17. *The Gardeners' Chronicle*, 27 February 1841, p. 135.
18. John Adair, *Hints on the Culture of Ornamental Exotic Plants in Ireland*, Dublin 1870, was largely rewritten as *Hints on the Culture of Ornamental Plants in Ireland*, Dublin 1878 (see p. 75). He suggested reading William Robinson's *Gleanings from French Gardens* (1868) and *The Parks, Promenades and Gardens of Paris* (1869).
19. Indian Army and Civil Service List, 1861–76.
20. Sir William Wilson Hunter, *A Life of the Earl of Mayo, fourth Viceroy of India*, London 1875, vol. 1, p. 173.
21. Mark Girouard, *The Victorian Country House*, Oxford 1971, p. 199.
22. *The Garden*, 28 September 1872, p. 267, and *The Gardeners' Chronicle*, 2 May 1885, p. 578.
23. Letter from the Knight of Kerry to *The Garden*, 27 July 1872, p. 72, and his obituary in *The Garden*, 30 October 1880, p. 169.
24. W. Watson, *The Gardeners' Chronicle*, 1 December 1906, p. 368, and J. W. Besant, *The Gardeners' Chronicle*, 26 June 1926, p. 461.
25. H. J. Elwes and A. Henry, *The Trees of Great Britain and Ireland*, Edinburgh 1912, vol. 6, p. 1,616.
26. See Sir William Stokes, *His Life & Work, 1804–1878*, London 1878, p. 189–91.
27. This has been communicated to us by Mrs Ralph J. Walker.
28. J. W. Besant, *The Gardeners' Chronicle*, 26 June 1926, p. 461.
29. Robinson, *The Wild Garden*, London 1870, p. 39.
30. *The Gardeners' Chronicle*, 7 August 1926, p. 110.
31. The owner of Garinish informs us that the island was visited some years ago by a great-niece of William Robinson, who informed him that Robinson had advised on the planting and layout of the island.
32. W. Watson, *The Gardeners' Chronicle*, 24 November 1906, p. 368.
33. ibid.
34. J. W. Besant, *The Gardeners' Chronicle*, 26 June 1926, p. 461.
35. Wyndham Fitzherbert, *The Gardeners' Chronicle*, 2 April 1910, p. 209.
36. This information has been communicated to us by Patricia Hutchinson of East Ardnagashel, near Bantry.
37. Ronald John Kaulback, *Tibetan Trek*, London 1934. See W. J. Bean, *Trees and Shrubs Hardy in the British Isles*, vol. 3, p. 285.
38. Wyndham Fitzherbert, *The Gardeners' Chronicle*, 8 December 1909, p. 245.
39. *The Garden*, 23 August 1813, p. 155.
40. *The Gardeners' Chronicle*, 2 May 1885, p. 578.
41. *The Garden*, 28 August 1909, p. 419.

42. *The Gardeners' Chronicle*, 26 December 1908, p. 148.
43. Letter from Gerard Leigh White to Richard Grove Annesley, 1920. Annes Grove MSS.
44. Field notes of F. Kingdon-Ward, 1924–5 expedition to Tibet.
45. Various letters, Annes Grove MSS.
46. *Irish Gardener and Horticultural Review*, 2 June 1929.
47. Edmund Spenser, 'Colin Clout's Come Home Again', lines 58–9.
48. *The Gardeners' Chronicle*, 1864, p. 1,179.
49. *The Gardeners' Chronicle*, 28 June 1887, p. 587.
50. *The Gardeners' Chronicle*, 14 July and 6 October 1883, pp. 53 and 444.
51. *Irish Gardening*, vol. 7, p. 69.
52. *The Garden*, 1875, vol. VIII, p. 385.
53. See Edward Malins and the Knight of Glin, *Lost Demesnes*, London 1976, p. 178.
54. *The Gardeners' Chronicle*, 6 September 1902, 1 August 1903, 12 September 1903, 12 July 1885, 18 May 1901, and *The Garden*, 13 August 1895, p. 75.
55. Sir Frederick Moore, 'Recollections of Mount Usher' in E. H. Walpole, *Mount Usher, 1868–1928*, Dublin 1928.
56. Lady Moore, 'The New Flora and Sylva', *A Letter from Ireland*, January 1929, p. 119.
57. Robinson, *The English Flower Garden*, 13th edn.
58. Guidebook to Mount Usher.
59. E. H. Walpole, *Mount Usher, 1868–1952*, Dublin 1928.
60. ibid.
61. ibid.
62. Colonel Charles Ball-Acton, *Colonel Ball-Acton*, privately printed, Guildford 1906.
63. F. W. Burbridge, 'An Irish Garden', *The Gardeners' Chronicle*, 17 June 1893.
64. ibid.
65. Lady Moore, 'The New Flora and Sylva', *A Letter from Ireland*, 1924, p. 120.
66. W. Watson, *The Gardeners' Chronicle*, 24 November 1906, p. 351.
67. *The Gardeners' Chronicle*, 17 June 1893.
68. Lady Moore, 'The New Flora and Sylva', *A Letter from Ireland*, 1924, p. 120.
69. *The Gardeners' Chronicle*, 17 June 1893.
70. Robinson, *The English Flower Garden*, London 1883, p. 95.
71. *The Gardeners' Chronicle*, 2 March 1901, p. 135.
72. *The Gardeners' Chronicle*, 30 May 1896, pp. 680 and 788.
73. *Country Life*, 1936, vol. 79, p. 224.
74. See Leslie Stringer, 'Rowallane', *RHS Journal*, 1956, vol. 81, p. 479.
75. According to Bean, including *Nothofagus antarctica*, a 'remarkable specimen with nine main stems and a wide spread'; also *N. dombeyi*, 66 ft by $7\frac{1}{4}$ ft (1966), *N. cunninghamii*, *N. fusca*, and *N. solandrii* var. *cliffortioides*.

Chapter 6

1. John Butler Yeats, *Early Memories*, Dundrum 1923, pp. 54–5.
2. W. B. Yeats. 'Reveries over Childhood', *Autobiographies*, London 1961, p. 21, refers to his great-uncle's death: 'after losing all his money, drowned himself, first taking off his rings and chain and watch as became a collector of many beautiful things'.
3. W. B. Yeats, 'Purgatory', *Collected Plays*, London 1952, p. 683.
4. Letter from Lissadell written by William Stokes, Physician-in-Ordinary to the Queen in Ireland and antiquarian, to his family, 1850. Quoted in William Stokes, *Sir William Stokes, His Life & Work, 1804–1878*, London 1878, p. 189.
5. The Rev. T. O. Rorke, *History of Sligo. Town and County*, Dublin 1889, pp. 11–13.
6. The story was told to Dr T. R. Henn by Maeve de Markievicz, the daughter of Constance de Markievicz. Perhaps the young Yeats took the bianconi car for part of the way—a form of transport named after Joseph Bianconi, the entrepreneur of horse-drawn side-cars who linked services of 4,000 miles across Ireland. He does not mention the incident in any of his published works.
7. W. B. Yeats, 'Autobiography', *Memoirs*, ed. Denis Donoughue, London 1972, p. 101. Merville is now Nazareth Houses, for old people and orphans.
8. Yeats to Eva Gore Booth, September 1916.
9. W. B. Yeats, *Collected Poems*, London 1950, pp. 263–64.
10. ibid., 'Towards the Break of Day', p. 208.
11. W. B. Yeats, 'Autobiography', *Memoirs*, p. 102.

12. There was an observatory founded by Edward Cooper in 1832, which predates the better-known telescope at Birr Castle.
13. W. M. Barry, *A Walking Tour round Ireland in 1865 by an Englishman*, London 1867, p. 84.
14. Planted *c*. 1860. See *The Irish Homestead*, 12 February 1898.
15. Lady Gregory, *Coole*, Dolmen Press, Dublin 1971, p. 101. The catalpa is a native of the eastern States of North America, not of the Pacific.
16. Quoted by Maurice Collis, *Somerville and Ross. A Biography*. London 1968, p. 129.
17. *Lady Gregory's Journals. 1916–1930*, ed. Lennox Robinson, London 1946, p. 22.
18. Lady Gregory, *Coole*, p. 94.
19. Anne Gregory, *Me and Nu: childhood at Coole*, Gerrards Cross 1970, p. 93.
20. Lady Gregory, article in *The Irish Homestead*, 19 February 1898.
21. W. B. Yeats, *Collected Poems*, p. 469.
22. James McGarry, *Place-Names in the Writings of W. B. Yeats*, ed. Edward Malins, Gerrards Cross 1976, p. 74 *et al*.
23. W. B. Yeats, *Collected Poems*, p. 238.
24. *The Dome*, 'Dust hath closed Helen's Eye', October 1899, USA.
25. *The Letters of W. B. Yeats*, ed. Allan Wade, London 1954, p. 652.
26. ibid., p. 659.
27. Foreword to *Thoor Ballylee—Home of William Butler Yeats*, ed. Liam Miller, Dublin 1965, from a paper given by Mary Hanley to the Kiltartan Society in 1961.
28. Sean O'Casey, *Inishfallen. Fare Thee Well*, London 1949, p. 146.
29. Lady Gregory, *Coole*, p. 94.
30. Letter to John Quinn, 10 February 1918.
31. De Burgh, *Landowners of Ireland*, 1878.
32. *Lady Gregory's Journals. 1916–1930*, ed. Lennox Robinson, London 1946, p. 34.
33. ibid.
34. ibid.
35. W. B. Yeats, *Collected Poems*, pp. 274–5.
36. This was the site finally chosen for the War Memorial Park of Remembrance, designed by Sir Edwin Lutyens. See p. 159.
37. James Pulham of Pulham & Sons, also worked at Batsford Park, Sandringham House, Waddesdon Manor, and Wisley (advised by Edward White) for the RHS.
38. The destruction of this statue, like that of the Nelson pillar in O'Connell Street may have been politically symbolical, but aesthetically and environmentally it was disastrous.
39. W. B. Yeats, *Collected Poems*, p. 227.
40. ibid., p. 347.
41. ibid., p. 399.

Chapter 7

1. Arthur Hellyer, *The Shell Guide to Gardens*, London 1977, p. 57, an excellent and authoritative work.
2. Unlike Colonel Hall-Walker (later Lord Wavertree), Lord Redesdale had experience of woodlands and forests in Japan and wrote *The Bamboo Garden*, a horticultural history of the plant. He was a friend of Lord Annesley to whom he sent bamboo plants.
3. *The Gardeners' Chronicle*, 29 October 1910 and 18 November 1911.
4. Minoru achieved unexpected fame when a colt named after him, owned and trained by Colonel Hall-Walker, won the Derby in 1909, his jockey wearing King Edward VII's colours.
5. *Account Book 1910–11*, National Botanic Garden, Glasnevin.
6. Called a Geisha House in the current guide.
7. The phrase is Barbara Jones's in *Follies and Grottoes*, London 1974, p. 440.
8. Sir Gardner Wilkinson, *Colour*, London 1858, p. 375.
9. Queen Victoria and the Prince Consort celebrated his last birthday at Killarney House. In the Queen's words, 'it was overpoweringly hot'. He died in December 1869.
10. Later the 3rd Baron Revelstoke, whose son is the present owner.
11. Lord Revelstoke, a classical scholar, used to consider Lambay as Ithaca, as also did Lord Lansdowne of Derreen. But the comparison is inappropriate as neither of these noble owners was returning like Ulysses to his island birthplace.

12. As in certain other places for which she designed gardens, Gertrude Jekyll never visited the site.

13. Quoted by Christopher Hussey, *The Life of Sir Edward Lutyens*, London 1950, p. 175, from notes of Lutyens written as a vote of thanks to T. H. Mawson after his lecture on garden design, given at the Architectural Association, 8 April 1908.

14. *The Architecture of Sir Edwin Lutyens*, London 1950, vol. 1, p. 46.

15. *The Gardeners' Chronicle*, 8 April 1911, XLIX, p. 211 and 6 May, p. 285.

16. Lutyens had seen similar *torri* at Villa Collazzi (Bombicci) near Florence, and in other Italian gardens where flowers had been displayed in this manner since Augustan times.

17. H. G. Wells, *Joan and Peter*, 1918, chapt. XII.

18. Christopher Hussey, *The Life of Sir Edwin Lutyens*, p. 260, implies that this inaccuracy in costing might have affected Lutyens's future prospects: 'The Planning Commission for New Delhi had doubts about Lutyens's appointment as architect for the new city, particularly with regard to his ability to control costs. One of the Commission, the Foreign Secretary (Lieutenant-Colonel Sir Henry McMahon K.C.I.E.) knew Lutyens personally and had some experience of how his enthusiasm was apt to prove expensive, having recommended him to the owner of Heywood for the designing of a garden terrace ...'. Lutyens's subsequent expenditure in New Delhi proved that their doubts were justified.

19. These words are inscribed below the memorial bust on St Stephen's Green to Thomas Kettle, poet, scholar-patriot, professor at University College, who was killed on active service in the First World War.

20. Acers of outstanding interest listed by A. J. Bean in *Trees and Shrubs in the British Isles* as coming from Dr Wilson to Lord Rosse are *Acer lawakamii*, *A. squamata*, *A. giraldii*, and *A. henryi*.

21. Similar to the fifteenth-century tower at Jerpoint Abbey and the keep at Blarney.

22. Edward Hyams, *Irish Gardens*, 1967, p. 54.

23. David Huntley, *Observations on Man*, 1749, 1st part, p. 208.

Bibliography

ADAIR, John. *Hints on the Culture of Ornamental Plants in Ireland*. London, 1870.

ALBERTI, Leon Battista. *De re aedificatoria*. Book V. Trans. James Leoni, London, 1955.

ANNESLEY, Earl. *Beautiful and Rare Trees and Plants*. Privately printed, 1903.

ANNESLEY, Mabel, Lady. *As the sight is bent*. London, 1964.

ARNOLD, Matthew. *Irish Essays*. London, 1891.

BALL-ACTON, Georgina. *Recollections of Colonel Ball-Acton*. Privately printed, 1906.

BALL, F. Elrington. *A History of the County of Dublin*. Dublin, 1902–20.

BARKER, Dudley R. *Prominent Edwardians*. London, 1906.

BEAN, W. J. *Trees and Shrubs Hardy in the British Isles*. Vols 1–3. London, 1970–6.

BETJEMAN, Sir John. *Collected Poems*. Boston, 1958.

BLOMFIELD, R. and THOMAS, Inigo F. *The Formal Garden in England*. London, 1897.

BURBIDGE, Frederick W. *The Gardens of the Sun*. London, 1880.

BUTLER, A. S. G. *The Architecture of Sir Edwin Lutyens*. Vols 1–3. London and New York, 1950.

BUTLER, John, Marquess of Ormonde. *Autumn in Sicily*. London, 1852.

CANE, Percy. *The Creative Art of Garden Design*. London, 1967.

CLONCURRY, Valentine, Lord. *Personal Recollections of the life and times, with extracts from the correspondence, of Valentine, Lord Cloncurry*. Dublin, 1849.

COLLIS, Maurice. *Somerville and Ross. A Biography*. London, 1968.

COLVIN, Howard. *A Biographical Dictionary of English Architects, 1660–1840*. London, 1954.

DE BOVET, Madame. *A Three Months' Tour of Ireland*. London, 1878.

DE BURGH (U. H. Hussey). *Landowners of Ireland*. London, 1878.

DUNRAVEN, 4th Earl of. *Past Times and pastimes*. London, 1878.

ELWES, A. J. and HENRY, A. *The Trees of Great Britain and Ireland*. Vols I–VII. London, 1906–13.

EVERETT, Katherine. *Bricks and Flowers*. London, 1949.

FFOLLIOTT, Rosemary. *The Pooles of Mayfield*. Dublin, 1958.

FINGALL, Countess of. *Memories. Seventy Years Young*. London, 1937.

FOTHERGILL, George A. (ed.) *A Gift to the Nation. The National Stud*. Limited edition, 1916.

FROUDE, J. A. *Short Studies on Great Subjects*. London, 1871.

FULLER, James Franklin. *Omniana: the autobiography of an Irish octogenarian*. London, 1916.

GILPIN, William Sawrey. *Practical Hints upon Landscape Gardening*. London, 1832.

GREGORY, Anne. *Me and Nu: childhood at Coole*. Gerrards Cross, 1970.

GREGORY, Lady. *Journals 1916–1930*. Ed. Lennox Robinson. London, 1946. *Coole*. London, 1971.

GUINNESS, Desmond and RYAN, William. *Irish Houses and Castles*. London, 1971.

HADFIELD, Miles. *Gardening in Britain*. London, 1965. *Landscape with Trees*. London, 1967.

HEAD, Sir Francis, Bart. *A Fortnight in Ireland*. London, 1852.

HEMPHILL, W. D. *Stereoscopic Illustrations of Clonmel*. Dublin, 1860.

HOEVER, Otto. *An Encyclopedia of Ironwork*. London, 1927.

HOLE, Samuel R., Dean of Rochester. *A Little Tour in Ireland by an Oxonian*. London, 1959.

HUGHES, John Arthur. *Garden Architecture and Landscape Gardening*. London, 1866.

HULBERT, W. H. *Ireland under Coercion*. London, 1888.

HUNTER, Sir William Wilson. *A Life of the Earl of Mayo, fourth Viceroy of India*. London, 1875.

HUSSEY, Christopher. *The Life of Sir Edwin Lutyens*. Vols 1–3. London, 1950.

HYMANS, Edward. *Irish Gardens*. London, 1967.

JEKYLL, Gertrude. *Colour Planning of the Garden*. London, 1924. *Garden Ornament*. London, 1918. *Wall and Water Gardens*. London, 1901. *Wood and Garden*. London, 1899.

LACY, Thomas. *Home Sketches*. London, 1852. *Sights and Scenes in the Fatherland*. London, 1863.

LOUDON, John Claudius. *An Encyclopaedia of Gardening*. London, 1822.

MACINTOSH, Charles. *The Book of the Garden*. Edinburgh and London, 1853.

MALINS, Edward and GLIN, The Knight of. *Lost Demesnes. Irish Landscape Gardening, 1660–1845*. London, 1976.

NIVEN, Ninian. *The Visitor's Companion to the Botanic Garden in Glasnevin.* Dublin, 1838. *A prospectus of the proposed public gardens at Monkstown Castle.* Dublin, 1839. *Redemption Thoughts.* Dublin, 1869.

O'CASEY, Sean. *Inishfallen. Fare Thee Well.* London, 1949.

O'LAVERTY, James. *History & Account of the Diocese of Down and Conor.* Dublin, 1878.

ORPEN, Goddard Henry. *The Orpen Family: life and writings of Richard Orpen of Killowen, Co. Kerry together with his forebears in England and brief notices of the various branches of the Orpen Family.* London, 1930.

PETO, Harold. *The Book of Iford.* Privately printed, 1917.

PHILLIPS, E. March and BOLTON, A. *The Gardens of Italy.* London, 1919.

PLINY, the Younger. *Letters.* Trans. William Melmoth. Loeb Library, 1915.

PREECE, John. *Gates of Veneto.* London, 1968.

ROBINSON, William. *The English Flower Garden.* London, 1883. *Gleanings from French Gardens.* London, 1868. *The Parks, Promenades and Gardens of Paris.* London, 1869. *The Wild Garden.* London, 1870.

RORKE, the Rev. Dr. T. *History of Sligo. Town & County.* Dublin, 1889.

ROSS-OF-BLADENSBURG, Sir John. *List of Trees and Shrubs grown in the grounds of Rostrevor House, Co. Down.* Dublin, 1911.

SEDDING, J. D. *Garden-Craft. Old and New.* London, 1895.

SENIOR, Nassau William. *Journals, Conversations & Essays relating to Ireland.* 2 vols. London, 1868.

SOMERVILLE, E. and ROSS, Martin. *Irish Memories.* London, 1925. *The Real Charlotte.* London, 1894.

STEPHEN, Oscar Leslie. *Sir Victor Brooke, Sportsman and Naturalist.* London, 1894.

STEWART, Edith, Marchioness of Londonderry. *Character and Tradition.* London, 1934. *Retrospect.* London, 1938.

STONES, Margaret and CURTIS, Winifred. *The endemic flora of Tasmania.* Parts I–V. London, 1971–6.

STOKES, William. *Sir William Stokes, his life & work. 1804–1878.* London, 1878.

TAYLOR, Geoffrey. *Some Nineteenth Century Gardeners.* London, 1951.

TUNNARD, Christopher. *Gardens in the Modern Landscape.* London, 1950.

VEITCH, James. *A Manual of Coniferae.* London, 1881.

WALPOLE, E. H. (ed.) *Recollections of Mount Usher 1868–1952.* Dublin, 1952.

WATKIN, David. *The Life and Works of C. R. Cockerell.* London, 1974.

WINGFIELD, Mervyn E., 7th Viscount Powerscourt. *A Description and History of Powerscourt.* London, 1903.

WINGFIELD, Sheila. *Real People.* London, 1952.

WODEHOUSE, Thomas, Baron Newton. *Lord Lansdowne a biography.* London, 1929.

YEATS, John Butler. *Early Memories.* London, 1923.

YEATS, W. B. *Autobiographies.* London, 1961. *The Letters of W. B. Yeats.* Ed. Allen Wade. London, 1954. *The Senate Speeches of W. B. Yeats.* Ed. Donald R. Pearce. London, 1961. *Collected Poems.* London, 1933.

Index

Index

187